T0321150

CYBER ENIGMA

UNRAVELING THE TERROR
IN THE CYBER WORLD

Cyber and its related technologies such as the Internet was introduced to the world only in late 1980s, and today it is unimaginable to think of a life without it. Despite being ubiquitous, cyber technology is still seen as an enigma by many, mainly due to its rapid development and the high level of science involved. In addition to the existing complexities of the technology, the level of threat matrix surrounding the cyber domain further leads to various misconceptions and exaggerations. Cyber technology is the future, thus forcing us to understand this complex domain to survive and evolve as technological beings.

To understand the enigma, the book analyzes and disentangles the issues related to cyber technology. The author unravels the threats that terrorize the cyber world and aims to decrypt its domain. It also presents the existing reality of cyber environment in India and charts out a few recommendations for enhancing the country's cyber security architecture. Further, the book delves into detailed analysis of various issues like hacking, dark web, cyber enabled terrorism and covert cyber capabilities of countries like the US and China.

E. Dilipraj is an Associate Fellow at the Centre for Air Power Studies (CAPS). This book is his maiden project in CAPS.

CYBER ENIGMA

UNRAVELING THE TERROR IN THE CYBER WORLD

E Dilipraj

Introduction by

Air Marshal Vinod Patney SYSM PVSM AVSM VrC (Retd)

Routledge
Taylor & Francis Group
LONDON AND NEW YORK

KW Publishers Pvt Ltd
New Delhi

in association with

Centre for Air Power Studies
New Delhi

First published 2019
by Routledge
2 Park Square, Milton Park, Abingdon, Oxon OX14 4RN

and by Routledge
52 Vanderbilt Avenue, New York, NY 10017

Routledge is an imprint of the Taylor & Francis Group, an informa business

British Library Cataloguing in Publication Data
A catalogue record for this book is available from the British Library

Library of Congress Cataloging in Publication Data
A catalog record for this book has been requested

ISBN: 978-0-367-32264-9 (hbk)
ISBN: 978-0-429-32556-4 (ebk)

Typeset in Adobe Garamond Pro
by KW Publishers, New Delhi 110002

KNOWLEDGE WORLD

CENTRE FOR AIR POWER STUDIES

VISION

To be an independent **centre of excellence on national security** contributing informed and considered research and analyses on relevant issues.

MISSION

To encourage independent and informed research and analyses on issues of relevance to national security and to create a pool of domain experts to provide considered inputs to decision-makers. Also, to foster informed public debate and opinion on relevant issues and to engage with other think-tanks and stakeholders within India and abroad to provide an Indian perspective.

Dedicated to my parents

Mr G. Emuraj and Ms E.Vanitharaj

CONTENTS

ACKNOWLEDGEMENT

I would like to express my heartfelt gratitude to all people who helped me through in the long journey of completing this book.

First and foremost, I would like to thank Late Air Commodore Jasjit Singh for giving me the opportunity to be part of this esteemed institution – Centre for Air Power Studies (CAPS).

Throughout the process of writing this book, Air Marshal Vinod Patney, Director General, CAPS has been my biggest source of encouragement. His valuable insight, enthusiasm and guidance had stirred up my confidence and passion in completing this book. I am indebted to Air Marshal Vinod Patney for moulding me as a research scholar.

My sincere thanks to Air Marshal Kishan Kumar Nohwar, Additional Director General, CAPS, for his encouraging words, support and for accepting nothing less than excellence from me.

A special thanks to all CAPS faculty who have been a huge source of encouragement by providing a glimmer of hope in this journey of success. Their reviews, suggestions, valuable comments and constructive criticism have enhanced my thought process and added value to the book.

Finally, my heartfelt love and gratitude to Ms Chandra Rekha for her unconditional love and moral support.

Thank you all once again.

With Regards
E.Dilipraj

PREFACE

Cyber and its related technologies such as Internet was introduced to the world only in late 1980s, and today it is unimaginable to think of a life without these all pervasive technologies. Despite being ubiquitous around the world, cyber technology is still seen as an enigma by many, mainly due to its rapid development and high level of science involved in it. In addition to the existing complexities of the technology, the level of threat matrix surrounding the cyber domain further lead to various misconceptions and exaggerations apart from elevating the complexity to a few notches above. It is evident that the world in the future is going to be fully dependent on the cyber technology and hence humans are forced to understand this complex domain in order to survive and evolve successfully as 'technological' beings.

It is in this context of understanding the enigma around the cyber domain, the book attempts to analyse and disentangle the various issues related to cyber technology. The book also attempts to unravel the various threats that terrorise the cyber world in detail by categorising them according to the perpetrators. The book aims to decrypt the cyber domain and at the same time exhibit the realities in terms of the threat vector, technological sophistication and the rapid development of the domain itself. The book also tries to present the existing reality of cyber environment in India and charts out a few recommendations and suggestions for enhancing the country's cyber security architecture.

The book has eight chapters. The first chapter "**Understanding the Cyber World**" is an introduction of the cyber world to the readers and explains how the cyber domain became a domain of warfare. This chapter also provides a few working definitions on the subject.

The second chapter on "**The Art of Phreaking, Hacking, Cracking...**" studies the history and evolution of hacking culture around the world in order to understand the practice and the people who practice it known as hackers. The chapter also covers a case study of various hacking incidents between India and Pakistan to understand the various types and methods of hacking capabilities in these two countries. The chapter also offer a few suggestions to effectively identify and use a country's hackers as force multipliers for enhancing the national security.

The third chapter on **"Deep and Dark Digital Ocean"** analyses the evolution of darker side of the internet that dwells in secret settings within the network. The chapter brings out the various illegal activities that are carried out in the dark web and also explores the various methods by which different countries around the world have managed to tackle this threat with appropriate cases as examples.

The fourth chapter on **"Cyber Enabled Terrorism"** explains how real world terrorists and other hostile non-state actors across the world are effectively misusing the sophisticated cyber technology for their evil missions and operations. The chapter identifies seven different purposes for which terrorists use cyber technology and all these methods are explained in detail with appropriate case studies and examples.

The fifth and sixth chapters explain in detail the covert cyber capabilities practiced and developed by two countries namely China and the United States respectively. The fifth chapter on **"Dragon's Fire in the Virtual World"** briefly studies the repressive cyber environment of China and also explores the covert offensive capabilities in the possession of the state's cyber agencies to act against its adversaries. The chapter also studies in detail the secret cyber units in the Chinese military and various private hackers groups operating from China with state support.

The sixth chapter on **"Eagle's Claw on Cyberspace"** is a detailed study on the various covert cyber capabilities existing with the United States. The chapter explains in detail a few covert programmes like X-Keyscore, Quantum, NSA ANT Catalogue, etc in an attempt to explain the level of sophistication existing with the nation states in terms of cyber capabilities. The chapter also has a case study on Stuxnet which is dubbed as the first cyber weapon of the world.

The seventh chapter on **"Cyber India: A Reality Check"** starts by covering in detail the history of computers in India and also explains the current cyber environment of the country in terms of its usage, security preparations, legal and policy support from government. The chapter also ventures into identifying the various threats to India's cyber security and the existing gaps in the country's preparation for a comprehensive cyber security. The chapter finally charts out few short term/ immediate measures in order to enhance the overall capability and security of the country in its cyber sphere.

The eighth and final chapter of the book titled "**The Need for Strategy in Cyberspace**", emphasises the need for a country to develop its own strategy in order to engage in the cyberspace. The chapter concludes with some suggestions and recommendations for enhancing India's overall cyber capabilities and security.

INTRODUCTION

Words and phrases like cyber, cyberspace, cyber world, cyber war, cyber-attacks, big data, internet of things and the like have caught the imagination of millions. In many quarters the words are met with wonder and even awe. The possible reason is that, to many, the cyber world represents an intangible, nebulous and unknown world. The title of the book is, therefore, appropriate as enigma is defined as 'a person or thing that is mysterious or difficult to understand'. Two other definitions merit mention. The cyber world is defined as 'the world of inter-computer communication' or 'a real or virtual world of information in cyber space'. Cyber space is the 'notional environment in which communications over computer networks occur'. The book aims to explain some of the mysteries of cyber space, its great value to mankind as well as how illicit activities which have spawned threaten to markedly reduce the value and even cause serious damage. Some remedial measures have also been suggested or indicated to protect the system.

The cyber world has witnessed an astronomical growth in the number of uses and number of users. The impact has been so great that, to a large and increasing extent, the real world is becoming dependent on the virtual world in cyber sphere. This includes the military, banking and commercial establishments, public utilities, manufacturing processes and many others that form part of the National Critical Information Infrastructure. Computers do improve the efficiency and effectiveness of the organisations and all users are increasingly relying on the magic of the computer world. The increasing dependence has given birth to cybercrime and the establishment of the underworld of cyber space also known as the 'Dark Web'. Cyber attacks can be very debilitating and impact our lives almost immediately. From the military point of view, cyber-attacks do not need a large body of soldiers but a single individual, who can cause great havoc whilst retaining the cloak of deniability. Cyber is now the fifth domain of warfare after land, sea, air and space and it is the only domain where significant damage can be caused without the use of bombs and rockets or other such destructive agents, that is, without the use of weapons that rely on kinetic energy.

Computers and information technology are powerful instruments and the basis of the internet. Today the internet has spread its tentacles worldwide. The introduction was humble but the progress has been epochal. The system received a fillip with the introduction of the World Wide Web that internet users are all too familiar with. The computers when combined with the internet spawned capabilities that quite literally altered our way of life in all its dimensions. The social media was also given a huge boost and we are only too well aware of the increasing power of social media.

It should have been expected that the internet powered world would not be allowed to have a smooth sailing. Soon computer freaks and hackers started to interfere in the functioning of what is proving to be a boon for mankind. Cyber defence and cyber offence techniques came into play and the dire process has accelerated with time. Thus the concept of cyber war was born and has already reached a level of maturity that is a matter of concern to all peace loving people. It is also interesting to note that the average time taken from the initiation of an attack to its detection is 205 days. Thus, there is inbuilt deniability and it is nearly impossible to pin point an attributable source. At the same time, public knowledge about the need for cybersecurity is rather low, in spite of the fact that cyber attacks could impact more people than any other form of attack apart from a nuclear attack.

In the recent past, attempts are being made to see if internet providers can defend themselves against an attack. The objective of the hackers seems to be to elicit the level of extant of defensive capability so that the internet can be targeted when ever required and disabled, to the extent that it can be done, at least temporarily. The plan is to use distributed denial of service (DDOS) by literally blasting very high levels of data on the site so that the site is saturated and the legitimate users are denied the use of the site. DDOS attempts to test capabilities, both offensive and defensive, continue apace and government agencies have to ensure that the internet has enough resilience to withstand the onslaught whenever it occurs. It is also on the cards that soon we will have deception techniques that rely on finesse rather than brute force to disable the internet. Data manipulations, data corruption, forging or altering documents to spread disinformation are some other evils that we have to contend with. That will compound the problem.

A question which comes up is that with the growing power of the internet, how is it that we are unable to stem the activities of the cyber criminals. The short answer is that in spite of having tremendous computer power that is now available, it is very difficult to keep track of or index all internet traffic. To put this point in the right perspective, as per the Cisco Visual Networking Index, by the end of 2016, it is estimated that the internet traffic will be 1.1 Zettabytes per year. One Zettabyte is the Arabic numeral one followed by 21 zeroes bytes. That is a huge size. It translates to internet traffic of 88.7 Exabytes per month, roughly 3 Exabytes per day, 125 petabytes per hour and 34.7 terabytes per second. These are mere statistics till it is appreciated that one terabyte is the equivalent of 4.5 million books of 200 pages each. The traffic every second is indeed very large and hard to imagine. Over and above this is the deep and dark digital ocean that cannot be accessed by conventional search engines. Such sites are used by the crooks of the world involved in all types of unsavoury activities. It is in everyone's interest, other than that of the criminals, to combat the vast den of illegal activities but so far little headway has been made. Admittedly the resources of the state are far greater but they have to be appropriately channelised. As the criminals have a global footprint, the international community should have joined hands but such unanimity is likely, if at all, only when the situation becomes far more dangerous than it is at present.

Terrorists have spread their tentacles far and wide and have now graduated to cyber terrorism. Terrorists need little infrastructure. They can operate from the comfort of an arm chair and from any location. They have anonymity and deniability on their side and secrecy is inbuilt. The global terror outfits have used all these advantages that accrue to them. That is the power of the internet. The terrorists can collect and collate information, discuss amongst one another, convey instructions, receive feedbacks and all this and more in total secrecy. They can also infiltrate on other websites to steal or amend information, and spread disinformation. Much worse, they can use and misuse the power of the social media. The state machinery is at a distinct disadvantage as cyber terrorism is far easier to prosecute than combating such terrorism. The state agencies must try harder and think of innovative approaches not only to contain this menace but also to be proactive. There are no easy answers but the quest for answers must gather pace.

China has the maximum internet users and the state ensures strict censorship to maintain surveillance on its own citizens. The internet is studiously monitored and the state controls the internet gateways. There are established rules on the use of the internet and they are implemented with very low tolerance. That is to be expected in a regime such as China. Firewalls are also used to its advantage and, apparently, the efforts have been quite successful. It is generally believed that China is actively pursuing the preparation for cyber war in its many dimensions. Hacking and breaking into websites and networks are apparently practiced regularly and with some success. The 'targets' have to find ways to deter such Chinese designs.

The US is the world leader in technology and the internet was born and nurtured in that country. The US is likely to remain the leader in the field and continues to govern the laws relating to the use of the internet either directly or indirectly. It is the global hub of internet traffic. One would assume that under such circumstances the US would have good defences against cyber attacks but successful hacking into US Government and other sites have occurred. No one can really claim to be immune from cyber attacks. Yet even though there are many instances of cyber attacks against the US, so far there has not been any really debilitating cyber strike. Is it because the attacks so far made have been mere probes or because the expertise of the attackers has not matured enough? The answer is elusive. The book gives a number of examples of cyber war and seen in totality they represent the state of the art at present.

India has the third largest number of internet users after China and US. Justifiably, it is considered as an IT superpower. We can be proud of our world renowned Information and Communication Technology industry. Yet we are amongst the most targeted countries as well. All types of cyber attacks are launched against our computers and communication networks. The US says that we are the 5th most snooped country. It is a dubious distinction that is quite avoidable. We have established necessary infrastructure to combat the menace but need more safeguards. Possibly we also need more committed people, more experts on cyber security and better training systems. Above all, we probably need an overarching strategy for cyber space.

Cyberspace remains largely unregulated. It is difficult to recommend enforceable and actionable regulations that will find favour with the international community. Cyber governance on a global platform is a subject of continued discussion in different fora but with little outcome. It is unlikely that such efforts will lead to the desired results in the near future. Hence we have to fend for ourselves. Any system for effective monitoring is likely to be intrusive and privacy issues will be involved but we have to sacrifice something for the national good. Internet traffic can only increase and, in time, we may need to have a cyber police force. If that is considered likely, it will be advantageous if we were to get off the block early and start thinking about it. Again, as a country our talents in the field of software are well recognised but not so in the hardware field. We need to correct that imbalance as danger often lurks in the hardware we import.

The subject is far too important and we should give it the attention it deserves. The starting point must be a basic knowledge on the subject. This book satisfies that need and more. Dilipraj has done extensive research and has written it in an easy to comprehend language. Many interesting details are mentioned and that makes for good reading whilst satisfying the major requirement of making the reader familiar with a topic that can only gain importance with time. I commend the book for the lay reader as well as the professional practitioners who will have to face the scourge of cyber attacks. Most importantly, the book should help the reader view the cyber world as less of an enigma.

Air Mshl **Vinod Patney** SYSM PVSM AVSM VrC (Retd)
Director General
Centre for Air Power Studies, New Delhi

UNDERSTANDING
THE CYBER WORLD

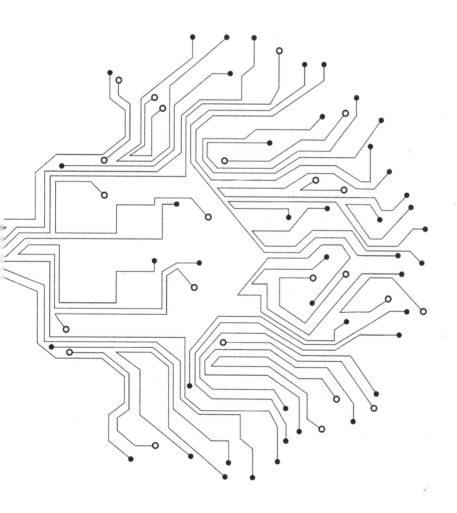

Throughout the history of mankind, no invention or discovery has been as irrepressible with regard to the nature of influence as cyber technology in the rapidly changing but in a more progressive atmosphere. Many inventions and discoveries from the ancient period since the stone age such as the discovery of the use of fire, invention of bow and arrow, invention of wheel and, in later centuries, the discovery of new continents , oil fields, and in recent times the invention of aircrafts, technology for dropping bombs/ missiles and rockets including invention of nuclear bombs, have all revolutionised the capability of humanity in various aspects and has contributed immensely in the evolution of the human race. However, cyber technology which was developed only in the later part of 20th century has rapidly penetrated into all walks of life and has become an indispensible part of human life throughout the world.

Computer technology along with high-end technologies such as personal computers, networking, internet, mobile phones, etc. have succeeded in establishing a gigantic virtual space within the real world. It is popularly referred to as the cyber world. This cyber world is expanding at an exponential rate with more and more new users being attracted to it for various reasons. Hence, due to the ever growing popularity, this domain ultimately has become an all pervasive medium for communication and connecting everyone around the world. Therefore, it is natural , that such an essential technology and network where the interests of a number of players are divergent and inconsistent with one another, is bound to face numerous conflicts with varying intensities that could result in serious repercussions in society in the real world. Hence, there is a pressing need to understand the cyber world in general and the various conflicts taking place in that sphere in particular, in order to facilitate, secure and refurbish the domain to be free of major conflicts at least in the future so that the human race would be able to depend on it more 'safely' than ever before.

In order to gain a better understanding of the growing relevance of cyber space to humanity in the present and future, this chapter introduces the cyber world by briefly looking into the evolution of cyber as a domain of conflict and warfare.

Evolution of Warfare

Evolution, the key for survival of mankind has never been without complexities and conflicts. A number of wars have taken place from time to time around the globe, fought by mankind for various reasons, but the mediums/domains in which these wars were fought varied from time to time depending upon the capability possessed by the human race at that particular period of time. In fact, conflicts have been one of the key factors that enabled mankind to evolve in thousands of years of existence in this world. These conflicts range from intra-personal, inter-personal, societal, intra-regional, inter-regional, intra-state, inter-state conflicts and so on. While all conflicts need not lead to a battle between the conflicting parties, the ones that do lead result in a catastrophe to either of the parties or to both in most cases.

Elaborating further on the after effects of conflicts it may be stated that a small scale conflict may not impact humanity as a whole, but conflicts fought on a large scale, usually involving two or more states and termed as 'Wars', might result in altering the future of mankind. In fact, human beings have been indulging in wars for centuries and the major reasons resulting in such wars could be invasion, colonisation, accession and/or conquering of land which was the most contested factor. Water bodies too, like rivers, seas and oceans, became the second domain for indulging in warfare when naval capabilities were developed way back in 3000 BC[1] or even before. It remained that way for centuries and several wars were fought across the world along these two domains with the objective to prove their supremacy in strategy from time to time. The never satisfying need to dominate and to have access to land and water led to major developments in the methods of fighting a war, type of weapons and tactics used during the land and naval warfare. However, there had been no drastic change in the domain of warfare itself until the early 20th century.

Invention of aircraft led to the opening of a new domain for warfare in air. Credited to have been invented by the Wright brothers with the successful test flight on December 17, 1903,[2] planes dominated in war and changed the whole scenario of warfare. It was utilised effectively during the 'Great War' or 'First World War (1914-1918)' in which aircrafts were used to drop troops or weapons. The countries in possession of aircrafts proved its effectiveness in several ways during aerial combat.[3] Eventually, with the aid of rapid advancement in aircraft technology, air power was used extensively during the 'Second World War', and it became the first big war covering the three domains - land, water and air. They were equally made use of for fighting between the armed forces of Allied and Axis Powers around the world.

Emergence of the Fourth Domain of Warfare

During the Second World War Germany, under the Nazis, developed and used rocket technology to drop bombs or missiles, using its V1 and successful V2 missiles.[4] After the victory of the Allies in the Second World War, the world witnessed the emergence of two Super Power Blocs led by USA and USSR. In spite of the fact that these two countries were allies during the war, they not only started having differences mainly on ideological issues but also had a lot of hostility and suspicion. They were keen to maintain *status quo* and fought many proxy wars at the cost of small and weak states and tried to establish one's superiority over the other by stockpiling nuclear weapons and deploying different kinds of missiles of various ranges apart from other conventional weapons deployed on land, in water and in air. They, thus, maintained power equilibrium between the two in the tri-domain warfare theatre and at the same time searched for ways and means to dominate the other.

This search during the 'Cold War' phase, led to the emergence of a new domain of warfare in the high-ground i.e. outer space, as a result of the growing capabilities to reach space by the two Power Blocs of the world. The USSR initially succeeded in the space race and went a step ahead of the USA with the successful launch of "Sputnik 1" satellite into space on October 04, 1957[5], thereby stimulating a burning desire for space exploration. Thus, the space race between the two World Powers began and escalated when the Soviets again successfully launched "Sputnik 2", this time with a living entity *"Laika"*, a dog, onboard the vessel into space on November 03, 1957.[6] The Americans on the other hand failed in their first attempt to launch their rocket named "Vanguard" on December 06, 1957. The Soviets were well ahead in the race in spite of the fact that Americans had the advantage of having a large number of German Rocket Scientists including Wernher von Braun with them who was the master mind of the Nazi Germany's Missile Programmes.[7] After almost a whole decade of trailing behind the Soviets, Americans finally got their opportunity to move ahead in the race when they successfully made their first manned mission to the Moon on July 20, 1969[8].

After a few years, space race between the two world powers began to dwindle due to various reasons ranging from requirements of huge financial investments for such projects, realisation of the need for cooperation than competition between countries, signing of various peace treaties between them and most importantly the emergence of USA as a single dominant power post Soviet disintegration. Although the space race did not lead to any direct confrontation between the two World Powers yet it led to awareness about the importance of space in the future years. This realisation also led to the development of interest in exploration of space domain among other countries that viewed space exploration as a matter of national pride and wanted to achieve a higher position in global order. Therefore, many countries began projects on space exploration and a few countries like India and China achieved a considerable success in this area.

The aspiration to conquer high grounds always existed not only among the two World Powers but also with other countries who worked with enthusiasm with the objective to achieve a superior position in the space domain. The advancement in this domain has not only led to enhancement of the technology used in the manufacture of missiles, aircrafts, air defence and missile defence technologies but also led to the development of space based weapon systems by countries like the USA, Russia and China, which has further widened the domain of space war. The catalogue of space weapon systems includes Anti-Satellite Missiles (ASAT) capability, Tactical High Energy Lasers, ICBMs, Orbital Re-entry Vehicles, and High-Altitude Weapons causing Electro Magnetic

Radiations. With these weapons already in operational stage and more projects being in various testing and development stages, it is an undeniable fact that space has become the fourth domain of warfare.

Evolution of the Fifth Domain of Warfare

While the four domains of warfare– land, water, air and space– were conceived exclusively for the purpose of warfare since the beginning, the field of cyber becoming the fifth domain of warfare cannot be ruled out. The capability to communicate and calculate has always been a distinctive factor which could differentiate mankind from other living entities on this planet. Apart from this, mankind by nature has the ability to invent new products and develop new technologies in all fields and it has remained consistent all through the evolution process. The desire for consistent innovation in the field of communications and calculation resulted in the development of computers and its related technologies. In view of the enormous interests in this field, funding dedicated to the development of computer and networking technology were made available by several players including military and private sector, and as a result it grew in a massive way within few decades of its emergence. Simultaneously, the concept of global networking of computers achieved through 'internet technology', combined with the widespread use of computers around the world, revolutionised the global communication system. Furthermore, a variety of services were offered through the internet and development of technology in the field of computers from personal computers, laptops, and palm tops led to a rapid growth in the number of users. This led to enormous increase in dependency on this all pervasive technology for all purposes. But it should be noted here that neither the computer and its related technologies nor internet were conceived with an aim to grow so big and confront so many security challenges during their developmental phases.

With the success of computers and commercialisation of internet in early 1990s, the usage of this all-encompassing technology increased radically as the preferred means for computing, data sharing and communication. Moreover, the invention of new portable devices like laptops and mobile phones has created a world of nomadic computing and communications systems. With billions of users and devices connected to one another along with billions of Giga Bytes (GB) of information stored, processed and shared in the networks, it can be said that mankind has succeeded in creating a 'Virtual World' with the help of computers, internet and other networks around the world. But this virtual world which is also known as the 'Cyber World' is the most vulnerable location for the new age conflicts which will not only affect the cyber environment but will also ruin the real world, depending on the magnitude of the conflict.

One important fact to be kept in view is that unlike the four domains of warfare where armed units or weapon systems are deployed to conduct warfare, the cyber domain just requires one individual with a computer and a sound knowledge of the cyber technology to cause enormous damage and loss to anyone. In other words the fifth domain of warfare enables individuals to become warriors even while enjoying the comfort of their homes/offices. This scenario appears more complex in view of the fact that this technology is open to all and anyone with the intention and capacity can start a cyber conflict to put forward his/her own interests. Therefore, the question before us is— how does a conflict in the cyber world affect the real world? In order to understand this and also to know why understanding cyber technology is very important for the safety and security of the real world, one has to understand how the real world is dependent on the cyber world.

Before the advent of computers, everyday work was being carried out either manually or with the help of multiple devices designed for specific purposes like abacus, calculators, typewriters, telegraphic machines, telephones, radios, etc. Moreover, where sensitive information was to be shared like in military, they followed its own reticent methods like encrypted letters, coded languages, Morse codes, dedicated radio frequencies and other conventional methods of information sharing. The military equipments and weapon systems were stand alone devices and did not have facility for networking. The weapon systems were operated manually, which not only required huge manpower but also consumed more time.

But the introduction of the computers and networking technology on commercial basis changed the whole scenario as it enabled to club all activities of calculations, computing and communications on one platform along with other activities such as knowledge gathering, data storage, information processing, and entertainment. The commercialisation of internet virtually reduced the size of the world and made it within the reach of one's finger tip through services varying from emails, websites, blogs, live chats, forums, file sharing, music and video streaming and more recently in connecting people across the globe through online social networking sites. With more and more services offered through the internet which help in easy communications and perform other functions is resulting in more and more users to adopt this technology every day. With the use of mobile communication equipments like laptops, cellular phones connected to the internet, this nomadic communication network has seen a major increase. With more than 3.4 billion users worldwide, internet is the biggest network in the world where enormous quantum of information is being stored, processed and shared, thereby becoming a vulnerable target for any cyber attack.

Computer and its related technologies made quick inroads into the sensitive sectors like banking, military, e-governance, nuclear, industrial and manufacturing establishments of countries and are offering a wide variety of services. These critical establishments, which form the backbone and are responsible for stability, satisfactory functioning and development of any country, are known as National Critical Information Infrastructure (NCII) and in recent years most of these NCIIs are completely relying on cyber technology for efficient functioning. More specifically, the Supervisory Control and Data Acquisition (SCADA)[9] systems and other industrial control systems used in almost all the NCIIs and industrial sectors, totally rely on cyber technology.

In fact, it is these SCADA systems which face the maximum threat in the cyber world. For instance, the STUXNET malware coding - allegedly to have been jointly developed by the US and Israel for targeting the nuclear establishments of Iran successfully disrupted the nuclear development program of Iran causing serious damage to the centrifuges in the Natanz Nuclear Enrichment Plant and delayed the whole process of Iran's Nuclear Development Programme.[10] This case is proof for the magnitude of damage that can be inflicted by a highly organised cyber attack on any country's NCII. Apart from these, almost all advanced military hardware like satellites, aircrafts, missiles, missile defence systems, ships, tanks, various radars, sensors, seekers and other detecting devices use cyber technology to enable it to function and communicate with one another thus forming a military network of devices for Network Centric Warfare capability. While such a holistic defence system is essential for any ambitious country, the fact is that all these devices and weapon systems which have different roles to play in their respective domains of warfare rely on cyber technology for their connectivity, communications, coordination, command, control and operations. This makes them vulnerable and disruptions in any area would affect the comprehensive warfare capability of the country in all its domains.

Therefore, a technology which was developed with the objective to enable mankind, save time and energy and to upgrade means of communications and computing has grown so huge in size and number, has influenced so deeply into the lifestyle of humans, that it has not only ended up in creating a virtual world but also opened a new front/domain of warfare.

Conflicts in the Cyber World

Mankind has developed military capabilities to defend its interests and to face threats making use of appropriate technologies available at that time; in the land in which we live, water ways and air which we use for transport and or even to fly to space beyond the planet. But this was not the case in respect of the cyber world as it was never conceived until recently as a domain of warfare. The cyber world remains vulnerable to various forms of conflicts within its sphere due to clash of interests between various groups involved in it and also due to lack of proper security mechanisms to safeguard the resources in this domain.

The cyber conflicts are categorised on the basis of the magnitude of the effects and the players involved in such attacks, which is similar to the categorisation done in respect of conventional warfare. For instance, in general, when there is a cyber conflict between two states or more, then the conflict is termed as cyber war, whereas, a similar conflict between a state and a non state actor/group is termed as cyber attack. The attempt of an individual to exploit a cyber infrastructure for personal financial gains is called as cyber crime but if the same individual or a group either representing a state or acting as non-state actor aims at exploiting the cyber infrastructure of a country's critical infrastructure then the act is categorised as cyber terrorism. However, there is always some ambiguity in defining any cyber conflict as there are no generally accepted definitions for these conflicts around the world and hence a cyber attack may be considered as a cyber war or even cyber terrorism depending on the interest/intention of the parties involved in it. Nevertheless in order to attain a basic understanding of these terminologies, a few working definitions are given below:

Richard A. Clarke, U.S. Government Security Expert, in his book "*Cyber War*" (May 2010), defines "cyber warfare" as:

> "*actions by a nation-state to penetrate another nation's computers or networks for the purposes of causing damage or disruption.*"[11]

And in 2004, Keith Lourdeau, the then FBI Deputy Assistant Director, Cyber Division, defined "cyber terrorism" in his testimony, in a Hearing on *Cyber Terrorism* before the Senate Judiciary Subcommittee on Terrorism, Technology, and Homeland Security as:

> "*a criminal act perpetrated by the use of computers and telecommunications capabilities, resulting in violence, destruction and/or disruption of services, where the intended purpose is to create fear by causing confusion and uncertainty within a given population, with the goal of influencing a government or population to conform to a particular political, social or ideological agenda.*"[12]

Generally cyber terrorism is misinterpreted as a cyber attack by terrorist organisations and the above definition proves that the general understanding is inaccurate in this regard but it also widens the scope of the definition. In other words, cyber terrorism is not only the act by conventional terrorists in the cyber world but a cyber operation by anybody ranging from an individual to a state with the intention of causing fear or terror on its target's cyber space and it can be termed as an act of cyber terrorism.

Similar to cyber warfare and cyber terrorism, the term cyber crime is also a term, which is ambiguous and difficult to define. However, there are a number of definitions around the term and some of the terms being used to define cyber crime include information offences, computer-related crimes, and computer crimes. But there is no one accepted definition for the term cyber crime. However, the UNDOC (United Nations Office on Drugs and Crime), report on cyber crime of the year 2013 elucidates various acts, which constitute Cyber Crime and could be used as template:

According to that report a cyber activity would be considered as "cyber crime" if it constitutes the following acts:

- *"Acts against the confidentiality, integrity and availability of computer data or systems like illegal access to a computer system, illegal access, interception or acquisition of computer data, illegal interference with a computer system or computer data, production, distribution or possession of computer misuse tools, breach of privacy or data protection measures.*
- *Acts related to computer for personal or financial gain or harm like computer related fraud or forgery, computer related identity offences, computer related copyright or trademark offences, sending or controlling sending of spam, computer related acts causing personal harm, computer related solicitation or 'grooming' of children.*
- *Acts related to computer content like acts involving computer related hate speech, computer related production, distribution or possession of child pornography, computer related acts in support of terrorism offences."[13]*

As evident, there is a lot of confusion in the mere definition of various forms of cyber conflicts, it becomes difficult for law enforcement agencies to identify and prosecute any such activity in the cyber arena. This also results in problems and frustration for law makers and policy makers of a state who are required to formulate appropriate policies and laws to secure their cyber space. As a result, cyber policies and cyber laws adopted by most states are vague. The gap between the rapidly advancing technologies in the cyber domain and the inadequate capability of the judicial and law enforcing agencies for one reason or the other is skilfully exploited and manipulated by the perpetrators of cyber attacks. This is one of the motivating factors for increase in the number of cyber incidences around the world and the prevailing persistent cyber threat.

With regard to cyber incidences and cyber threats, it often raises a question in one's mind as to who is responsible for such activities or in simple terms who are the perpetrators. As mentioned earlier, anybody with the intention and technological capabilities can cause a destructive cyber attack irrespective of whether it is an individual or a group or even if a state is involved. Therefore, the perpetrators of a cyber attack can be a state, an organisation, a group of people known or unknown to each other or even an individual. If a state conducts an openly declared cyber attack against another state, then it can be categorised as a cyber war and an act of war in general will be handled by the cyber security personnel of the state, including the conventional armed forces, but such an event is a rare case scenario. In reality, all cyber activities are conducted in stealth mode irrespective of its perpetrators by concealing their identity facilitated by the technology which makes it difficult to identify the source of threats in the cyber realm. Different players make use of technology for different purposes but end up terrorising the cyber world. Citing some of the examples as to how different players in the cyber arena use covert means to terrorise are given below:

- Countries use cyber technology to conduct cyber skirmishes and sabotage, cyber surveillance and espionage, cyber propaganda and psychological operations.

- Non-state actors/ terrorists use cyber technology for covert communications, coordination and planning of terror attacks, propaganda, training, recruitment etc.
- Multinational business organisations use this technology for their motivated false propaganda and, to conduct espionage on the activities of their rivals.
- Individuals and small groups of people use this technology with the objective to make financial gains through cyber crime, to sabotage rivals, to fight covertly against a bigger adversary and sometimes for fun.

Apart from these persistent cyber threats from different players, there are also other threats like rampant spread of malwares and existence of cyber weapons, existence of secret locations like dark web which is also known as the underworld of the cyber space– which are causing huge adverse impact on cyber security and global security on the whole. Thus, it would be prudent and absolutely necessary to understand the different kinds of cyber security threats caused by several players and the threats which exist by design, in order to enable one to effectively tackle and overcome these risks at least in the future.

Therefore, the subsequent chapters of the book would dwell in detail about the various cyber security threats which are caused by the different players like hackers, non-state actors/ terrorists, nation-states, and also analyse the kind of security risks that exist in the form of deep and dark web. Before summarising the findings and analyse what could be the strategy to be followed in the cyber world in the coming future, one of the chapters would discuss in detail about India's engagement with the cyber world and analyse its experience starting from the history to the current scenario in the country related to cyber sector.

Notes

1. "History of Boats and Ships", in http://www.historyworld.net/wrldhis/plaintexthistories.asp?historyid=aa14, accessed on September 08, 2012.
2. "The Road to Kitty Hawk", in http://www.wright-brothers.org/History_Wing/History_of_the_Airplane/Century_Before/Road_to_Kitty_Hawk/Road_to_Kitty_Hawk.htm, accessed on September 09, 2012.

3. Cox, Sebastian and Gray, Peter, "*Air Power History: Turning points from Kitty Hawk to Kosovo*", Frank Cass Publications, 2002.

4. "Guided Missiles", *Popular Science and Technology Series*, Defence Research and Development Organisation, 1990.

5. "A Brief History of Space Exploration", http://www.aerospace.org/education/inspiring-the-next-generation/space-primer/a-brief-history-of-space-exploration/, accessed on September 10, 2012.

6. "Animals as cold warriors: Missiles, Medicine and Man's best friend", in http://www.nlm.nih.gov/exhibition/animals/laika.html, accessed on September 11, 2012.

7. "Dr. Wernher von Braun", MSFC History Office, NASA, https://history.msfc.nasa.gov/vonbraun/bio.html, accessed on September 11, 2012.

8. "Moon Landing", in http://en.wikipedia.org/wiki/Moon_landing, accessed on September 12, 2012.

9. SCADA (supervisory control and data acquisition) is an industrial control system at the core of many modern industries such as manufacturing, energy, water, power, transportation and many more. SCADA systems deploy multiple technologies that allow organizations to monitor, gather, and process data as well as send commands to those points that are transmitting data. SCADA systems range from simple configurations to large, complex projects. Most SCADA systems utilize HMI (human-machine interface) software that allows users to interact with and control the machines and devices that the HMI is connected to such as valves, pumps, motors, and much more. SCADA software receives its information from RTUs (remote terminal units) or PLCs (programmable logic controllers) which can receive their information from sensors or manually inputted values. From here, the data can be used to effectively monitor, collect and analyze data, which can potentially reduce waste and improve efficiency resulting in savings of both time and money.

10. Mueller, Paul and Yadegari, Babak. "The Stuxnet Worm", The University of Arizona, 2012.

11. Richard A. Clarke and Robert A. Knake , "*Cyber War – The Next Threat to National Security and What to do about it?*", (Harper Collins, 2010).

12. Hearing before U.S. Senate Judiciary Subcommittee on Terrorism, Technology, and Homeland Security on February 24, 2004) (Statement of Keith Lourdeau, FBI Deputy Assistant Director, Cyber Division).

13. "Comprehensive Study on Cybercrime", *Report by United Nations Office on Drugs and Crime*, 2013, Vienna.

2

THE ART OF PHREAKING, HACKING, CRACKING…

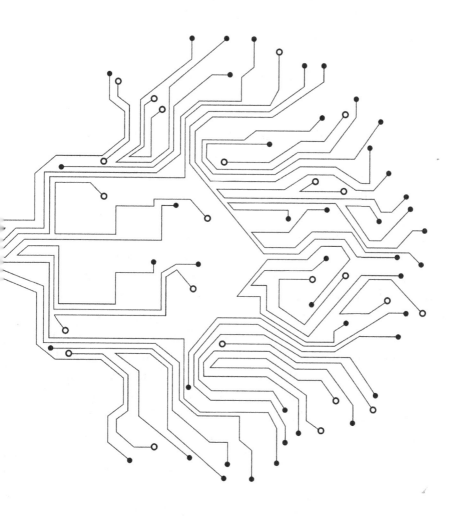

The previous chapter dealt about the basics and the evolution of cyber as a domain of conflict. The current chapter would analyse the evolution and growth of hackers as a subculture within the global society especially among the cyber community. The analysis in this chapter would begin with the history of hacking and cover the various phases of evolution of this art over the years. This would be followed by a case study of a series of hacking incidents involving India and Pakistan and conclude highlighting a few pointers with a view to bring the hackers into the mainstream environment.

During the process of evolution and development of mankind, the natural feeling of curiosity has played a major role in advancing the process of development through a step by step process. This fact was also elucidated by Walt Disney, one of the most creative minds the world has seen, when he said that:

"We keep moving forward, opening new doors, and doing new things, because we're curious and curiosity keeps leading us down new paths."

It is the curiosity of mankind and the burning desire to bring consistent improvements in their lives which have led to inventions and discoveries based on their needs from time to time. As a result of this, mankind today stands in a much more technologically evolved and advanced stage of development. Even otherwise, all human beings have a natural habit filled with curiosity to study, learn, understand, explore, discover, or invent anything new to improve their lives whatever might be their field of interest. Any new product which is the outcome of thinking and the research carried out by curious minds, opens up new possibilities for further exploration – a process which forms a chain reaction. One example of such an outcome is the rapid development of telecommunication technology which has revolutionised the world since its introduction and enabled to connect with each other easily.

The telecommunication technology has undergone massive upgradation beyond recognition in a short span, as a result of research carried out by enthusiastic minds who wanted to consistently improve the mode of communication. When the telecommunication networks were established and made operational, efforts were made by techno-savvy individuals and engineers in the telecommunication and related fields around the world to explore this new technology, albeit with varying intentions. Such explorations into this highly technological and complex field of virtual networks led to the creation of 'hackers' and several 'hacking' incidents Although the terms hacking and hackers have acquired a negative connotation over a period of time due to various reasons, it was not the case when it all began.

Tracing the History

It is well known that the United States of America is the most advanced country in regard to modern technology, especially after the World War II. Before the introduction of computer networks and the establishment of global internet, people were using another network, which was globally connected and fully operational – the telephone network. The network of telephone connections was in fact the first 'real-time' global communication system which was available for commercial purposes. The fact that modern technology was associated with this complex network had intrigued many curious 'techno-freak' minds in the society who wanted to understand the system, an aspect which can be attributed to the basic human tendency to explore. This led to the development of many methods and tricks to play around with the telephone network, though nobody knows or could be certain as to when or who started it, but apparently it was in the late 1960s. This routine of meddling with the telephone network or exploiting the technical loopholes in the telephone network is recognised as 'Phreaking'.

Phreaking

An act which was started for fun, gradually became a hobby for those interested in tampering telephone networks or in general modern technology. A famous phone phreak 'Mark Bernay', explains about the thrill he was getting while doing such things: "the kick was to find out how to beat the system, how to get at things one was not supposed to know , how to do things with the system that one was not supposed to be able to do."[1] As the number of the phone phreak enthusiasts expanded, they started to discuss and share new techniques that would emerge from time to time with other groups across the country by making free phone calls using various methods of phreaking. Thus, over a period of time, underground syndicates of phone phreaks also came into existence which started working to put forward their economic interests.

The fundamental idea for any phone phreak was to develop new methods to make free calls (irrespective of whether it is a privately owned phone or a public pay phone) by somehow evading the system set up by the companies managing the telecommunication network. Phone phreaks with higher technological capabilities were able to do much more than making free calls. For instance, a famous phone phreak John Draper aka *Captain Crunch* was able to "send his voice around the world and for this purpose, he sent his voice towards east from one phone using satellite facilities, and simultaneously sent his voice towards west through cable and established communication around the world when both the phones rang simultaneously and on picking them up he heard his own voice which travelled both ways around the world from his location and came back to himself."[2] This may not amuse many, as many of us in our childhood would have tried and succeeded to make call from one phone to the other phone in the same room using that particular telephone network, but the method used by *Captain Crunch* to make such calls was the most important aspect as he did not use the dial pad on either of the phones to make the calls and he was also able to route his calls, one through the cables and the other through satellite without any assistance from the phone companies.

The phone phreaks employed many methods to carry out their act of phreaking such as whistling, using specially engineered devices/boxes, methods like loop-arounds, etc. Among all, the first and most interesting method used was whistling into the mouthpiece of a telephone to make free calls. Joe Engressia aka *Jollybubble* who was visually challenged, was considered by the phone phreaking community as the prime mover in this trade, as he was the first person to discover that by whistling the required quality of sound at the right frequency into the phone's mouthpiece could enable one to make free calls. Even though this was becoming a popular method among the phone phreak enthusiasts, it remained hard for them to determine the right frequency for manual whistling. At that time John Draper aka *Captain Crunch* came to the rescue of phone phreaks by discovering that a toy whistle which was being given as a freebie along with 'Captain Crunch' cereal packet had the proper pitch of 2600Hz – the frequency which was needed to phreak the telephone sets. He had not only found the right whistles, but also annexed the name of the product as his pseudonym.

Figure 2.1: Cap'n Crunch Whistle

Source: http://sites.psu.edu/thedeepweb/2015/09/17/captain-crunch-and-his-toy-whistle/. Accessed on February 11, 2016.

Another popular method used for phone phreaking was loop-around which was mainly popularised by the phone phreak Mark Bernay. In simple terms a loop-around is the unauthorised utilisation of a test circuit which has two phones at different terminals that was set up by the phone company to test their circuit line to remote offices without any need for a person to be present at the other terminal. The phone phreaks exploited this facility meant for testing and began to use these lines as party lines, chat rooms or for alternate phone number.[3]

However, the golden age of phone phreaking began after the invention of 'Blue Box in the late 1960s. It was a cleverly engineered device which can be utilised to trick the phone company's long distance switching systems to allow the Blue Box user to make free long distance calls. According to Ron Rosenbaum, the author of the first article that exposed Blue Box to the general public, Al Gilbertson (not real name) is credited to have invented that device.[4] The blue box, at times also referred as M-F-ers, is a multi-frequency device. At a time when long distance calls were too expensive, this phone phreaking device became an immediate hit among the phone phreaking enthusiasts. In the 1970s and 80s many such devices like the Blue Box were invented by phone phreaks with different features. [See Appendix 1 for the list of devices and its features].

While phreaking remained a widespread hobby among the technical enthusiasts, the fact that such a technology exists to evade the telephone systems attracted many underground groups towards the phone phreaks. The technical expertise of many phone phreaks was used by underground groups and drug cartels to make sure that their illegal activities remain untraceable. It is reported that a Las Vegas syndicate ordered a thousand beeper boxes to enable them to keep the lines open for them for hours from coast to coast to place bets, which would be expensive otherwise if they had to pay for the calls. At times, phone phreaks would even get bulk orders for Blue Boxes worth US$300,000 from such underground groups.[5]

A few phone phreaks, who were attracted by the money involved in it, helped the underground groups. A few others, who were aware of the illegality and legal repercussions stayed away from such illegal activities. The telephone companies like Ma Bell and AT&T were aware of the illegal activities of phone phreaks and the consequent loss in revenue. Companies in association with the law enforcement agencies nabbed phone phreaks from time to time who indulged in illegal activities. It was a cat and mouse game. A few other phone phreaks who were attracted towards the technological aspect alone involved in the trade kept on exploring more new technologies as and when they were introduced. One such fascinating technological product which was introduced in the 1970s was the technology for data processors/ computers.

Although the initial models of computers in the 1970s were not user friendly as it is today, the scope about their tremendous potential in several fields attracted techno-freaks towards these devices. They developed interests to explore these devices and look for ways to tamper with them. Even the famous phone phreaks like Mark Barney and Al Gilbertson started meddling with the computers and they found that it perfectly suited to carry on their trade. In fact, the feeling of attraction for a techno-freak to tamper was not limited to a particular device/system like the telephone and its network, but on all automatic electronic equipments. Berney had once quoted about his fascination towards playing with automatic electronic equipments as: "*there are lots of things you can play with. Things break down in interesting ways.*"[6] The sense of curiosity and attraction to explore the computer technology, which was considered to be the technology of the future, brought not only the phone phreaks but also many others into the world of 'computer freaking'.

Computer Freaking

As computers became an enigma among techno-freaks, everybody was interested to either explore or exploit this modern machine and understand its functioning. The meddling with the early day computers by techno-freaks was known as computer freaking and it attracted more people. As computers were not easily available in the 1970s, a group of computer enthusiasts would gather in a common place, mostly in a garage, to meddle with the computer device that they would have to acquire somehow. As the number of enthusiasts grew, few computer freaks organised a bigger gathering of fellow computer freaks on March 05, 1975 and that convention was called "Home Brew Computer Club".[7]

Figure 2.2: Invitation poster for the first Homebrew Computer Club meeting

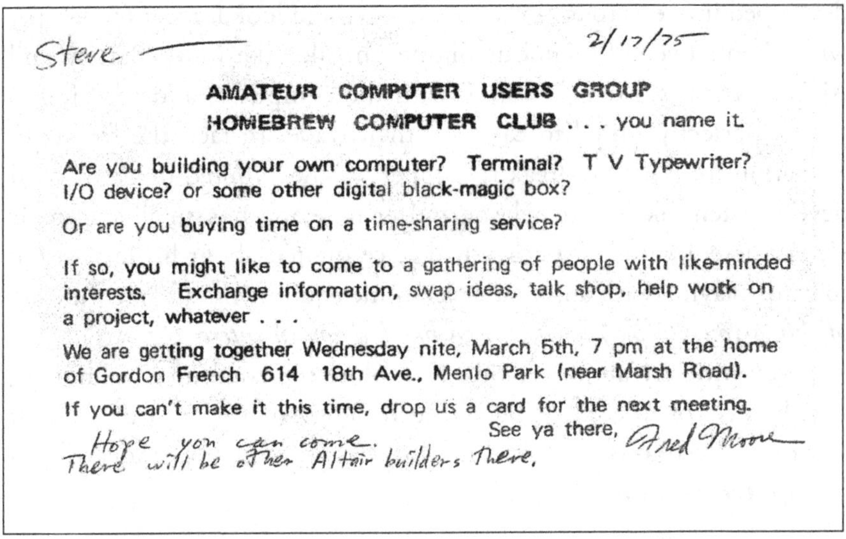

Steve —

2/17/75

AMATEUR COMPUTER USERS GROUP

HOMEBREW COMPUTER CLUB . . . you name it.

Are you building your own computer? Terminal? T V Typewriter? I/O device? or some other digital black-magic box?

Or are you buying time on a time-sharing service?

If so, you might like to come to a gathering of people with like-minded interests. Exchange information, swap ideas, talk shop, help work on a project, whatever . . .

We are getting together Wednesday nite, March 5th, 7 pm at the home of Gordon French 614 18th Ave., Menlo Park (near Marsh Road).

If you can't make it this time, drop us a card for the next meeting.

See ya there, Fred Moore

Hope you can come. There will be other Altair builders there.

Source: https://en.wikipedia.org/wiki/Homebrew_Computer_Club. Accessed on February 23, 2016.

This club, during its existence till 1986, contributed immensely to the development of computer system and enabled the setting up of as many as 23 computer companies by the members of this club including 'Apple Computers', which was established jointly by Steve Wozniac and Steve Jobs, who were also members of this club.[8]

The different methods and techniques developed by the computer freaks to meddle with the computer devices and to customise the machine to suit their interest was called as "hack", a word or a jargon which emerged from the 'Tech Model Railroad Club' of Massachusetts Institute of Technology (MIT) in the 1960s. It was from this jargon, the words '**Hacking**' and '**Hacker**' emerged at a later stage and gained popularity through media.

Hacking

Throughout 1970s the act of computer freaking, which from now on would be addressed as hacking, spread and attracted a large number of techno-freaks, and as a result created a sort of sub-culture in the society which was popularly came to be known as 'Hackers' culture'. The hackers considered their culture as a counter-culture to that of the computer engineers who were professionally more sophisticated and had better resources. The development of personal computers by companies like IBM, Radio shack, etc. in early 1980s, gave a big boost to the activities of hackers as computers were available more easily to them and helped in the development of their skills and fulfilled their aspirations. The 1980s is reported to be the golden age of hacking because computers were no more a rare product. Apart from this, availability of devices like modems, which enabled computers to communicate using telephone lines, were widely available and significantly extended the reach of a hacker.[10]

A hacker spends a lot of time to understand how computer systems, including computer hardware, operating system software, application programs, and networks function. Hackers believe that it is essential to acquire knowledge about the systems – and about the world of computer – by dismantling the system to see how they work, and apply this knowledge to create new and even more interesting products or devices.[11] Hackers, by and large, are persons who learn themselves. Apart from this, there are also opportunities for sharing of information (development of new techniques and methods) amongst its community, which is evident from the various conventions beginning from Home Brew Computer Club to the 21st century hackers conferences like the DEFCON, ShmooCon, ToorCon, etc. Therefore, hackers are consider themselves as well as expected to be treated as the true native habitants of the cyber world.[12]

Although 1980s is known as the golden age of hacking, their image took a beating in view of their reported activities during the same period. To start with, a movie named 'Wargames' was released in theatres in 1983, which had a storyline about a teenage whiz kid from America who hacks the super computer of a nuclear missile base of the country and almost starts a global nuclear war. Though articles about hackers and their activities would appear in journals and magazines from time to time before the release of the movie, it did not have much of an impact as the number of readers who went through these articles was nothing as compared to the viewership of this movie. Apart from this, the visual impact of the movie created a sort of phobia in the minds of the general public towards the activities of hackers. After the release of the movie, more articles and news on hackers and hacking with adverse impact led to the negative image of hackers.

A hacker is defined as a person who enjoys exploring the details of programmable systems and finds appropriate methods to stretch their capabilities.[13] Hacking can be defined as the thrill of exploration and the excitement of learning how something works in order to modify or improve it.[14] However, due to the negative publicity through popular media and exaggeration of journalists about their activities, the definition of hacker underwent changes and he is described as an inquisitive malicious meddler of computers who tries to collect information by poking around. Such perception towards them was unacceptable to the traditional hackers who felt that traditional hacking is completely different from the widespread perception now existing in the minds of the people. Therefore, the hacking community came up with another jargon in 1985 known as '**Cracker**', which became acceptable after it was inducted in the 3rd edition of 'The New Hacker's Dictionary' edited by Eric S. Raymond.[15]

By definition, a Cracker is one who breaks the security of a system. This term was coined in 1985 by traditional hackers in their defence against the misuse of the term by journalists in a negative sense. While it is expected that any real hacker could have done some kind of cracking for the sake of it without any bad motives and came to know many of the basic techniques, anyone who passed the 'larval stage'[16] is expected to have outgrown the desire to do so except for immediate, benign, practical reasons (for example, if it's necessary to get around some security in order to get some work done). Practically, there is far less overlapping between the activities hacker and cracker contrary to the perception of general public who are being misled by sensational journalism.[17]

Cracking is the act of breaking into a computer system and that is what a cracker does. Contrary to widespread belief, this does not usually involve some mysterious leap of 'hackerly' brilliance, but require persistence and the dogged repetition of a handful of fairly well-known tricks that exploit common weaknesses in the security of target systems.[18]

Therefore, after realising the growth of the culture of hacking and cracking and anticipating its adverse impacts on the society in the future, the US government passed a law in the Congress which was known as the Computer Fraud and Abuse Act in 1986.[19]

Apart from this, in the late 1980s a philosophical divide started emerging within the hacking community itself as an increasing number of hackers were no longer satisfied with exploration of the systems merely to learn how they worked but wanted to use their skills for individual gain. This view was expressed by Kevin Mitnik, probably one of the most popular hacker, who stated that:

> *"Hackers are breaking the systems for profit. Before, it was about intellectual curiosity and pursuit of knowledge and thrill, and now hacking is big business..."*[20]

The factor which differentiated or was instrumental in creating the difference between traditional hackers and the new group of hackers which emerged was what the hackers refer to as "the hacker ethics". It is a loosely binding couple of ethical rules conceived by the early hackers in order to regulate their operations and to make sure that their activities do not cause damage to the computer resources. The hacker ethics are the following:

- The belief that information-sharing is a powerful positive good, and that it is an ethical duty of hackers to share their expertise by writing open-source code and facilitating access to information and to computing resources wherever possible.
- The belief that system-cracking for fun and exploration is ethically OK as long as the cracker commits no theft, vandalism, or breach of confidentiality.[21]

Both the ethical principles are widely, but not universally, accepted by hackers. Most hackers subscribe to the first hacker ethic and many act on it by writing and giving away open-source software. A few go further and assert that *all* information should be free and *any* proprietary control of it is bad, a philosophy which has created disputes between hackers and business oriented information companies and defenders of intellectual property rights. As regards the second it is more controversial as some people consider the act of cracking itself to be unethical, like breaking and entering. There are also some with the belief that 'ethical' cracking excludes destruction and at least moderates the behaviour of people who see themselves as `benign'/harmless crackers. Keeping this in view, it could be one of the highest forms of 'hackerly' courtesy to (a) break into a system, and then (b) explain to the concerned authorities about the vulnerability and exactly how it was done and how the hole can be plugged.[22] A widely followed practice which many hackers practice using various techniques like exploiting zero day vulnerabilities to hack into systems, networks and software and then report it back to the authorities in most cases for monetary benefits and in a few cases for nothing but for the sake of enhancing security. However, this aspect is again exploited by crackers, as many crack into the vulnerabilities existing in the systems and software only for their monetary and other gains rather than raising an alarm according to the hacker ethics.

There was an increasing number of new breed of unethical hackers or hackers with their own interpretation of ethics who were driven by self interest and monetary gains and directed their knowledge and skill towards illegal pursuits, including activities like distribution of pirated commercial software, games and malwares. During the period from late 1980s to 1990s, the hackers community started fragmenting based on their intentions, and like-minded hackers started forming separate groups which eventually led to the formation of 'electronic gangs' driven by their selfish interests.[23] Many such gangs which were motivated by economic and political interests started to use their skills to tap sensitive information stored in large institutions, like government departments, educational centres, banks, research facilities, etc. Eventually, as it happens with the regular gangs in the real world, it didn't take long for the gangs to fight amongst themselves which further escalated the fear and aversion towards hackers in the minds of the public as they witnessed disruption of phone networks and other public networks getting jammed from time to time. As a result, hacking too ventured into the murky path like phone phreaking.

In the 1990scomputers became a household device and with the commercialisation and spread of internet globally, leading to hacking becoming a global activity. Though hackers were active across the world even before the internet was established at the global level, the fact that internet provided connectivity and transfer of data in real-time and facilitated easy access to the hackers throughout the world. This also enabled them to make contact with their peers beyond the borders of states. As a result, all forms of hacking started to spread rapidly across the globe and it became a part of everyone's life as media reported instances about the disturbances the crackers had caused to the public through their actions like web defacements, denial of service, spreading malwares, stealing information, breaking into sensitive networks, and by conducting other forms of cyber attacks to promote their selfish interests.

Therefore, having understood the history of hacking and hackers themselves, it would be appropriate to classify hackers based on their intentions for hacking. The said classification of hackers is as follows:

Figure 2.3: Intent based Classification of Hackers

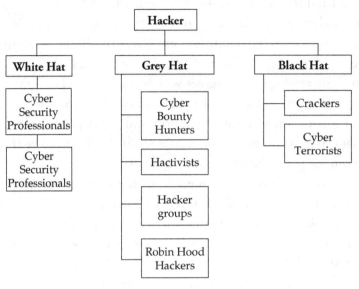

Source: Author's own.

It should also be noted here that for a hacker his/her skills in the trade is the most important asset and all hackers do not possess identical or similar level of skills in the trade and therefore, every hacker or a cracker cannot accomplish all the tasks he/she like to perform. Based on their level of skills, the hackers are generally classified between the two extremes of a script kiddie and an elite hacker.

A script kiddie is a cracker/ hacker at the lowest level with limited technical expertise using easy-to-operate, pre-configured, and/or automated tools to conduct disruptive activities against networked systems. They do mischief with scripts and programmes written by others, often without understanding the full details about the material they are using.[24] An elite hacker has a social status among hackers as he/she has higher skills in the trade and are capable of accomplishing highly complex hacking tasks. Elite hackers continue to maintain connections with their peers and any newly discovered exploits are circulated among this group of hackers/crackers.[25]

Hacking at present has become a problem which the global population has to contend with everyday, in the current globalised world. Hackers across the world operate and conduct their operations with different motives including vendetta, jokes/hoaxes/prank, terrorism, political and military espionage, monetary benefits, hate, etc. The law enforcement agencies on the other hand are in constant pursuit of the hackers with the objective to bring them before law. However, this cat and mouse game will continue despite implementation of strong legislations or even after establishment of several new security roadblocks to prevent hacking, as long as computers and technology driven communication systems is available for utilisation at our disposal. However, it is also in a way helping the evolution process of the domain as hackers push for new innovations while they exploit and devalue the older ones. Thus, the best way in this case is not to find ways to eliminate hacking rather to bring the hackers in to the mainstream and focus their energy and skill towards development.

Case Study: An Analysis of Hacking Incidents between India and Pakistan

In the wake of 21st century, the world of cyber began to spread its roots deep into the society and penetrated into the lives of the people so much so that the internet became an indispensable part of every citizens' life, thus, upgrading them to the status of 'netizens'. Moreover, technology in cyberspace gained dynamism, increasing the population of netizens. This became dexterously possible in cyberspace not because all the citizens became technically sound but mainly because the cyber technology became more user friendly. Nevertheless, the right of 'freedom to express' was readily available in cyberspace by virtue of very low level of restrictions and legal barriers applicable from the governments of the countries barring a few countries like China and Iran.

The users of cyberspace range from young kids looking for information for school assignments to business tycoons looking for more profits, from government's e-governance services for the public to terrorists/non-state actors using it for their online communications and covert operations. As a result, in due course of time this unregulated space of cyber became the mine of information worth great billions, opening a battleground for the netizens to acquire such vast information and also to some to sabotage the same to fulfil their selfish motives. The important feature of this battle was that it did not require an army to fight but an individual capable of writing few lines of codes, one who has only minimum level of expertise in the cyber technology could wage a war against a country.

This form of battle among the netizens in cyberspace is described with various names like cyber crime, cyber war and cyber terrorism depending on the nature of the perpetrators, their intentions and the consequences of their activities. This is also the preferred form of fight against the public, the government and their perceived enemies by an individual in view of the following reasons; low level of restrictions and legal barriers, anonymity and no casualties, and most importantly indispensability of only minimal resources and the need of infinitesimal number of people with little expertise. Almost all the countries of the world face this challenge in their respective cyberspace on regular basis and it is more often experienced in the networks of the rival states. In addition, citizens of a country who are unable to express their hatred and fight against their rival state brazenly, find cyberspace a suitable option to vent out their anger and hatred as it provides them a natural aegis and anonymity along with the weapon of technology. In this regard no country is an exception to this cyber hatred contest including India and Pakistan.

India and Pakistan

The South Asian neighbours have fought three major conventional wars in 1947-48, 1965, 1971 and a limited war in 1999 ever since their independence in 1947, until the end of the 20th century. During the end of the 20th century, the tensions between the two nations increased to its highest level as both the countries annexed the tag of 'States with nuclear weapon' after successfully conducting nuclear tests for military purpose one after the other. Although the nuclear deterrence and other international pressures has barred these two countries from going to another major war in the later scenarios, the hatred in the minds of the citizens of these two countries has only increased. This hatred is aggravated further when the state sponsored terrorism from Pakistan became the highest national security threat for India and the Indian armed forces were busy retaliating to such threats.

The Fce Breaker

As discussed in the earlier chapter throughout the history of computers, the said technology advanced rapidly but almost without any regulations making it vulnerable to the misuse for immoral and anti-social purposes. As a result, this became the attractive medium for people to express their views and emotions to their targeted audience all over the world. Cyber attacks started spreading globally and the number of incidents increased over a period of time. It also reached India on June 3, 1998 when the Indian website owned by 'Bhabha Atomic Research Centre' (BARC) came under cyber attack by a group called as 'milw0rm'. The attack was caused by hacking the website of BARC and defacing the same. It was also found that the attackers had downloaded five mega bytes of emails and data from the database.[26] The attackers in the defaced website sent out a message that the attack was in response to the testing of nuclear weapons by India on May 11 and 13, 1998. The defaced website of BARC had the following message from the hackers:

> "*Nuclear Tests in India. This page has been hacked in protest of a nuclear race between India, Pakistan and China. It is the world's concern that such actions must be put to end since nobody wants yet another world war. I hope you understand that our intentions were good, thus no damage has been done to this system. No files have been copied or deleted, and main file has been just renamed. Stop the Nuclear Race! We Don't Want a Nuclear Holocaust*".[27]

At first, it was believed that these attacks were by the Pakistani hackers backed by ISI but later after a thorough investigation it was revealed that these hackers were individuals who only had developed contacts within themselves through internet and are operating with their pseudo names and belonged to different nations. The group consisted of teenagers who went by the aliases of JR, Keystroke, ExtreemUK, savec0re, and VeNoMouS.[28] VeNoMouS, 18, hailed from New Zealand, ExtreemUK and JR, 15, from England, Keystroke, 16, from the US and Savec0re, 17, from Russia.[29]

Although the first major cyber attack faced by an important Indian website was not by Pakistani hackers, the initial blame on them which came out as an immediate response from the Indian side clearly exhibits the level of suspicion in the minds of the people for obvious reasons. However, this first major attack on an important Indian website which was proved to be an act not by Pakistani hackers but this incident clearly became an ice-breaking ground that paved the way for future cyber attacks between the netizens of the two countries. After this incident, in the year 1999 there were four incidents of attacks on Indian cyber networks that were recorded and the investigations revealed that these were carried out from Pakistan. The number of attacks increased drastically to seventy-two in the year 2000 and there were also reports confirming about seven attacks in 1999 and 18 attacks in 2000 on the Pakistani networks carried out from India.[30] Thus, a mutual hacking clash began without much fanfare through the cables between the netizens of India and Pakistan.

The saga of hacking tussle continued even in the 21st century where the first half of 2001 witnessed 150 attacks defacing websites on the Indian side and similar attacks took place in the Pakistani side also but its number was comparatively a little less.[31] This act of hacking attacks from both sides has kept increasing every year and the victims of this cyber skirmishers were the key websites of both the countries. Mr. Munawar Iqbal, President of Pakistan Computer Association (PCA) in an interview stated that:

> *"As per my information there are two groups of hackers from both countries: one is called the Indian Cyber Army and the other is known as the Pakistan Cyber Army. Both are in competition to hack each other's websites. It is totally illegal, and should be stopped in the greater regional and international interest, as well as that of both countries' people."* [32]

Later on, many new hacking groups started emerging and displaying their skills to hack the networks. One of the most notorious and dangerous group originated from Pakistan out of these groups was the 'Z Company Hackers Crew' (ZHC) which has a record of attacking 1846 Indian websites of both government and civilian in one day on May 29, 2009.[33] There are also other hackers groups like 'Pakistani Hackers Club' (PHC) whose founder is claimed to be from Karachi and the 'G-Force' which is believed to consist eight members basically from Lahore.[34]

The Indian side, also witnessed the emergence of many groups out of which H2O or the 'Hindustan Hackers Organisation'[35] is very famous among the cyber hacking community and another group called 'TEAM NUTS' which did a record hacking and defacement of 57 commercial sites in Pakistan in one day in 2010.[36]

The Spill Over Effect

As the hacking feud which was fed by hatred and anger growing progressively among the private hackers groups from India and Pakistan, it led to increase in the number of cyber attacks carried out by them. Although this became a daily occurrence in both the countries, it remained unrecognised or not even taken into consideration as a threat to national security by either Indian or Pakistan government. But the spill over effect of this cyber feud soon came to the limelight as it was too important to be ignored.

As the various cyber hacking groups in both the countries were waiting for their opportunity to sabotage the other nation in a massive way, the D-Day finally arrived on November 26, 2010, the second anniversary of the 26/11 Mumbai terror attacks. On this day the members of the Indian Cyber Army (ICA) launched an all out attack on 870 Pakistani websites out of which 34 were crucial government websites belonging to Pakistan Navy, Maritime Security Agency, Foreign Ministry, Chief Minister of Sind, etc. The ICA spokesperson stated that *"Our objective of launching cyber attacks was to pay our homage to the martyrs of 26/11,"* in the website called Hacker Regiment.[37]

This act of ICA instigated the hackers groups in Pakistan, and their most powerful group called Pakistan Cyber Army retaliated with a similar all out attack on December 03, 2010 on the 39th anniversary of the 1971 Indo-Pak war by attacking 270 Indian websites out of which the worst affected was the website of Central Bureau of Investigation (CBI) which remained offline for almost one month since the attack before being brought back with great difficulty.[38] The whole software had to be tested and revalidated again before making it available online. It was later identified by the Department of Electronics and Information Technology that the hackers who attacked CBI website were based in Peshawar and it is also believed that they had used an Indian Air Force website as a back gate to enter the CBI website which shared the same database and became the biggest security lapse.[39] The hacked CBI website had the message saying:

> *"This attempt is in response to the Pakistani websites hacked by 'Indian Cyber Army'. We told you before too... we are sleeping but not dead.. Remember PCA (Pakistan Cyber Army)! back off kids or we will smoke your d00rs off like we did before.. lets see what your investigating agency so called CBI can do for you or for us! Haha.. one more attempt from your side.. We got your every website lying around here like its our local server! Buahahaha...so we would like to say to your 31337 hackers and your 31337 NIC team go and read some more books... you guys are seriously bunch of script_kiddies!.. you know nothing rite now..got r00t access to NTC server? Wtf mass defacements...how about something like this...a planned attack! Haha...btw we got r00t to your NIC too :P. Your filtering sucks... have fun! And DO NOT DISTURB... we got better things to do.. :D.. stop complaining about Pakistani websites security.. secure your own ass first..thats what intelligent people do!..lol..tata.:D".*[40]

In retaliation, the ICA attacked and defaced the website of Oil and Natural Gas Regulatory Agency (ONGA), the counterpart of ONGC of India in Pakistan on December 04, 2010.[41] The defaced website of ONGA had the following message:

"You Have Been Hacked by the INDIAN CYBER ARMY This Is a Retaliation of Hacking 'CBI."[42]

Pakistani Government sources claimed that the attack on their 870 websites on November 26, 2010 were planned and executed by India's technical intelligence agency called the "National Technical Research Organisation" (NTRO) by hiring hackers for their offensive cyber operations which could never be proved. Similarly, India also accused Pakistan's ISI for the attack on December 3, 2010 on their 270 websites and most importantly regarding the website of CBI which was the most affected. India also claimed that ISI had recruited hackers for waging a cyber war against India.

The series of attacks made by the Indian and Pakistani hackers groups on the cyber networks of each others during the month of November and December 2010 was considered to be one of the major cyber attacks that have ever taken place between any two countries of the world without the support of the government. Nevertheless, the series of attacks was just seen as a prelude to a much bigger battle in cyber space between India and Pakistan in the future.

The series of attacks carried out by the private hacking groups of both India and Pakistan on the websites of each other invited the attention of the respective governments. Immediately after the attacks were carried out, Mr. Sachin Pilot; India's then Minister of State for Communication and Information Technology, called a multi-level meeting of various agencies like CBI, NTRO and National Informatics Centre (NIC) and discussed this issue.[43] Although the series of hacking incidents faded away for a while after the intervention of respective governments, the hacking groups of both the countries claimed that they have access to cyber networks of their enemies more easily.

"We still own many servers of Pakistan and are prepared to respond to any attack from the PCA or any other Pakistani hacker group," says 'Disfigure' a hacker from the ICA[44].

Although many small cyber skirmishes and hacking were taking place after the major cyber clash between the hackers of India and Pakistan, they were not considered harmful. The atmosphere suddenly became intense on January 26, 2012 when India was all geared up to celebrate its 63rd Republic Day. An India based hackers group called 'Jaguar Hacker' defaced 21 Pakistani websites and posted a message saying:

"Noth(i)ng Personal But It's Just That Today Is Our Republic Day.. :).Don't worry nothing has been deleted... Just Index page renamed (sic),"[45]

In retaliation to this, the famous hacking group from Pakistan 'Z Company Hacking Crew' hacked about 400 websites of India and posted:

"You claim to be the largest democracy in the world but when it comes to Kashmir and Kashmiri people you tend to forget all your democratic principles. You kill our fathers, our brothers, shoot down teenagers point blank and detain them under draconian laws like PSA without even giving them a fair trial, you rape our sisters and mothers. After years of atrocities and oppression we say that we will Rise and Rise Again ... Until Lambs become Lions !!!(sic)".[46]

According to sources in Global Cyber Security Response Team (GCSRT), Bangalore, a total of 2118 Indian websites were hacked including the website of Central Bank of India on January 26, 2014. Pakistani hackers with the handle "StrikerRude", "KashmirCyberArmy", "PakCyber Expert", "HUnter Gujar" claimed responsibility for the hacking attacks and their operation was named "#OP26jan".[47] However, a majority of websites were restored within a few hours after the attacks. In retaliation to this an Indian cyber hackers group called "Indian Cyber Rakshak" hacked more than 100 Pakistani websites on January 29, 2014.[48]

This saga of hacking websites of each other continues between Indian and Pakistani hackers fuelled by mutual hatred and vendetta and also to exhibit their hacking skills under the garb of exhibiting patriotism and nationalism.

Why Does this Matter so Much?

The series of hacking attacks between India and Pakistan (by the various hacking groups of these countries) are not a surprise to the cyber technology management groups as they encounter such activities regularly. According to the annual report from Computer Emergency Response Team of India (CERT-in), the agency has tracked around 25,037 instances of defacements of Indian websites including a number of government websites and other attacks in the year 2014, which amounts to approximately 68 hacking instances on an average per day. In spite of all these reports, it is unfortunate to know from many independent cyber security observers in India that although there are regular reports of hacking incidents, the government organisations are not vigilant enough to take necessary steps to improve the security of Indian cyber networks. It has been reported that out of 7,000 Indian government websites, only 3,192 have been audited for information technology (IT) security, while 3,556 other websites are still being audited. Yash Kadakia, head of Security Brigade, a government-empanelled security auditor says that:

> *"According to our data, about half of the government websites are vulnerable to cyber attacks. Most of the government websites do not have proper security checks in place."*[49]

Similar level of lethargy prevails on the Pakistani side too in securing their cyber infrastructure. When enquired about the steps taken for management of security to the Pakistani cyber networks, a senior official in the Electronic Government Directorate (EGD), the agency officially responsible for monitoring the hacking saga in Pakistan said:

> *"The government has so far secured only 33 websites belonging to government ministries and departments, out of thousands of official government websites. And there is no system that can't be hacked. You can break any kind of lock, and the same is the case with hacking websites. The government never demonstrates seriousness in dealing with the hacking problem, which poses a constant threat to all state and privately-run websites"*[50].

While aggression is the only tactic followed by the hackers groups in both the countries, on the contrary, the security providers of the cyber space has always been found to be lacking in their vigilance with a view to provide security to the cyber networks and infrastructure of their countries. Sunil Abraham, Executive Director of the Bangalore-based 'Centre for Internet and Society' said during an interview to 'Al Jazeera' that:

"The Indian government has a very low level of cyber awareness and cyber security. We don't take cyber security as seriously as the rest of the world."

The problem of cyber attacks by the hacking groups would not be a big problem if it would stop with the hacking and defacing of websites. But in reality it moves on to the next levels. The same group who carry out hacking and defacing of websites would even involve in cyber espionage and data mining against their enemies. These groups may also offer their expertise to any terrorist organisations in return for monetary benefits and other forms of remuneration. A cyber security professional working with one of India's intelligence agencies said:

"We once sat down to check the Delhi [internet] Backbone. We found thousands of systems compromised. All were government's systems, ", "Research and Analysis Wing, Intelligence Bureau, Military Intelligence... we don't realise how much damage has already happened."[51]

The lack of awareness and lethargic approach in monitoring and providing security to the cyber networks in India led to thousands of computers across the country being compromised. The infection could range from small Viruses, Botnets[52] to that of Stuxnet[53] level malwares which can hamper the total operations of the network connected to the compromised computer.

The list of new malwares such as Stuxnet, Flame[54], Duqu[55] etc. and many more are under the process of coding and their abilities to operate as a cyber weapon are incredible and at the same time the consequences could be unbearable if not properly protected. Assuming that the hackers groups get access to these kinds of malwares/ cyber weapons, then the situation would be extremely dangerous from the point of view of national security as the threat they pose is equivalent to terrorists getting access to nuclear weapons. While talking about the same, Mr. Sachin Pilot, the then Minister of State for Communications and Information Technology said that:

> *"The entire economies of some countries have been paralysed by viruses from across the border. We have to make ourselves more resilient," "Power, telecom, defence; these areas are on top of our agenda."*[56]

The Crescendo

A careful study of the series of hacking incidences on websites and network of one another by the private hacking groups of India and Pakistan would reveal a basic fact that something which started as a minor display of hatred has now taken the shape of a large scale act in the form of personal revenge, economic profits, a race to show off technical supremacy and anti-national propaganda.

This was very much evident from one unfortunate event that disturbed the internal security of India in August 2012. The Indian government was alerted after the exodus of thousands of people from North East gathered in railway stations of south Indian cities especially Bengaluru after being threatened by SMSes and violent morphed pictures which were being circulated on more than 100 websites. The SMSes threatened the people from North East living in various cities in India of a targeted attack on them and asking them to go back to their homelands whereas the pictures circulated in the internet was of some violent bloodshed images that happened elsewhere. Out of the various SMSes that were in circulation, one SMS said:

> *"It is a request to everyone to call back their relatives, sons and daughters in Bangalore as soon as possible. Last night four north-eastern guys were killed by Muslims in Bangalore (two Manipuri, two Nepali). Two Nepali girls*

were kidnapped from Brigade Road. The reports say that from August 20, marking Ramzan, after 2 pm they are going to attack every North-eastern person. The riot started was because of the situation in Assam."[57]

Another SMS said:

"Many Northeast students staying in Pune were beaten up by miscreants believed to be Muslims following the Assam riots. Heard that it is happening in Muslim areas like Mumbai, Andhra Pradesh, Bangalore. At Neelasandra two boys were killed and one near passport office."[58]

The Government of India reacted soon in this case and a 43-page report was prepared by intelligence agencies in collaboration with National Technical Research Organization (NTRO) and India Computer Emergency Response Team (CERT-IN) which traced several doctored images to Pakistan. The origins of these morphed images were later traced specifically to Lahore, Rawalpindi and other Pakistani cities by the Indian Intelligence agencies.

"From all available forensic evidence, we are fairly convinced that all those postings came from Pakistan,"

said an official of National Technical Research Organisation (NTRO). Another senior official who is involved in India's Pakistan watch for several years said:

"It has been happening for several months now. This is a low cost, very effective way of destabilising us," "They don't need to send terrorists and explosives to create mayhem. Internet has been a very effective platform for instigating communal divisions in India. They also have a multiplier effect, first resulting in anger and hatred, then riots and, finally, many taking to terrorism."[59]

This act of involvement of Pakistan based elements is intolerable and is seen as cyber terrorism and cyber psychological warfare against

India to cause internal security disturbances and eventually create a big crisis in the country. This incident which created a major imbalance in the internal security of the country is the biggest example about the adverse effects of misuse of cyber technology and hacking skills.

For India, it is not only Pakistan that challenges its security on the cyber front but there is also a Red Giant Cyber Dragon – China against India, which has more advanced and organised form of cyber army with them, with which it even challenges United States through cyber espionage operations like 'Titan Rain'.[60] It is believed that Chinese cyber warfare policy is based on 6th century B.C., Chinese strategist Sun Tzu: "The art of fighting without fighting". There are instances between India and China where officials in the Indian government have alleged that the attacks on Indian government networks, such as that of the Indian National Security Council, have originated from China. According to the Indian government, Chinese hackers are experts in operating Botnets. Fears of Chinese cyber espionage have resulted in blocking of deals with Chinese telecoms, like Huawei, keeping in view its ties with the Chinese military.[61] India's intelligence agencies raised several warning about Huawei's penetration into Indian telecom. Their worst fear is that the Chinese firm could be a Trojan horse, meant to infiltrate India's network in peacetime and disable it through remote 'kill switches' during wartime, through hidden 'trapdoors' and malicious programmes that could then open a channel back to its designers.[62] The cyber attacks which was witnessed in 2010 on the computer systems of India's National Security Adviser's (NSA) office, Indian Air Force and Indian Navy are suspected to have been made from China. In each case, it opened up several small windows through which classified documents and presentations were whisked away. At this juncture, Pakistan's attachment towards China is an important factor and this could become deadly for India if they both join hands in the future for cyber offensive operations against India.

What could be done?

In order to avoid any mishaps, Indian government should take measures by identifying the real people behind these hacking sagas on the Indian side and rehabilitate those who deserve and recruit them to her cyber security infrastructure. As most of the hackers are teenagers, this act of converting the 'Black Hat Hackers' or 'Grey Hat Hackers' into 'White Hat Hackers' would be the right step for the government to get hold of them and mould them. This will not only give a future to such youngsters but will also create a strong cyber security culture in the country.

India's Information Technology sector is a significant contributor to the economy of the country, and the country is one of the leaders in this sector in the world. The country has enough young IT talents who, unfortunately, remain scattered across India's huge landmass. In fact, most of these talented young minds are in contact with one another through various platforms on internet. They operate in the cyber space with strange pseudonyms and with different agendas. Although a few wander as black hat hackers, there are many more prospective young vibrant brains which, when harnessed, could prove to be potential assets to the country. The Government of India needs to tap these young talented individuals to overcome its shortage of a highly skilled workforce of cyber security experts. While this seems to be an easy enough strategy, the question remains as to how this talent can be identified from amongst India's huge population. The answer could be by conducting a nation-wide talent hunt through 'Cyber competitions'.

The Path Weavers

This is not a new technique as it is being followed by many leading countries of the world, like USA and China. On May 08, 2009, the White House came up with a proposal for conducting a nation-wide cyber challenge with the aim of finding and developing 10,000 cyber security specialists to help the United States regain the lead in cyberspace.[63] In the same proposal, the following statement by Jim Gosler, NSA Visiting Scientist and the founding Director of the CIA's Clandestine Information Technology Office, was highlighted:

> "There are about 1,000 security people in the US who have the specialised security skills to operate effectively in cyberspace. We need 10,000 to 30,000".[64]

It was also mentioned in the proposal that such competitions would act as a diversion to young talented people from going astray. This competition was conducted by the government of USA in association with SANS Institute, a leading institution in Information Security Training and Security Certification in the world.

In fact, there is a possibility that the Americans could have borrowed this idea of conducting nationwide cyber challenge from the Asian giant and India's neighbour, China. The practice of conducting such cyber competitions in China is prevalent since early 21st century and they have a more structured approach to it. China's approach is in two stages: one at the regional level and then at the national level. The People's Liberation Army (PLA) conducts these competitions on behalf of the Chinese government. As a first step, the PLA invites young talented people to participate at the regional level cyber competitions which are conducted in all the military regions of the country. In the second stage, the top few contenders of every region are formed as a team and made to represent the region in the nation-wide competition.[65]

The victorious talented lot is then tapped by the PLA to work for them either as private operatives or recruited into their cyber armies, i.e. Unit 61398. The most popular case of one such identified talent of China is Tan Dailin[66] who operated with the pseudonym "*Wicked Rose*" and who, at the young age of 20, was the leader of a private hacking unit from China called Network Crack Program Hacker (NCPH). '*Wicked Rose* was the champion of the national cyber challenge of China held in the year 2005. After his victory, he started operating with few other cyber experts as a team known as NCPH. He was sponsored by the PLA for his missions and the group was an expert in exploiting "Zero-day vulnerabilities" in Microsoft Office software and they were also experts in building Trojans. Using this technique they were able to make a number of successful attacks on their targets, including the critical infrastructure of the US and were able to extract thousands of documents for their commanders in the PLA.[67] (See Chapter 5 for more information on Tan Dailin and NCPH).

The Way Ahead

Although India does not support or encourage such covert cyber operations by any individual/groups, yet the above mentioned methods can be taken as an example to understand the ability of young minds in this highly technical and complex domain. Though a few cyber related competitions are conducted by a few Indian educational institutions, universities and on the sidelines of high level cyber conferences, their reach and level of testing is far below the required standards. However, if such competitions are conducted on a larger scale by the government, it might have a nation-wide reach and participation from all parts of the country that would enable the Indian government to identify and exploit the hidden talent. There are a number of pro-Indian hacker groups in the country who have been involved in hacking wars with their counterparts from Pakistan, China and other countries. The talents of such hackers would be a potential asset for the country if harnessed properly, or else they could end up being an embarrassment for India.

However, mere identification of talents will not be enough for the country to get the desired results. The government needs to take steps to form a framework which would enable the identified talented youth to be groomed and put their skills to use for preserving our national interest, which in turn would serve the purpose of defending the cyber space of the country. The proposed National Cyber Security Coordination Centre (NCCC), operating under the Prime Minister's Office could be made as the nodal agency to undertake this onerous task of enhancing India's cyber security by identifying, grooming and producing highly skilled cyber warriors for the country. The proposed technical university by the state-run telecom service company, BSNL, can also be involved in the process to provide technical training and grooming the identified talented youth.[68]

Another strategy to hunt for talented youth for enhancing cyber security of the country is to announce rewards to experts who can help solve complex cyber problems. Again taking an instance from the US, where the federal government in early 2016 announced its "first Cyber Bug Bounty Program in the history of the federal government," officially inviting hackers to take up the challenge. Dubbed "Hack the Pentagon," the bug bounty program invited the hackers and security researchers only from the United States to target its networks as well as the public faced websites which were registered under DoD.[69] The programme got an overwhelming support with around 1,400 white hat hackers participating and identifying more than 100 bugs in the networks and also received awards up to US$15,000 for disclosing most destructive vulnerabilities in the DoDs networks.[70] Such 'Capture the flag' style programmes initiated by the Indian government will not only help the government to reach out to the right talents but will also help identify loopholes in the country's defensive systems which could be plugged to enhance the country's cyber networks. As the saying goes in the Indian Armed forces *"Catch them young"*, the same approach has to be followed in the cyber domain, which will not only provide an effective offensive and defensive cyber capability in the future but would also help turn the evil of hacking to a strength for the country.

Notes

1. Ron Rosenbaum, Secrets of the Little Blue Box", *Esquire*, October 1971, p. 222.
2. Ibid., p.121.
3. "Telephone Loop Lines", http://home.ptd.net/~n3cvj/looplines.htm, accessed on February 13, 2016.
4. Rosenbaum, n.1.
5. Ibid.
6. Ibid.
7. Steven Levy, *"Hackers: Heroes of the Computer Revolution"*, Dell Publishing, 1984.
8. "The Secret History of Hacking", *Discovery Channel* (2001; the US: Discovery channel, 2001), DVD.
9. Robert Trigaux, "Hackers: The Underbelly of Cyberspace", *St.Petersburg Times*, June 14, 1998, http://www.sptimes.com/Hackers/underbelly_of_cyberspace.html, accessed on February 23, 2016.
10. Clarke, Zuley, James Clawson, and Maria Cordell, "A Brief History of Hacking" (Thesis, Georgia Tech, November 2003), p.1.
11. Steven Levy, *"Hackers: Heroes of the Computer Revolution"*, Dell Publishing, 1984.
12. Jarkko Moilanen, "Realms of Cyber warriors – Definitions and Applications" (Master's Thesis, University of Tampere, August 2009), p.15.
13. Eric S. Raymond, *"The New Hacker's Dictionary"*, 3rd edition, MIT Press, 1993.
14. Clarke, n.10.

15. Raymond, n.13.
16. A period of monomaniacal concentration on coding apparently passed through by all fledgling hackers. Common symptoms include the perpetration of more than one 36-hour hacking run in a given week. Neglect of all other activities including usual basics like food, sleep, and personal hygiene and a chronic case of advanced bleary-eye. It could last from 6 months to 2 years, while the apparent median being around 18 months. A few afflicted ones could never resume more 'normal' life, but the ordeal seems to be necessary to produce really wizardly programmers.
17. Ibid.
18. Ibid.
19. Jose Pagliery, "The evolution of hacking", *CNN*, June 5, 2015, http://edition.cnn.com/2015/03/11/tech/computer-hacking-history/, accessed on February 26, 2016.
20. Gerry Smith, "Kevin Mitnick, Former Fugitive Hacker, Laments How The Game Has Changed", *The Huffington Post*, August 16, 2011, http://www.huffingtonpost.com/2011/08/16/kevin-mitnick-hacker-book_n_928107.html?ir=India&adsSiteOverride=in, accessed on January 10, 2015.
21. Ibid.
22. Ibid.
23. Clarke, n.10.
24. Ibid.
25. Douglas Thomas, *"Hacker Culture"*, (Minnesota: University of Minnesota Press, 2002).
26. http://ces.iisc.ernet.in/hpg/envis/doc98html/miscbarc69.html, accessed on 3/09/2012, 11:30 am
27. http://www.youtube.com/watch?v=XcL9EqUbg4Y, accessed on September 3, 2012.
28. William C Boni and Gerald L. Kovacich, *I-way robbery*. (UK: Butterworth-Heinemann, 1999) p. 142.
29. Ibid.
30. Iftikar Alam, "Pakistan India cyber war begins", *The Nation*, December 05, 2010.
31. Alamzeb Khan, "Pakistan Cyber warfare and Internet Hacking", http://www.simple-talk.com/opinion/opinion-pieces/pakistan-cyber-warfare-and-internet-hacking/, accessed on January 17, 2012.
32. Ibid.
33. Waqas, "1846 Government & Civilian Websites Hacked by Company Hacking Crew", *Hackread*, https://www.hackread.com/1846-government-civilian-websites-hacked-by-z-company-hacking-crew/, accessed on December 10, 2012.
34. Iftikar Alam, n. 30.
35. Ibid.
36. Mohit Kumar, "57 Pakistani websites Hacked By Team Nuts", December 06, 2010, http://thehackernews.com/2010/12/57-pakistani-websites-hacked-by-team.html, accessed on December 6, 2012.

37. Sandeep Unnithan, "Inside the Indo Pak cyber wars", *India Today*, March 18, 2011, http://indiatoday.intoday.in/story/cyberspace-china-india/1/226396.html, accessed on February 18, 2016.
38. Ibid.
39. Alamzeb Khan, "Pakistan Cyber warfare and Internet Hacking", January 17, 2012, http://www.simple-talk.com/opinion/opinion-pieces/pakistan-cyber-warfare-and-internet-hacking/, accessed on August 6, 2013.
40. www.cbi.gov.in/index.php, accessed on December 3, 2013.
41. Iftikar Alam, n. 30.
42. Indian Cyber Army Hack Ogra.org.pk, *The Hacker News*, December 04, 2010, http://thehackernews.com/2010/12/indian-cyber-army-hack-ograorgpk.html, accessed on February 26, 2016.
43. Unnithan, n. 37.
44. Ibid.
45. "Indo-Pak Cyber War on Jan 26", *Mid Day*, January 28, 2012, http://www.mid-day.com/news/2012/jan/280112-Indo-Pak-cyber-war-on-Jan-26.htm , accessed on July 14, 2014.
46. Ibid.
47. "More than 2000 Indian websites hacked", *The Hindu*, January 29, 2014, http://www.thehindu.com/news/national/more-than-2000-indian-websites-hacked/article5627784.ece, accessed on February 27, 2016.
48. "Hitting back, Indian hackers deface Pakistani websites", *The Hindu,* January 30, 2014, http://www.thehindu.com/sci-tech/technology/internet/hitting-back-indian-hackers-deface-pakistani-websites/article5630449.ece, accessed on February 28, 2016.
49. Piyali Mandal, "Half the govt websites in India are prone to cyber attacks", *Business Standard*, January 6, 2013.
50. Alamzeb Khan, n. 39.
51. Fitter, Pierre Mario, "Stuxnet attack wakes India up to threat to critical infrastructure", *India Today*, September 5, 2012.
52. The term bot is short for robot. Criminals distribute malicious software (also known as malware) that can turn your computer into a bot (also known as a zombie). When this occurs, your computer can perform automated tasks over the Internet, without you knowing it. Criminals typically use bots to infect large number of computers. These computers form a network, or a botnet.
53. See chapter titled "Eagles Claw on Cyberspace" to know more about Stuxnet malware.
54. Flame is modular computer malware discovered in 2012 that attacks computers running the Microsoft Windows operating system. The program is being used for targeted cyber espionage in Middle Eastern countries.
55. Duqu is a computer worm discovered on September 1, 2011, thought to be related to the Stuxnet worm. The Laboratory of Cryptography and System Security of the Budapest University of Technology and Economics in Hungary discovered the

threat, analysed the malware, and wrote a 60-page report naming the threat Duqu. Duqu got its name from the prefix "~DQ" it gives to the names of files it creates.

56. Ibid.

57. "TRAI tracking panic-spreading SMS"; *The New Indian Express,* August 17, 2012.

58. Ibid.

59. "Exodus of northeast people: Eight Pakistani sites identified for spreading rumours", *The Times of India,* August 20, 2012. http://timesofindia.indiatimes.com/india/Exodus-of-northeast-people-Eight-Pakistani-sites-identified-for-spreading-rumours/articleshow/15563233.cms, accessed on March 2, 2016.

60. Nathan Thornburgh, "Inside the Chinese Hack attack"; *TIME,* Thursday, August 25, 2005.

61. Indrani Bagchi, "China mounts cyber attacks on Indian sites"; *The Times of India,* May 5, 2008.

62. Unnithan, n.37.

63. "The United States Cyber Challenge", *The White House Files,* May 8, 2009.

64. Ibid.

65. Ken Dunham and Jim Melnick, "Wicked Rose and the NCPH Hacking Group", *An iDefence Research Report,* 2007.

66. More details about Tan Dailin and NCPH can be found in the chapter titled "Dragon's Fire in the Virtual World".

67. Ken Dunham, n. 67.

68. "BSNL to open technical university, offer cyber security training", *Times of India,* April 13, 2014, http://timesofindia.indiatimes.com/tech/jobs/BSNL-to-open-technical-university-offer-cybersecurity-training/articleshow/33700956.cms, accessed on March 8, 2016.

69. "Statement by Pentagon Press Secretary Peter Cook on DoD's "Hack the Pentagon" Cybersecurity Initiative", *U.S. Department of Defence,* Press Release No. NR-070-16, March 02, 2016, http://www.defense.gov/News/News-Releases/News-Release-View/Article/684106/statement-by-pentagon-press-secretary-peter-cook-on-dods-hack-the-pentagon-cybe, accessed on March 8, 2016.

70. Mohit Kumar, "Hack the Pentagon: Hackers find over 100 Bugs in U.S. Defence Systems", The Hacker News, June 14, 2016, http://thehackernews.com/2016/06/hackpentagon.html, accessed on June 20, 2016.

3

DEEP AND DARK
DIGITAL OCEAN

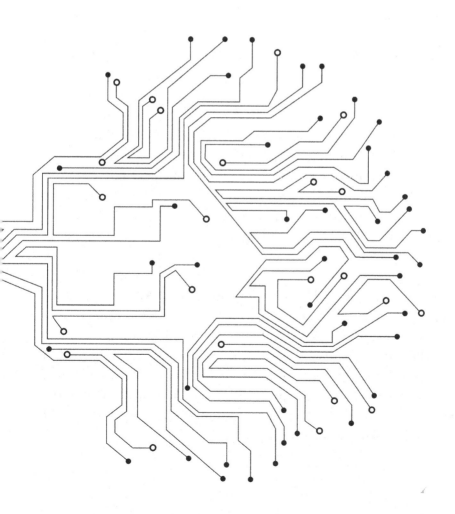

The previous chapter dealt with the menace of hacking and how hackers are disturbing the global cyber community and at the same time indirectly aiding the advancement of cyber technologies by technologically invalidating the existing ones. This chapter is discussing the details of the inert threat existing in the cyber domain, specifically in the internet in the form of deep and dark web. Starting with a brief history of internet, the chapter would then cover the aspects of deep and dark web. It would also explain the method for accessing these deep web resources through The Onion Routing (TOR) and would finally analyse the threats caused by the existence of such dark spaces on the internet to the global community.

How it Started?

"The Internet is the first thing that humanity has built that humanity doesn't understand, the largest experiment in anarchy that we have ever had."[1]
— Eric Schmidt[2]

Starting as a mere concept named "Galactic Network" by J.C.R. Licklider of MIT in August 1962, the 'internet' has revolutionised the way this world communicates within the past few decades. Having been technically nurtured in Defence Advanced Research Projects Agency (DARPA) from early 1960s to late 1970s, internet, i.e. the then ARPANET has undergone various phases starting with the sending of host-to-host message with mere packet switching technology in extreme low speed (2.4 kbps – 50 kbps) in 1969, to the advancement of Host-to-Host protocol of ARPANET called "Network Control Protocol" (NCP) in 1970, to the introduction of 'electronic mail' service in 1972 for easy coordination mechanism in ARPANET which took off as the largest network application for over a decade. Later, due to the inability of NCP to adapt to open-architecture network environment which would globalise the network, a new protocol called Transmission Control Protocol/Internet Protocol was developed.[3]

While file transfer and remote login (Telnet) were very important applications, electronic mail was probably the most significant innovation which expanded new methods of communication with each other by providing a model in the building of the Internet itself. Slowly a number of proposals started pooling in that would help to expand the applications of internet, including packet based voice communication (the precursor of Internet telephony), various models of file and disk sharing, and early "worm" programmes that showed the concept of malware agents. Thus, internet which was initially designed for one application, i.e. file sharing, became a platform for conceiving many applications in it which became a reality when 'World Wide Web' (WWW) was introduced. While Ethernet technology was developed in 1973, this technology coupled with the widespread developments of LANs (Local Area Network), PCs (Personal Computer) and Workstations, led the nascent internet to flourish in 1980s.[4]

As a result of the increase in the scale of operation of the Internet many issues pertaining to the management came up and were resolved. To begin with, the hosts were assigned names (early URLs) which made it unnecessary to remember the host's numeric addresses. Next as the number of users increased, the simple single distributed algorithm routing technique based routers were replaced with a hierarchal model routing based routers which permitted different regions to use a different Interior Gateway Protocol (IGP), so that different requirements for cost, rapid reconfiguration, robustness and scale are accommodated. Along with the evolving internet, supporting operating system was also developed that helped in the widespread adoption of internet. Soon after the transfer of ARPANET from NCP to TCP/IP on January 1, 1983, ARPANET was split into a MILNET supporting military operational requirements and an ARPANET supporting research needs thus forming a precursor for the civilian use of internet. Consequently, by 1985, Internet became well established as a technology that supports a broad community of researchers and developers, and was also used by other communities for daily communications through computer especially the electronic mails.[5]

As the development of DARPA's ARPANET was making progress on one side, many more agencies which were able to secure funding started developing their own networks on the lines of ARPANET. The U.S. Department of Energy (DoE) established MFENet for its researchers in Magnetic Fusion Energy, whereupon DoE's High Energy Physicists responded by building HEPNet. Space Physicists from NASA followed with SPAN, the academic and industrial Computer Science community with an initial grant from the U.S. National Science Foundation (NSF) and established CSNET. Apart from these networks, one another landmark network that was developed was NSFNET with TCP/IP protocol which during its lifetime grew to 45 mbps links with over 50,000 networks on all the seven continents and even in outer space. As a result of the successful development of various networks by the US and other international government funded agencies, commercial sectors around the world also started showing interest in this technology during late 1980s which opened the way for commercialisation of internet in early 1990s.[6]

Although initial commercialisation of internet was restricted only to the vendors and buyers of military related technology, their hard work in successfully achieving interoperability among their products widened the scope for internet to spread in other fields as well. Therefore on October 24, 1995 the Federal Networking council (FNC) passed a resolution defining the term 'internet'. The definition is as follows:

"The Federal Networking Council (FNC) agrees that the following language reflects our definition of the term "Internet"."Internet" refers to the global information system that —

- *is logically linked together by a globally unique address space based on the Internet Protocol (IP) or its subsequent extensions/follow-ons;*
- *is able to support communications using the Transmission Control Protocol/Internet Protocol (TCP/IP) suite or its subsequent extensions/ follow-ons, and/or other IP-compatible protocols; and*
- *provides, uses or makes accessible, either publicly or privately, high level services layered on the communications and related infrastructure described herein."[7]*

It developed from a concept which was conceived in the era of timesharing,[8] prolonged its stay and expanded its borders by adapting itself to function and grew along with the new developments in the computer technology like personal computer, client-server, peer-to-peer computing, network computing, Local Area Networks (LAN) and also by supporting wide range of functions from file sharing and remote login to resource sharing and collaboration, and has spawned from electronic mail and later to the World Wide Web. The scope for adaptability combined with the huge investment from commercial sector into this successful promising technology made internet to become a 'commodity' from its initial status of 'luxury'. Also, the availability of this all pervasive technology (internet), along with powerful affordable computing and communications devices in portable form (i.e., laptop computers, PDAs, cellular phones), has created a new paradigm of widespread nomadic computing and communications system.[9]

Figure 3.1: Top Significant Events in the History of Internet

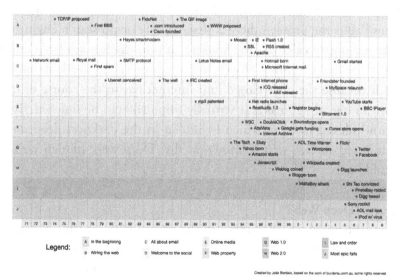

Source: http://joaobordalo.com/articles/2009/05/22/moments-in-the-internet-history. Accessed on March 10, 2015.

Even during its experimental phase, as a developing technology, internet had attracted thousands of users. Later on, in due course of time when it was more commercialised, the number of users multiplied to millions keeping in view the prospects of internet as a platform for networking, communication, gathering of knowledge, research and entertainment with the invention of several new applications like, e-mail, websites, blogs, chat rooms, immediate messages, music and video sharing, online news media, and more recently social networking which transformed internet into an absolute necessity. This is clear from the fact that within a span of two decades after commercialisation, internet attracted more than 3.6 billion users around the world.[10] As internet has drastically reduced the cost and time for communication more people started embracing this technology. After 2005, the number of users increased to more than 3.6 billion mainly due to the expansion of social networking, online shopping and other forms of easy communications including Video Voice over Internet Protocol (VVoIP) services like Skype. Moreover, the amount of information available in the indexed internet is estimated roughly to be more than 5 million terabytes according to Google which includes texts, pdfs, images and videos.[11] But the problem here is that nobody or no search engine can either accurately calculate the amount of information available online or find the exact number of websites, blogs or videos available online. This is because the once closed knit internet has in the course of time grown so big which makes it virtually impossible to be indexed. Thus, the un-indexed internet which is hidden in the darkness deep under the indexed surface web is known as the 'Deep web, hidden web, or Invisible web'.

What is 'Deep Web'?
During the initial period of internet, the information available in the web was very little which could easily be indexed and the users were also able to access them easily. But later on the situation underwent a change as the usage of internet expanded and as a result indexing of information in the internet was based on queries entered in search engines. The conventional

search engines which were operational in early days were able to retrieve static pages but proved inefficient while retrieving dynamic pages. A static page is a webpage which has static content and is also linked to other pages on the internet and on the other hand a dynamic page has dynamic content which changes from time to time, linked to a particular webpage and can be retrieved only through targeted queries or keywords. This created a gap between the static and dynamic web pages in the internet and the gap started to widen more progressively. Therefore, in 1994, Dr. Jill Ellsworth coined the phrase 'Invisible Web' to refer to information that was 'invisible' to queries of the conventional search engines used at that period of time.[12]

Later, in 2001, Michael K Bergman, a web scientist coined another term 'Deep Web' in his paper titled "The Deep Web: Surfacing the Hidden Value". His definition for the term deep web was no different from Ellsworth's term of 'invisible web', but he avoided using this term because his main aim was to discover automated means for identifying deep web sites and directing queries to them in order to make these invisible pages visible on the surface web. He also tried to quantify the size of the deep web and to characterise the quality of content in the deep web. As Bergman's paper was the first extensive research on the invisible/ deep web and also because it became widely famous among the web research community the term "Deep Web" prevailed over 'invisible web' to refer to the un-indexed sources of the web. Therefore, the definition of the term 'deep web' would be as follows:

The information content on the internet (web pages, documents, files, images, etc) which are:

- *inaccessible through direct queries in the conventional search engines,*
- *which can be accessed only through targeted queries or keywords,*
- *which are not indexed or which are unable to be indexed by the conventional search engines, and*
- *which are protected by security mechanisms like login ids, passwords, membership registrations and fees.*

In short, the information content on the internet which cannot be accessed directly through conventional search engines but requires some targeted approach is called 'deep web' or 'invisible web' or 'hidden web'.

In order to understand the concept in a better way, let us consider the example of one well known deep web resource in the internet: "JSTOR". JSTOR is widely used in academic digital library of books, journals and primary sources that started in 1995. Since then, it has a huge collection of articles and books in various formats which can be downloaded by its users by getting access through membership and fees. Any queries on the search engines for the articles available in JSTOR would take us to the JSTOR's page but one cannot download the articles directly by just reaching those pages without paying the fees and getting the membership. Moreover, since JSTOR became famous over the years, the search engines have adopted their crawlers to accommodate the web pages of JSTOR in their results whereas there are several other web pages like JSTOR with enormous quantum of information content which are still hidden or invisible from the crawlers and spiders of search engines. Although the search engines like Google, Bing, Yahoo, etc. are constantly altering their algorithms to make their crawlers reach the deepest point possible in order to retrieve information and most importantly to index them in their results, yet the internet is becoming bigger every minute and is paving the way for deeper web resources which are hidden from the eyes of the search engines. Figure 3.2 shows what happens in one minute on internet.

Figure 3.2: What Happens in an Internet Minute?

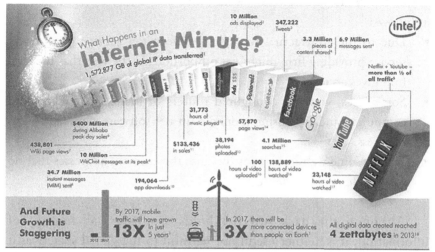

Source: http://www.intel.com/content/www/us/en/communications/internet-minute-infographic.html. Accessed on March 14, 2014.

While the data showed in figure 3.2 is just a sample taking the traffic data of few websites into consideration, the real magnitude of information being processed in a minute is much bigger than any estimate.

Dark Web, Dark Net & Dark Internet – Definitions and Concepts

The fancy internet/ surface net which provide its users with all information and entertainment also has another dark face. The dark side of the internet is that it includes several pornographic websites, forums, chats, explosives courses, hackers, assassins, human trafficking, black markets of weapons and drugs, etc. which are hidden in secret web links. This part of the internet which causes grave danger to the world cyber community and also to the global security in general is a part of the deep web and is called 'Dark web'. The term 'Dark Web' is often confused with two other similar terminologies 'Dark Net' and Dark Internet', which are also somehow related to internet.

The Dark Internet refers to *the network hosts on the internet that can no longer be accessed through conventional methods or those old network hosts which are lost due to the advancement and chaos in the internet.* The causes for the loss of network hosts which create this dark internet are as follows:

- Due to the contractual wrangles between net service providers a service providing firm might cut off portions of the web that the rival firm gives access to.
- Sometimes, wrongly configured routers or malicious hackers and computer vandals abusing loopholes in net software can lead to loss of access.
- Finally, some websites are lost because they use old addresses that no router references anymore.[13]

Although the dark internet holds a substantial amount of information, it is neither useful nor harmful to the global society as it is no longer accessible, also it need not be termed as a part of the deep web for the same reason.

While Dark Internet is inaccessible or totally out of the scene, what about the Dark Net? The 'Dark Net' can be defined as *a private network interlinked through internet using non-standard protocols and ports which are basically connected through peer-to peer connections mostly based on trust.* It is an anonymous network as the IP addresses of the users are not publically shared. Also, many dark nets require software like Freenet, GNUnet, retroshare, syndie to be installed in order to have access to them. Although, dark net is also a part of the deep web, but it is more of a cluster of private networks unlike the dark web which is more public. Also the concept of search engines does not exist in the dark net because every network is private and connected through peer-to-peer basis. While the dark net is basically used for file sharing purposes, it is mostly used for illegal activities and dissident political communications posing a threat to the global security.

Having defined the dark net and the dark internet now, the 'Dark Web' can be defined as *the portion of the deep web which contains generally illegal and anti-social information and can be accessed either through conventional browsers or specialised browsers for accessing the secretive web links.*

Figure 3.3: Artistic Image Showing the Deep and Dark Web

Source: http://davidenewmedia.wordpress.com/workingterms/darkweb/. Accessed on March 16, 2014.

In recent years, dark web is moving towards more secret locations in response to the crackdown by the government agencies on them. The dark web is a lucrative location for criminals and other anti-social elements as it provides them a natural cover from the government agencies. Moreover, the unaccounted huge economy involved in the dark web is like a treasure hunt for perverted minds. Also the existence of black markets of drugs, weapons, fake IDs, human organs, human trafficking, etc. requires anonymous location for them to operate without the fear and monitoring of the government agencies. Therefore, in recent years, more and more dark web sites are turning towards secret domains like 'onion' sites which cannot be accessed through conventional browsing methods. Thus, before going in detail about the terror in the deep and dark web, it is imperative to know how to have access to these secretive dark websites in the deep web.

The Onion Routing

Being a global public medium meant for interaction, any information on the internet is traceable to its origin or can be interrupted to cause damage to the information. This vulnerability was not acceptable by many users of the internet and therefore the need for having a secured encrypted method for networking was felt which would not only keep the data safe but also safeguard the anonymity of the users.

Thus, 'The Onion Routing Project' (TOR Project) was conceived with initial sponsorship from the US Naval Research Laboratory. Its current sponsors include US Department of State Bureau of Democracy, Human Rights, and Labour, SRI International, National Science Foundation, Radio Free Asia, The Ford Foundation, Google Summer of Code, an anonymous North American ISP, and more than 4,300 personal donations from individuals.[14] The current Tor Project claims that it is a non-profit organisation which works towards privacy and security on the Internet.[15]

Tor and its Operations

Tor is a free software bundle which can be downloaded from its official website www.torproject.org. Its initial release was on September 20, 2002 and it is a cross-platform software which can work on almost all operating systems. The Tor bundle uses Mozilla Firefox as the embedded browser for accessing the internet. The onion routing (Tor) gets its name from its encryption method, where layers of encryptions are stacked one above the other like an onion in order to make anonymous communications and also to hide the origination node of the communication. Any communication on the internet has two parts: the data payload and the header for routing. The conventional encryption software were able to encrypt the data payload but failed in hiding the header, whereas Tor is different from previous encryption software in a way that it can not only encrypt the data payload but can also hide the header which is used for routing thus erasing the cyber footprint of any communication and creating more privacy, security and anonymity to its users.[16]

When a user is connecting through the tor bundle, the user's system becomes a tor client and it obtains a list of tor nodes from a directory server through an encrypted link. The tor nodes are nothing but various users (tor clients) around the world who have volunteered their systems to act as a transit for the tor network.

Figure 3.4: Pictorial Representation of Tor Connection (circuit) is Made in a Tor Network

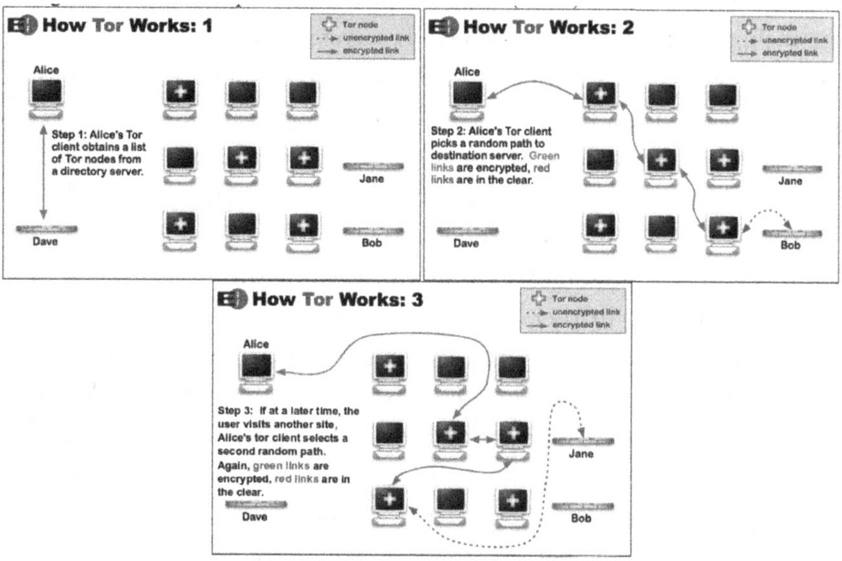

Source: "Tor: Overview", http://www.torproject.org.in/about/overview.html.en. Accessed on March 16, 2014.

When a request is made from the user to connect to a website, the software builds its own encrypted random path called circuit across the tor nodes to reach the destination. The circuit extends one hop at a time i.e. each node only knows from where it takes the relay and where it has to pass on the relay and so no node in the whole circuit is aware of the whole path any data packet has taken. Also each hop has its own encryption key which masks the path of the data packet. Once a circuit is established any kind of communications can be made or variety of software can be deployed through the tor network. Also, in order to be more efficient, the tor network uses the established circuit only for a certain period of time and for requests received later a new circuit gets connected to its destination which delinks the data path of earlier actions of the user from the path of the new requests and hence erases the footprint.

Hidden Services in the Tor Network

Apart from providing the function of an anonymous browser bundle tor software also offers other hidden services like web publishing and instant messaging service through anonymous servers configured exclusively for these hidden service purposes. This hidden service helps the tor users to publish a website in the tor network where users can publish materials and access the information online from these websites without any kind of censorships. Moreover, because of the anonymity provided by the tor network neither the users will know the owner of the site or the owner will know who is posting information or accessing the site.

Before moving further in discussing how the hidden services work, it is essential to know why the users of internet require such hidden services or in general why do users wish to be anonymous while going online. The answer to this question in simple terms is "fear of being identified". In the real world people have a personal and a professional life likewise, in the virtual /cyber world too, the users have their own personal and professional identity which most of them would like to keep delinked from the other. This is because of the kind of activities they carry out with their personal identities. For example, a person who is working in a government establishment may not like or agree with all the policies of the ruling government. But since his career is based on it he/she would remain silent in the real world without showing his dissatisfaction. When the same person goes online and when he/she knows that they can share anything without revealing their identity, they create their discrete personal online identity to share their dissatisfaction through social networks, forums or chat rooms, etc. But they may not link their professional identity to this personal identity in order to remain clean and unnoticed. Also more crooked minded people use this anonymity provided by internet for more crooked reasons and to be hidden from being identified in the real world. This remains the case for all other anonymous users of internet and its hidden services by its users around the world.

While the fear of being identified remains the main intention for anonymity by the users, the technology that allows them to be anonymous works as follows. The hidden services works on "rendezvous points" through which tor users connect to the hidden services offered in the tor network, each without knowing the other's network identity.

"The hidden services in the tor network have to advertise themselves to the clients about their existence because they are hidden unlike the services in the public internet where the websites are well connected and have a user friendly URL. Therefore, the service randomly picks some relays, builds circuits to them, and asks them to act as introduction points by telling them its public key. The hidden service assembles a hidden service descriptor, containing its public key and a summary of each introduction point, and signs this descriptor with its private key. It uploads that descriptor to a distributed hash table. The descriptor will be found by clients requesting abc.onion where 'abc' is a 16 character name derived from the service's public key."[17]

Figure 3.5: Tor Hidden Services Protocol Step 1 & 2

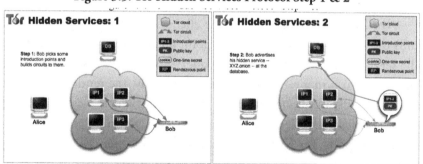

Source: "Tor: Hidden Service Protocol", in http://www.torproject.org.in/docs/hidden-services.html.en. Accessed on March 17, 2014.

"After establishing the connection, the client downloads the descriptor from the distributed hash table. The client will come to know the set of introduction points and the right public keys to use from the descriptor for abc.onion. Simultaneously the client also creates a circuit to another randomly picked relay and asks it to act as rendezvous point by telling it a one-time secret. When the descriptor is present and the rendezvous point is ready, the client assembles an introduce message and sends it to one of the introduction points, requesting it be delivered to the hidden service. As the communication is carried out in the tor network, the client's IP address cannot be related with the introduced message and thus the client remains anonymous."[18]

Figure 3.6: Tor Hidden Services Protocol Step 3 & 4

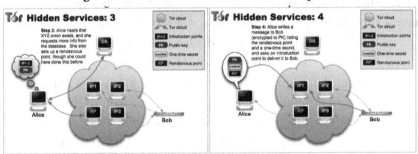

Source: "Tor: Hidden Service Protocol", in http://www.torproject.org.in/docs/hidden-services.html.en. Accessed on March 17, 2014.

"The hidden service decrypts the client's introduction message and finds the address of the rendezvous point and the one-time secret in it. The service creates a circuit to the rendezvous point and sends the one-time secret to it in a rendezvous message. Finally, the rendezvous point notifies the client about successful connection which was established which enables both client and hidden service to use their circuits to the rendezvous point for communicating with each other. The rendezvous point simply relays (end-to-end encrypted) messages from client to service and vice versa."[19] Generally, a complete connection between a client and the hidden service consists of 6 relays: 3 of them picked up by the client with the third being the rendezvous point and the other 3 picked up by the hidden service.

Figure 3.7: Tor Hidden Services Protocol Step 5 & 6

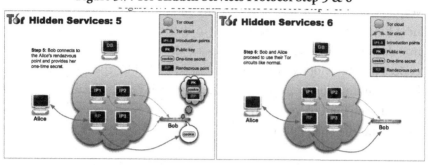

Source: "Tor: Hidden Service Protocol", in http://www.torproject.org.in/docs/hidden-services.html.en. Accessed on March 17, 2014.

The Onion Websites

The hidden service supported by the tor network attracts many users around the world, who wish to hide from government monitoring or bypass any kind of censorships, to publish their '.onion' websites which can be categorised under various fields ranging from encrypted mails services, hidden social networking, whistleblowers sites like Wikileaks, online shopping, to the murky sites like black market of drugs and weapons, hitman services, adult pornography, cyber laundering, etc. Most of the onion sites are instable in nature as they do not exist in a particular URL for long time. A list of active onion websites' URLs in the tor network during the conduct of this study are available in Appendix 2.

The table in Appendix 2 is the list of most popular onion sites active in the tor network. It is virtually impossible to list out the whole directory of onion sites as their numbers are beyond estimation as well the URLs of many web pages are yet to be found. The problem here is that the proportion of the dark web is much bigger and it is growing every minute in its size, depth, number of users and also in terms of services offered by these web pages.

Terror in the Deep and Dark Web

As the dark web is growing in its size and usage it is offering a variety of services to its users. But the nature of the service offered in this dark web is a threat to the real world as most of them are illegal ranging from drugs, weapons, hitmen to that of pornography and money laundering. Although these kinds of services are prohibited in the real world, the natural cover provided by these hidden services increase the magnitude of usage of these services online. More and more users are attracted by the single fact that they can anonymously use these services for their personal gains. A deeper look into the kind of terror existing in these dark web services would help understand the real danger.

Black Markets

Similar to the online shopping facilities offered in the internet/ surface net, the dark net also offers its users with number of deep and dark online markets where the only difference is the products sold through them. While books, clothing, watches, footwear, jewellery etc., are the usual products for sale in the surface net, the deep web/ dark web online markets are filled with products like drugs (stimulants, psychedelics, prescription, precursors, ecstasy, dissociatives, cannabies, steriods/PEDs,etc), arms, weapons, ammunitions, fake IDs, stolen electronic goods, stolen or skimmed credit card details, stolen art works, banned books, and other illegal products. Few dark web market pages like "Silk Road" offer a holistic service of sale of various products while few other web pages like "only.Cigs"[20] offer only particular products. 'only.Cigs' is a deep web market which offers its users all brands of cigarettes around the world and 'Silk Road' is the most popular and the most notorious black market in the dark web.

'Silk Road' is dubbed as the 'ebay of deep web' by its users as its service is similar to that of ebay of the surface net. Anybody who has a product for sale can register themselves in the 'silk road' webpage and can post a picture of the product and the pricing in the appropriate product category. Any user who wishes to buy the product can login and purchase the product by making the payment to the webpage. Every vendor has their own track record for credibility and authenticity which increases the trust factor among the buyers who purchase a product from a vendor. The fact that all payments are through crypto currency: 'Bitcoins'[21] makes the conditions favourable for its users in order to avoid the involvement of any financial agency to oversee the whole process. Also the products are delivered either at doorstep or at a pickup point. The service is offered all around the world expect for few constraints by some vendors for delivery to some parts of the world.

During the conduct of this study 'Silk Road' offered a variety of products categorised under various categories like alcohol, apparel, art, biotic materials, books, computer equipment, custom orders, digital goods, drug paraphernalia, drugs (stimulants, psychedelics, prescription, precursors, ecstasy, dissociatives, cannabies, steriods/PEDs), electronics, erotica, forgeries, hardware, herbs and supplements, jewellery, lab supplies, lottery and games, medicine, money, packaging, services and writing.[22] Similarly, there are many more web pages in the deep and dark web which offer similar products to its users. There are also web pages like "UK Guns and Ammo Store"[23] exclusively for the sale of arms and ammunitions in the dark web. In general, it can be stated that almost 30 percent of the dark web resources are filled with these online black markets of illegal products which pollute the society and can cause serious damage to the stability of the society.

Adult Content

Although, the surface net also has a number of pornographic sites, the dark web pornographic content is much bigger in size and cruder in nature. Most of this dark web adult content can only be accessed by becoming a registered user or by paying some fees to the web pages. Apart from the web pages, there are also forums and chat rooms like "Dark Nexus"[24] in the deep web where its users can discuss their evil thoughts with one another. The adult content pages constitute more than 40 percent of the dark web while most of its contents are videos.

Fake IDs, Middle Man Services and Other Financial Services

The deep web is also the hub of other illegal activities like making of fake IDs, sale of counterfeit banknotes, stolen credit/ debit cards, PayPal accounts, etc. There are many web pages in which fake IDs can be ordered, made and delivered for a particular price. The fake IDs include Passports,

Driver's Licence, Identification Cards, etc. Stolen or Skimmed Credit/ Debit cards, counterfeit banknotes are the other fancy products that are sold in the deep web through many web pages.

Few other pages offer some sort of service of middle man to its users where the individual would claim to offer help to the users for all sorts of illegal activities for a certain price. A few web pages are also dedicated to 'Assassination Services' where the user has to give the name, and other details of the person to be assassinated and pay for the service or in some cases even worse, where the users are asked to bet on few people's date of death and anybody who guesses it right would be rewarded.[25]

While many web pages do not support negotiations, a few web pages give the option of negotiable price. In a few web pages the buyer has to directly place the order and wait for the product to be delivered, while in others, if the vendor is an individual, e-mail id of the vendor is given so that the user can contact the vendor directly through e-mail and place the order after price negotiations. These forms of web pages which offer fake IDs, counterfeit banknotes, stolen credit/ debit cards and other financial and services of middleman constitute around 10 percent of the dark web resources and are mostly owned and operated by individuals or a small group of people who wish to make huge money in the shortest way possible.

Other dark web contents include forums and chat rooms where likeminded people discuss their evil ideas among themselves. It also includes the sale of banned books, training materials for making explosives and other chemical components including RDX, etc. In addition to this many terrorists literature and other forms of anti-social literatures which are appealing to likeminded readers are also found in this web. Besides that, betting on sports, illegal gambling and lottery are also a part of the dark web financial services. Furthermore, there are also more gruesome web pages which offer its readers with results of banned and cruel medical tests conducted on people, which provide human organs for sale and much more.[26]

Implications of Deep and Dark Web on Global Security

From the above description about the deep and dark web it is obvious that they pose a serious threat to the security in the cyber/ virtual world, but it should also be noted that on a longer run, the services provided in the deep web especially in the space of dark web poses a greater threat to global security.

How Does the Deep and Dark Web Affect the Global Security?

First, the hidden services which offer easy access to encrypted e-mails, forums, chats and other forms of file sharing services provide a safe haven for the terrorists and other non-state actors to communicate within themselves without any monitoring by f the government intelligence agencies. While the contents of the internet/ surface net are being monitored regularly by the intelligence agencies of the world to spot the existence of any suspected terrorists, the deep web with its hidden services provide the hiding ground for them. Moreover, since the location of the user is masked while using the hidden services with proper precautions, this facility enables terrorists to be more active on the deep web without the fear of being caught. Therefore, the deep web acts like a 'Pandora's Box' which provides them anything and everything from encrypted means of communication, file sharing, training grounds, knowledge sharing, recruitment, to planning and coordination. They also attract funds for their organisation and their cause by using these hidden services of the deep web by accepting bitcoin donations which they would in turn be used in purchasing weapons in the dark web black markets and use it against the society. For instance, "Fund the Islamic Struggle without Leaving a Trace" is a webpage in the deep web which invites donations for Jihad through bitcoin transactions to a particular bitcoin address.[27]

Secondly, the services and resources of the deep web and dark web are already a lucrative target for the black hat hackers, cyber thieves and other anti-social elements who concentrate their efforts in robbing the economy of the deep web for their personal financial gains. As most of the transactions in the deep web are through virtual currencies like bitcoins and through online money transactions like PayPal, these services are under heavy cyber attacks by the hackers and cyber thieves to steal the wealth available on various web pages and from various virtual currency miners, stock holders and account holders. Also the deep web virtual economy poses a grave threat to the economy of the real world as it is very unstable and also because of the fact that it does not have any accountability. Therefore, the deep web services acts as a lucrative safe house for the anti-social elements to carry out their cyber laundering (online money laundering), through gambling, betting, lottery and even through direct encrypted transactions in the dark web. Furthermore, the issue of cloned and skimmed credit/debit cards details and other financial details being sold in the deep web creates chaos in the real world banking system. If this situation continues, it can also be stated that the theft of bank details and credit/ debit card details will increase in the future.

Thirdly, the dark web in particular is a great threat to the future generation users. The human psychology is such that the mind would get easily attracted towards shortcuts, easier ways out, easy money and sinful temptations and hence the future generations who are kids could be attracted towards the dark web easily thereby changing the mindset of a whole generation. This will result in the way internet is being used in the future as a hub for illegal activities as the user does not have to fear of being caught. As a result more and more cyber criminals/terrorists will be produced who will pose a great danger to the cyber security of the world. Apart from this, the uninterrupted sale of drugs and weapons, arms and ammunitions, fake IDs, etc in the dark web would result in the increase of drug addicts and juvenile criminals in the future. Also, the existence of huge amounts of adult content materials like extreme, sickening and disgusting pornography which can easily be accessed in the dark web might foster a culture of perverted and criminal sexual behaviour resulting in creating wrong ideologies and criminal thoughts in the minds of the kids. Also the factor of easy and widespread access to such obnoxious content might in future even treat behaviour that is considered heinous at present as normal. Such effect on the psyche of future generations will subsequently affect social cognition and society as a whole.

Finally, internet security and on the whole cyber security is at stake due to the ill effects of deep and dark web. While the international community is still lobbying support for different models of Internet governance, the existence of the deep web and its enormous resources and services creates a bigger problem for the administrators who would govern the internet in the future. It also intensifies the debate between open source and restricted access, censorship, monitoring, surveillance and other forms of supervisory and regulatory mechanisms imposed on the internet.

How is it Being Tackled?

Although it might seem that it is impossible to do anything against the deep web by the security agencies because of the way it has created deep inroads in to the lives of netizens around the world, still the security agencies are trying their best to bring order to this chaotic deep space. It has to be stated that they have tasted success in some cases but are still struggling on many other fronts.

For instance, in August 2013, almost 50 percent of the known onion deep web pages completely vanished from the deep web network due to the crack down on a hosting operation in Ireland. The hosting operation named as 'Freedom Hosting' was hacked using the 'javascript exploit' in the Firefox browser version 17 which was embedded in the tor browser bundle at that time and was taken down by the Federal Bureau of Investigation (FBI) of the US. Also, the owner of the Freedom Hosting infrastructure *Eric Eoin Marques* was arrested and extradited from Ireland to the US. His infrastructure which hosted many of the onion sites utilised 550 servers around Europe and offered space to anyone who wanted it, with a promise to never look at the contents personally. The hosting service was targeted by FBI because it was diagnosed that this infrastructure was the major hub in distributing child porn in the dark web.[28]

Later in another instance, the black market giant in the deep web, 'Silk Road' was taken down on October 2, 2013 by FBI in an operation conducted after years of painstaking process of piecing together the cyber footprints of the operator of the website and it also resulted in arresting the main operator '*Ross William Ulbricht*' aka '*Dread Pirate Roberts* (DPR)'. Apart from this the FBI also seized more than 26,000 bitcoins worth US$3.6 million from accounts on Silk Road. Also they had seized 144,000 BTC worth US$28 million that belonged to Ulbricht.[29] Subsequently on December 2, 2013 three more administrators of the site were also arrested. [30] As a result of bringing the whole dark net black market giant to a standstill, FBI proved to the world that even the deep web can be traced, tracked, monitored and controlled by the law enforcing agencies. Also, *Ross William Ulbricht* was sentenced to life imprisonment without an option for parole by Judge *Katherine B. Forrest,* in a Federal District Court in Manhattan in May 2015.[31]

Post closure of Silk Road website, 'Silk Road 2.0', a replica of the original however was resurrected by former associates of Ulbricht and it started functioning usually and with more security mechanisms than they were having earlier from early November, 2013. This again did not last long as the FBI was determined to take them down again, which they did by taking down the website and arrested *Blake Benthall* aka *Defcon,* the alleged operator of Silk Road 2.0 on November 05, 2014.[32] Post the arrest Manhattan US Attorney Preet Bharara stated that:

> *"Let's be clear—this Silk Road, in whatever form, is the road to prison. Those looking to follow in the footsteps of alleged cybercriminals should understand that we will return as many times as necessary to shut down noxious online criminal bazaars. We don't get tired."[33]*

FBI might have managed to take down the illegal black market giant of the deep web in the TOR network, however, there are a number of other websites of various magnitude that are responsible for terrorising the society with their illegal operations. Also many of the dark net sites which were brought down due the shutdown of Freedom Hosting service changed their hosting space and resurfaced again later in the dark web. Therefore, it should be understood that it is impossible for the government agencies of one country to tackle the problems of the global internet which is too big for any country. Also many legal issues would surface between countries during the various stages of investigation in any particular case. Additionally, the level of technicalities involved in the process makes the issue more complex as it was evident in the Silk Road case where the Federal agents of the US had to take aid from Carnegie Mellon University in cracking the TOR network due to lack of technical sophistication within the agency.

Therefore, this cat and mouse game between the law enforcing agencies of various countries and the criminals dwelling in the deep and dark web will continue even in the near future until the cyber space becomes a well governed space with proper state regulations in place, which at present is a hypothetical scenario.

Notes

1. http://www.brainyquote.com/quotes/keywords/internet.html, accessed on March 9, 2014.
2. Eric Emerson Schmidt (born April 27, 1955) is an American software engineer, businessman, and was the executive chairman of Google. He is member of the President's Council of Advisors on Science and Technology (PCAST) for the US President Barak Obama. In 2013, Forbes ranked Schmidt as the 138th-richest person in the world, with an estimated wealth of US$8.3 billion.
3. Leiner et al., "Brief History of the Internet", *Internet Society*, 2013.
4. Ibid.
5. Cohen, Raphael, "Internet History", *International Journal of Technoethics*, 2(2), 45-64, April-June 2011.
6. Leiner et al, "Brief History of the Internet", *Internet Society*, 2013.
7. Ibid.
8. In later 1960s and 70s timesharing system enabled many users to share computer resources simultaneously. In the timesharing mode, the computer spends a fixed amount of time on one program before proceeding to another. Each user is allocated a tiny slice of time (say, two milliseconds). The computer performs whatever operations it can for that user in the allocated time and then utilises the next allocated time for the other users. Although this concept seems similar to multiprogramming, in multiprogramming, the computer works on one program until it reaches a logical stopping point, such as an input/output event, while for timesharing system, every job is allocated a specific small time period.
9. Cohen, Raphael, "Internet History", *International Journal of Technoethics*, 2(2), 45-64, April-June 2011.
10. http://www.internetworldstats.com/stats.htm, accessed on June 11, 2016.
11. http://www.wisegeek.org/how-big-is-the-internet.htm, accessed on March 11, 2014.
12. Bergman, Michael K. White Paper: "The Deep Web: Surfacing Hidden Value", *Journal of Electronic Publishing*, Volume 7, Issue 1, August 2001.

13. "Expedition to the Lost Net", *BBC News*, December 26, 2001, in http://news.bbc. co.uk/2/hi/science/nature/1721006.stm, accessed on March 15, 2014.
14. "Tor: Sponsors", http://www.torproject.org.in/about/sponsors.html.en, accessed on March 16, 2014.
15. "Tor: Overview", http://www.torproject.org.in/about/overview.html.en, accessed on March 16, 2014.
16. "Tor: Overview", http://www.torproject.org.in/about/overview.html.en, accessed on March 16, 2014.
17. "Tor: Hidden Service Protocol", in http://www.torproject.org.in/docs/hidden-services.html.en, accessed on March 17, 2014.
18. Ibid.
19. Ibid.
20. http://cigs7cviqbi4bvuy.onion/, accessed on March 21, 2014.
21. Bitcoin is a digital currency mined using cryptographic techniques. It is used as a peer-to-peer payment system which was introduced by Satoshi Nakamoto in 2009. It is now being used as the money for major transactions in the internet.
22. http://silkroad6ownowfk.onion/login, accessed on March 21, 2014.
23. http://tuu66yxvrnn3of7l.onion/, accessed on March 21, 2014.
24. http://e266al32vpuorbyg.onion/, accessed on March 22, 2014.
25. http://assmkedzgorodn7o.onion/, accessed on March 23, 2014.
26. https://torlinkbgs6aabns.onion.to/, accessed on March 24, 2014.
27. http://teir4baj5mpvkg5n.onion/, accessed on March 25, 2014.
28. "The Ultimate Guide to the Deep Web", in http://www.sickchirpse.com/deep-web-guide/, accessed on March 24, 2014.
29. Lee, Dave, "Silk Road: How FBI closed in on suspect Ross Ulbricht", *BBC*, October 2, 2013, in http://www.bbc.com/news/technology-24371894, accessed on March 26, 2014.
30. Greenberg, Andy, "Feds Indict Three More Alleged Employees Of Silk Road's Dread Pirate Roberts", *Forbes,* December 12, 2013, in http://www.forbes.com/ sites/andygreenberg/2013/12/20/feds-indict-three-more-alleged-employees-of-the-silk-roads-dread-pirate-roberts/, accessed on March 27, 2014.
31. Mohit Kumar, "Silk Road Matermind Ross Ulbricht Sentenced to Life in Prison", *The Hacker News*, May 29, 2015, http://thehackernews.com/2015/05/ silkroadrossulbricht.html, accessed on July 26, 2015.
32. Mohit Kumar, "FBI Seize silk Road 2.0 Servers; Admin Arrested", *The Hacker News*, November 6, 2014, http://thehackernews.com/2014/11/ fbiseizesilkroad20serversadmin.html, accessed on December 18, 2014.
33. "Operator of Silk Road 2.0 Website Charged in Manhattan Federal Court", *Press Release*, Federal Bureau of Investigation, November 06, 2014, https://www.fbi. gov/contact-us/field-offices/newyork/news/press-releases/operator-of-silk-road-2.0-website-charged-in-manhattan-federal-court, accessed on December 18, 2014.

CYBER ENABLED TERRORISM

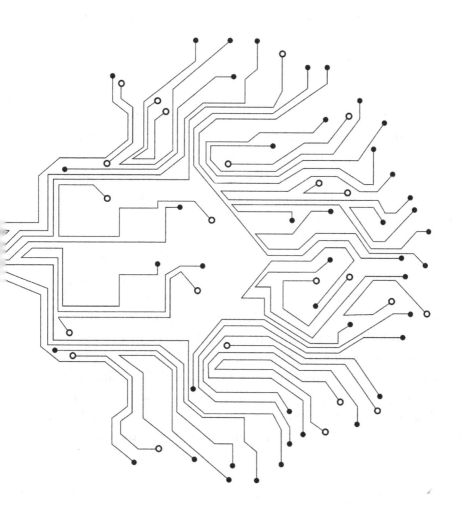

After the analysis on the inert threat posed by the deep and dark web in the internet to the global security in the previous chapter, this chapter would concentrate on the issue of terrorism in the cyber space. Like the hackers community, terrorists are also part of the category of non-state actors who are able to utilise and manipulate the technological advances of the cyber domain for satisfying their political ambitions. This chapter would cover the rationale for terrorists to use cyberspace, the vulnerabilities in cyber space that are well exploited by the terrorists and most important the various objectives for which the terrorists exploit the cyber resources for their evil missions.

Computer hacking results in financial losses and hassles. The objectives of terrorist groups are more serious. This is not to say that cyber groups can't access a telephone switch in Manhattan on a day like 9/11, shut it down, and therefore cause more casualties.[1]

— Kevin Metnik[2]

The most dreaded evil of the world– terrorism - stretches its tentacles terrorising the society and aims to achieve their goals and objectives of the people attached to them. The presence of terrorists in society is difficult to trace as they merge themselves neatly into the lifestyle of the society and when they surface, they exhibit their true repulsive and unethical intentions which are evident from the several attacks of terrorists all around the world.

The presence of terrorists is also prevalent in the cyber world, or in other words in the world of computers especially internet owing to the fact that it provides a secret place for terrorists to exist virtually. Contrary to the popular belief that terrorists would cause chaos in the virtual world by attacking computer networks, including internet, it however remained unnoticed for a long time that more than a physical attack, the terrorists would make use of the pool of information readily available on the internet and get assistance from other technological upgradations of the cyber world to aid and conduct their evil missions. In other words, terrorists would use and abuse the internet and cyber resources in general for their own benefit rather than destroying the same physically or virtually.

The fact that ready availability of internet and technologies in the cyber world are being exploited by terrorists for their missions is very much evident from the effective use of the domain by Islamic State terrorists, several reports of 9/11 which stated that *Al–Qaeda* used the technology of 'steganography' to send their mission plans hidden inside many normal pictures.[3] After 2001 and the commencement of 'Global War on Terror' led by US, many countries jumped into the bandwagon and took major steps for curbing terrorism with great effort. Although some of the countries do not have the need or power to fight in the terrorist hubs, they have raised their voice in international forums in support of curbing terrorism and have assured their diplomatic support for the global cause. As a result of such strict efforts from time to time from countries, the terrorists and the terrorist organisations felt the heat and are forced to retreat and reduce their operations in the open world. However, their activities and presence continue in the virtual world and in fact it expanded along with the expansion of the cyber world in terms of social networking and other forms of easy communications offered through advanced technologies of the internet all of which have worked in their favour.

The presence of terrorist groups in the cyber world is not a new phenomenon as they existed and used the resources of the internet since its invention. It has been recorded that way back in 1998, around half of the 30 organisations designated as "Foreign Terrorist Organizations" under the 'U.S. Anti-terrorism and Effective Death Penalty Act of 1996' maintained websites; by 2000, virtually all terrorists groups were found to have established their presence on the internet.[4] A study conducted by "United States Institute of Peace" in 2003-2004 revealed that hundreds of websites were found to be serving terrorists and their supporters on the internet. The number of users kept increasing over the years and also spread from mere presence of websites to other forms of communications like mailing, chatting, social networking, etc. Their operational capabilities also widened from conducting psychological warfare to gathering information/ data mining, from training to fund raising, from propaganda to recruiting and from networking to planning and coordinating terrorist acts. Therefore, in order to eradicate terrorism from the face of the world, it is not only enough to take strong action in the real world but it is also essential to understand the activities being undertaken by terrorists in the complex cyber world by identifying, analysing illustrating and countering the ways in which the various terrorists and the terrorist organisations around the world exploit the unique attributes of internet and manipulate the technological advancements in cyber space to promote their evil efforts.

Vulnerabilities in Cyber Space

The cyber world, especially internet, provides virtually anything to its users. Cyberspace is far more important than web emails and social networks. It is a digital medium through which it is possible to conduct all human activities from communication, calculation, to making a decision and its implementation. Its working involves wide range of products, software, hardware, chips to satellites, structures and management procedures and people, from developers to end-users. The origin of internet was in 1960s, commissioned by the United States government to build robust, fault-tolerant, and computer networks. The funding from the U.S. government formed the backbone of the National Science Foundation in the 1980s. Funding for the development of internet for commercial purposes led to worldwide participation in the development of new networking technologies, and merger of many networks. The commercialisation of what was by the 1990s an international network, made it popular and its incorporation into virtually every aspect of modern human life. As on March 2016, more than 3.6 billion people use the services of the internet.

Since its introduction, the internet has grown rapidly in a big way in terms of number of users, the quantum of information stored, development of new methods for processing data and sharing, different types of techniques for communications and as a medium of education, entertainment, etc. While all these advantages of the internet attract more users and facilitate their work, there are also very important disadvantages or vulnerabilities which has to be faced while using the internet. These are manipulated by malevolent minds for their selfish gains and terrorising acts.

Gabriel Weimann, a noted expert in the field of cyber security, in his paper has listed out the vulnerabilities of internet that provides an ideal arena in many ways for several activities by extremists/terrorists. According to Weimann, internet offers:

- Easy access,
- Little or no regulation, censorship, or other forms of government control,
- Potentially huge audiences spread throughout the world,
- Anonymity of communication that reduces the risk of being caught,
- Fast flow of information,
- Inexpensive development and maintenance of a web presence,
- Interactive platform,
- A multimedia environment, and
- The ability to shape coverage in the traditional mass media, which increasingly use the internet as a source for their stories.[5]

Internet is an unbiased technology and provides uniform service to all its users around the globe. It acts as a convenient and easy medium for collection of information in a short span of time with a minimal effort – without ever moving from a place – for all its users. The terrorists use this feature of the internet to gather information and conduct virtual reconnaissance for their operations. The investigations on 26/11 Mumbai terror attack by Lashkar-e-Taiba (LeT) terrorists, showcased how they used 'Google Earth' application to pre-plan their attack so precisely from entry to exit points in order to cause maximum damage and inflict a major impact on the society.[6]Moreover, internet has no centralised governance in either technological implementation or policies for access and usage and each constituent network sets its own standards It is neither owned by any one individual, organisation or a country nor has regulations, censorships and other forms of binding government laws and rules applied to it except in the case of few countries like China, Iran and Cuba where censorships are strictly followed. This void of any kind of binding regulations and globally accepted governance provides free access to terrorists to act independently in the realm of internet.

Internet also provides a great form of anonymity as there is no verification on the credibility of the user's personal information like name, address, etc. and there are many encrypted methods in which information can be shared using numerous encryption software that are freely available on the internet. Though the user's IP address could be traced the recent developments in technology has given away for terrorists and other users' fraudulent methods to evade tracing by using proxies and masking software. This anonymity aids the terrorists to actively be present and communicate in the virtual world without fear of being caught by the law enforcing agencies for any of their illegal and immoral activities on the internet. To create a website on the internet or to be present on it via other forms like blogs, forums, chat rooms, social networks, etc. has become so easy in recent years that according to www.worldwidewebsize.com, there were 4.04 billion pages available on the internet as of June 20, 2016.[7] Almost all the terrorist organisations, irrespective of their ideologies, have presence on the internet in the form of website, forum, blogs, etc. But they are unable to be pinned down due to the anonymity provided by the internet. The terrorists use a series of encryption methods, they keep shifting their virtual location from one place to another randomly, also use social networking and other easy means of communication which makes it almost impossible to trace.

Figure 4.1: Size of the Indexed World Wide Web

The size of the indexed World Wide Web
(Number of webpages)

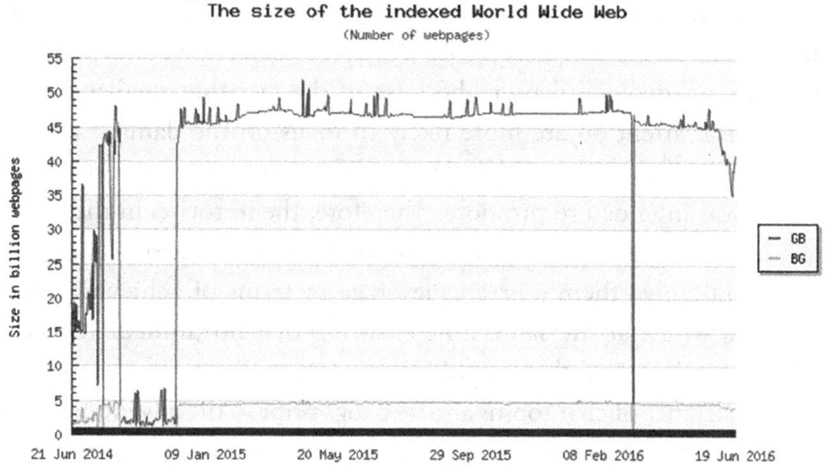

GB = Sorted on Google and Bing BG = Sorted on Bing and Google
Source: http://www.worldwidewebsize.com/, accessed on August 20, 2016.

In the initial period, transmission of information to the right parties at the right time required a great deal of effort and there was always a fear of leak of secrets. But in the age of information, the internet offers a rapid flow of information across the globe in no time which can also be encrypted to avoid leakage of secrets and moreover this information can be transmitted to infinite number of parties at the same time. With the advanced technology of multimedia applications, the information is made more attractive with a combination of texts, high graphics, audio and video in order to make it appealing to a larger audience. According to the report of International Telecommunication Union (ITU), out of the 7.4 billion population of the world, there are 3.6 billion internet users.[8] Though the rest 3.8 billion population claim to be not using internet, the impact of the information made on the 3.6 billion of the internet users gets multiplied when it reaches the rest of non-users as they are informed by the media. The enormous numbers of audience on the internet serve a great deal for the terrorists as they can easily communicate to any one or a group or to the whole lot without much hassle. Moreover, the information can be sent at a lightning speed in an attractive multimedia format that would attract most people.

In recent years, the terrorists have clearly understood the fact that acts of violence are not necessarily the most effective ways of making a political or ideological point because of the fact that media, public and political attention are more likely to focus on the damage caused (destruction of property and/or loss of life) than whatever 'cause' the violence was intended to promote. Therefore, the terrorists in the cyber realm are focusing to increase their ability to affect a wider population which would give them a greater leverage in terms of achieving their objectives, whilst at the same time ensuring that no immediate long-term damage is caused that would overshadow the issue.

The existence of chat rooms and web logs prior to the advent of social networking was effectively used by terrorists as interactive platforms in order to reach their supporters and sympathizers around the world to communicate and spread their cause. These interactive forums were used by the cyber terrorists as virtual propaganda fields, publicity platforms and command transfer networks. The lack of time for the mass media to investigate a story by themselves due to competition among various networks is used by the cyber terrorists to make a fake story which go viral by posting hoax news on the internet as the mass media often rely on internet for news. The stories which are baseless and fake, gain authenticity and eventually attain a level of credibility as it is circulated more and more on the internet. This act of cyber propaganda helps the cyber terrorists to gain an upper hand in manipulating the mass media to sensationalise a spurious issue.

The cyber world is certainly affected by vulnerabilities that are efficiently used by terrorists. The cyber world is still in the evolving phase and this process of evolution would continue in the 21st century too. For the successful evolution of the cyber world, it becomes very important to understand the methods by which the vulnerabilities of cyberspace are being used by terrorists. It is equally important to understand the ways in which they use the internet for their virtual operations and their level of expertise to manipulate the technological advancement towards their immoral cause.

How Terrorists Use Internet and Operate Virtually

Today, almost all the banned and active terrorist organisations of the world, irrespective of their size, operating location and capability, have their presence in the cyber world. Their presence is in the form of websites which are multilingual at times and some organisations have more than one website. They are also present in the social networking sites, chat rooms, forums and other public interactive platforms that would help them reach the society with stealth. The use of internet by terrorist organisations resembles the use of the medium by traditional political organisations, for instance, raising funds and disseminating propaganda. Others, however, are much more unusual and distinctive, such as hiding instructions, manuals and directions in coded messages or encrypted files. Although the internet is exploited by the non-state actors in all possible ways, the following are the seven important purposes for which the terrorists use internet:

- Networking of their organisation.
- Publicity and propaganda.
- Psychological warfare.
- Fundraising.
- Data collection and information dissemination.
- Recruitment and mobilisation.
- Planning and coordination.

Networking of their Organisation

Like all organisations, terrorists' organisations also have their own hierarchy and command and control structure in order to maintain their cadres, pass orders, messages, information to carry out their missions and also to suffice the needs and goals of the organisation. But due to the crackdown of government agencies on terrorist organisations around the world, it has become difficult for the terrorists to meet at a single place to discuss their goals, missions, plans and methods. Moreover, the geographical distance between one unit of a terrorist organisation to another unit requires some common networking medium for them to be linked with one another. Therefore, they opt for easier means of communication technologies to keep their networking tight enough to run their organisation and also keep their command chain unbroken as ever before.

The new communication technologies in the digital medium – especially use of computers – have some special advantages of their own that prove to be a boon for these terrorists.

- First, these communications made through computers (like e-mails, Immediate messages, chats, forums, videoconferencing, etc.) reduce transmission time as most of them work in real time. Therefore, it enables to provide contact with their dispersed organisational actors swiftly and to coordinate effectively.

- Secondly, these new technologies are available at a very cheap price, which helps the organisations reduce their financial burdens. [9]

- Third, although there is possibility of being caught if their cyber footprint is traced, the sender and the receiver never have to come out of their hiding in order to send/receive their messages. Moreover, while proper encryption methods are used while communicating, the problem of cyber foot print is also taken care of.

- Fourth, and the most important advantage, is that by adapting to the modern cyber methods of communications, the terrorists have increased the variety and complexity of the information that can be shared.[10]

Moreover as the terrorist leaders are always on the run, fearing the security agencies, their meetings with their followers are conducted through video conferencing services like Skype, VOIP services and satellite phone to keep their hierarchy, command and control systems in order, as well as not being exposed to the government agencies. Also, the modern communication technology helps these organisations to enhance their links for sharing of common knowledge and resources with other similar organisations that share similar ideologies, goals and ambitions.

Publicity and Propaganda

There is no doubt that the penetration of internet into the daily lives of people has drastically reduced their workload with its hassle-free e-services, but at the same time it has also opened new channels for the terrorists to reach the people in order to publicise and proliferate their ideas and motives in an attempt to gather support for themselves. Before the age of internet, traditional media like television, radio and print media were the only ways of publicity and propaganda that existed as options for the terrorists. But these mediums of publicity were all heavily monitored and protected by the laws of the government and its agencies. Therefore, uncensored internet became a boon for terrorists to communicate with their targeted audiences easily, bypassing all the laws and the vigilant eyes of the law enforcing agencies.

The terrorists and terrorist organisations use their websites and other platforms of internet to post messages, videos, make statements and other forms of multimedia communications to justify their violent actions, blame their enemies, gain sympathy, gather support and popularise their ideas and movement among the public. The fact that terrorists now have direct control over the content of their message offers opportunity for them to shape how they are to be perceived by different target audiences and to manipulate their own image and also the image of their enemies. This is evident from the lines of *Ayman al-Zawahiri*, senior *Al-Qaeda* leader's letter to the late leader of *Al-Qaeda* during operations in Iraq in July 2005, stating that "*I say to you: that we are in a battle and that more than half of this battle is taking place in the battlefield of the media.*"[11]

The websites of the terrorist organisations are the main source of publicity and propaganda. These sites contain all the information about the organisation from its history, leaders, ideology, agenda, publications, and speeches of its leaders, popular statements made by its leaders and photo and video galleries. Many sites offer multilingual services in order to widen its international audience. English language is most popularly used in these types of sites along with their local language, to cover the international audience. For example, "*Hezbollah*" a banned organisation by the United States, the Netherlands, Bahrain, the United Kingdom, Australia, Canada and Israel,[12] hosts a website with URL: http://www.moqawama.org/ which is well structured with well formed graphics and multimedia. The website is multilingual, providing its information in French, English, Spanish and Arabic. It has got a huge collection of propaganda photos and videos which get updated every day. The videos are collection of speeches of all its leaders and other Shia Islamic leaders in support of the organisation's Shia Islamic ideology. This website also contains a huge photo gallery with the photos of its leaders, the organisation's achievements and many incidents and events. In spite of its links to a banned organisation, this website's appearance at the outset appears deceptive like a news website.

It is not only the idea of *Hezbollah* to host websites on their own for publicity and propaganda, but this remains the modus operandi of almost all the banned/terrorist organisations in the world to host their own websites to create a direct contact with their targeted audiences. Author *Gabriel Weimann*, in his paper states that all active terrorist organisations maintain web sites, and many maintain more than one web site and use several different languages.[13] But, there are also cases where the websites are not officially owned by the terrorist organisations but are owned by some of its sympathisers, supporters or followers which create confusion for the government agencies and other online terrorist tracking and monitoring agencies to identify the real plans of the terrorists.

Table 4.1: A Table showing various banned/terrorist organisations around the world and their respective Official Website URLs at the time of this work.

Name of the Organisation	URL of their Official Website
Hamas	www.hamasinfo.net
AlAqsa Martyrs Brigades	www.fatehorg.ps
Fatah Tanzim	www.theisraelproject.org
Popular Front for the Liberation of Palestine (PFLP)	http://pflp.ps/english/
People's Mujahedin of Iran	www.mojahedin.org
Kurdish Worker's Party	http://www.pkkonline.com/en/
Liberation Tigers of Tamil Eelam	http://www.eelamweb.com/

Japanese Supreme Truth (AumShinrikyo)	http://english.aleph.to/
Hizb-ul-Mujehideen	http://hizbulmujahideen.webs.com/
Jamatud Dawa	http://jamatdawa.net/
Khalistan Movement	http://www.khalistan.net/ http://sikhfreedom.com/
ArmateCorsa (the Corsican army)	http://www.armata-corsa.com/
Armed Revolutionary Forces of Colombia	http://www.farc-ep.co/

Although websites play a major role in the publicity and propaganda for the terrorists, there are also other platforms on the internet which offer much more attractive and interactive modes of communication to their targeted audiences. These platforms include chat room, blogs, forums, online journals, social networks and video hosting which are highly unregulated. All these platforms of publicity and propaganda help the terrorist reach their audience directly with messages to influence them with their ideas. The chat rooms and forums provide a free hangout for the terrorists to influence the minds of the younger generation around the world, who ignorantly fall into the trap. There are a large number of groups in these chat rooms and forums which are dedicated to various terrorist outfits and each group has got a sizeable number of followers. The followers of these groups in the chat rooms and forums fall in the category of sympathisers and supporters that would turn into active followers at any point of time. Talking of chat rooms, Gary Bunt has stated that: *"Chat rooms are often unregulated and unmonitored by scholars and clerics, can provide a virtual hangout for teenage and young-adult Muslims, and are sometimes rife with anti-kuffer (nonbeliever) sentiment"*[14].

The blogs owned by the terrorists are being used as mini websites to the utmost level possible with almost similar functions as a website. There are also journals published online by the terrorist organisations at regular intervals for hard-core followers, supporters and sympathisers. For instance, "Inspire" is an English language online magazine published in the Arabian Peninsula by *Al-Qaeda.* This magazine is considered to be a political warfare tool targeting the American and other Western governments, with the intention of inspiring home-grown terrorism. This tactic is used to generate over-reaction by the governments on its Muslim population with threats of individual jihadist attacks. The editor of this journal, *Anwar al-Awlaki,* is a member of *Al-Qaeda* in the Arabian Peninsula (AQAP) and also *Al-Qaeda* in the Islamic Maghreb (AQIM).

The video hosting sites like www.youtube.com play a major role in the act of propaganda for the terrorists as it provides them with the fastest method of communication to the whole world. These video hosting sites are used to post videos which are very gruesome in nature, and also videos of speeches of terrorist leaders. For instance, the beheadings of *Wall Street Journal* Reporter Daniel Pearl in February 2004 and Nick Berg, an American seeking employment in Iraq in May 2004, were broadcasted via videos posted on Islamic websites and then broadcasted and reported via mainstream media. In August 2005, the self-proclaimed "Jihad Brigades in Palestine" claimed missile attack on a Jewish settlement in Gaza by posting a video to a German server that allowed visitors to upload materials and also showed apparent members setting up a missile, readying it for launch and firing it off.[15] Also, the terrorists post videos, messages on their websites and on other video hosting sites that describe the plight of their women who were sexually abused[16], in order to gain sympathy for themselves and to justify their violent actions. The video hosting is an important strategy followed by Islamic State (IS) terrorists and their videos are known for their sleek productions. There are unaccounted number of videos posted every day on these video hosting sites all around the world and anyone who has a basic understanding of computers and internet can get access to these videos, but it is very difficult for the governments or the law enforcing agencies to track down every video and to remove it from the site. This provides a natural stealth for the terrorists and terrorist organisations to host their videos for publicity and propaganda.

The social networking websites are inclusive in nature, which encompasses all the attributes of internet communications like messaging, photos and video sharing, posting of message to one another and file sharing. Every feed in these social networks is considered important when it is related to any sensitive issue which is happening around the world and there are several examples that one could quote from various events happening around the world. Therefore, these social networking websites are a boon for the terrorists to contact, share and use it as a publicity and propaganda platform. Out of the numerous examples, a classic example in the Indian context would be the case of Mahdi Biswas, who was operating the infamous twitter handle 'Shami Witness', alleging his loyalty with the Islamic State terrorist organisation and indulging in propaganda.

The absence of any restrictions in these social networking websites helps the supporters and sympathisers of any terrorist organisation to be in contact with one another and to share their ideologies openly on a public forum. Hence, it could be stated that the recent developments in the world of internet, with its comprehensive mechanism, can be credited for not only reducing the size of the world and saving time but at the same time has also added complexities for the law enforcing agencies who has to monitor and control the spread of publicity and propaganda of terrorists who use the virtual media.

Psychological Warfare

Terrorism has always been accompanied by a form of psychological warfare which helps the terrorists gain a certain level of deterrence among the public. The basic idea for the terrorist to wage psychological warfare is to create fear among the public about the violence and other brutal consequences that could be the result of any possible terrorist attack. It is also sometimes used by the terrorist groups as a shield to cover their own incapability, for which they use publicity and propaganda to exaggerate their potential and try to create panic among the public. In simple terms, psychological warfare in the cyber world is used by the terrorists to create 'cyber fear' among the public. While talking about the same/ author *Thomas* in his paper "*Al-Qaeda* and the Internet" argues that:

Cyber fear is generated by the fact that what a computer attack could do (i.e., bring down airliners, ruin critical infrastructure, destroy the stock market, reveal state secrets, etc.) is too often associated with what will happen . . . It is clear that the Internet empowers small groups and makes them appear much more capable than they might actually be, even turning bluster into a type of virtual fear. The net allows terrorists to amplify the consequences of their activities with follow-on messages and threats directly to the population at large, even though the terrorist group may be totally impotent. In effect, the Internet allows a person or group to appear to be larger or more important or threatening than they really are.[17]

The internet, with its highly advanced communication technologies and multimedia environment, creates a favourable situation for the terrorists to amplify their potential for an attack. The video hosting websites are explicitly used as a main platform for the psychological warfare by the terrorists by posting videos of recorded terrorist activities along with messages that would explain a terror plot to frighten society. A terrifying example would be the case of *The Wall Street Journal* reporter Daniel Pearl's video (being beheaded by *Al-Qaeda* in Pakistan in 2002). By releasing this propaganda video, the actual aim of *Al-Qaeda* was to frighten the American government and other Americans living in the Muslim world as the video ends with the scrolling of following verses of warning:

"We assure Americans that they shall never be safe on the Muslim Land of Pakistan. And if our demands are not met this scene shall be repeated again and again..."[18]

Another similar example would be the event that took place in Iraq with the kidnap and murder of Liverpudlian Kenneth Bigley who was a citizen of UK. He was kidnapped from his house in Baghdad, along with two American colleagues Armstrong and Hensley, on September 16, 2004. On September 18, the Tawhid and Jihad group, allegedly headed by Abu Musab al-Zarqawi, released a video of the three men kneeling in front of a Tawhid and Jihad banner and the kidnappers said they would kill the men within 48 hours if their demands for the release of Iraqi women prisoners held by coalition forces were not met. Armstrong was beheaded on September 20 when the deadline expired, and Hensley also faced the same fate 24 hours later. Videos of these killings were posted on the internet shortly after the events took place.

A second video was released by Bigley's captors on 22 September. In this video Bigley is shown pleading for his life; he directly petitions the British Prime Minister saying,

I need you to help me now, Mr Blair, because you are the only person on God's earth who can help me.[19]

The video was posted on a number of Islamist websites and shown on Arab satellite television station "Al-Jazeera". A third video was released on 29 September showing Bigley, wearing an orange boiler suit, chained inside a small chicken-wire cage. In this video, Bigley is heard saying,

"Tony Blair is lying. He doesn't care about me. I'm just one person."[20]

Bigley was beheaded on 7 October, 2004. The kidnappers filmed Bigley's murder and these images were subsequently posted on a number of Islamist sites. According to news reports, the video shows Bigley reading out a statement, before one of the kidnappers steps forward and cuts off his head with a knife.

The jihadis produce videos in a professional manner that are released through media outlets such as the Al-Sahab Institute for Media Production (video production arm of *Al-Qaeda*) and appear frequently on the public media like Al-Jazeera channel as well as the web.[21] These videos and messages have dual impact of spreading anxiety among the public while simultaneously boosting morale among supporters, sympathizers and likeminded groups. The theory behind filming the violence and uploading videos on the internet is to make a bigger impact of their capabilities and exaggerate their abilities.

Apart from video hosting method of psychological warfare, the terrorists also use internet for their long term achievements to threaten the people of a country by spreading disinformation, delivering threats and dissemination of horrific images over the internet. The appropriate example would be the case of serious internal security disturbance in India in August 2012 due to a covert psychological warfare by unidentified miscreants from Pakistan. Indian government was alerted of the exodus after thousands of North East people gathered in the railway stations of various cities all over the country after being threatened by a series of SMSes and violent morphed pictures that were being circulated on more than 100 websites. The SMSes threatened the North East people living in various cities in India of a targeted attack on them and asking them to go back to their homeland whereas the pictures circulated on the internet were of some violent bloodshed image which were mostly doctored using advanced computer software. Out of the various SMSes that were in circulation, one such SMS read:

"It is a request to everyone to call back their relatives, sons and daughters in Bangalore as soon as possible. Last night four north-eastern guys were killed by Muslims in Bangalore (two Manipuri, two Nepali). Two Nepali girls were kidnapped from Brigade Road. The reports say that from August 20, marking Ramzan, after 2 pm they are going to attack every North-eastern person. The riot started was because of the situation in Assam."[22]

Another SMS read:

"Many Northeast students staying in Pune were beaten up by miscreants believed to be Muslims following the Assam riots. Heard that it is happening in Muslim areas like Mumbai, Andhra Pradesh, and Bangalore. At Neelasandra two boys were killed and one near passport office."[23]

Most of the online content was posted from July 13, 2012 and fake profiles were created for spreading morphed pictures. The government of India reacted soon in this matter and a 43-page report was prepared by intelligence agencies along with National Technical Research Organization (NTRO) and India Computer Emergency Response Team (CERT-IN) which traced the origin of several doctored images to Pakistan. The report noted that social media, e-mails, internet chat rooms and Voice Over Internet Protocol (VOIP) calls were profusely being used to spread disinformation and rumours to provoke unrest in the Indian state of Assam and other parts of the country. The origins of these morphed images were later traced back to Lahore, Rawalpindi and other Pakistani cities by the Indian Intelligence agencies. This act of unnecessary involvement by Pakistan based elements was seen as cyber terrorism and cyber psychological warfare against India in order to cause internal security disturbance and eventually to create a huge crisis in the country.

These acts of spreading disinformation, delivering threats and dissemination of horrific images and videos over the internet creates a persistent threat among public regarding any untoward incident that might happen in the society. Therefore, the terrorists gain advantage in achieving their demands by terrorising the public not by means of explosion of bombs or by other conventional attacks but by virtually warning the public regarding the untoward consequences that they have to face if their demands are not met.

Fundraising

"…money is the oxygen of terrorism. Without the means to raise and move money around the world, terrorists cannot function."[24]
— Colin Powell, Former United States Secretary of State.

Organisations around the world function with numerous purposes and ideologies but the general rule is that irrespective of their ideologies, purposes and demands, they all need funds to survive and operate to achieve their goals. The terrorist organisations are no exception to this rule as "they need substantial funds for planning terrorist attacks, training and recruiting operatives, disseminating propaganda, providing transportation, preserving channels of communication, supporting satellite organisations and subsidising living costs of terrorist operatives."[25] It is for this reason the terrorist organisations around the world use all possible overt and covert means of fundraising techniques. One of the covert means of fundraising used by them is to annex the cyber technology for raising, transaction and circulation of funds to meet their organisation's financial demands. The financial support is requested through charities online, indulging in credit/debit card frauds, laundering money through online gambling, using peer-to-peer transaction services, misusing and stealing digital currencies and mobile financing are some of the most commonly used tactics to launder money in the virtual world by the non-state actors.

For instance, it has been estimated that of *Al-Qaeda's* total income, about 10 percent is being spent on operational costs and the rest 90 percent goes on the cost of administering and maintaining the organisation. In order to meet their financial needs, especially after the crackdown by the global forces on their overt methods of fundraising which depended deeply on donations, *Al-Qaeda* has shifted to more covert methods, or in other words virtual methods, by which "its global fundraising network is built upon foundation of charities, non-governmental organisations and other financial institutions that uses websites and internet based chat rooms and forums."[26] Analysts found *Al-Qaeda* and few humanitarian relief agencies using the same bank account numbers on numerous occasions.

The Sunni extremist group *Hizabut-Tahrir* uses an integrated web of internet sites like http://www.hizbuttahrir.org/, http://www.hizb-australia.org/, http://hizb-america.org/ and http://www.hizb.org.uk/ from Europe to Africa to call for the return of an Islamic caliphate. "The website deceives its visitors by stating that it desires to help return of an Islamic caliphate by peaceful means and the supporters are encouraged to assist the effort by monetary support, scholarly verdicts and encouraging others to support jihad. The Russian breakaway republic of Chechnya had used the internet to publicise banks and bank account numbers to which its supporters and sympathisers could contribute."[27]

Al-Qaeda faction in Iraq, during the Iraq war, was reported making online appeals for new fundraising ideas. In an Arabic statement posted on *Al-Qaeda* in Iraq's online forum, website administrator *Seif Saad* lamented the state of the group's finances and launched an urgent appeal for money to "feed the widows and the orphans" of *mujahedeen,* or holy warriors. He stated that *"A few days ago a brother was martyred, leaving behind a wife and children. There is no need to explain how we were running here and there to collect money for their minimum requirements of life".*[28] This is one of the tactics of online fundraising by the terrorist organisations by trying to pose a sympathetic image for their slain fighters and their family and attract more funds for its organisations. In general, most of the websites and blogs owned by the terrorist organisations or their supporters have a column for accepting donations to their organisation and their cause.

Apart from these methods of fundraising, the terrorist organisations also use the illegal method of money laundering in its digital version to fulfil their financial needs which is called the online money laundering/ cyber laundering. Money laundering over the internet is carried out through fake online auctions, online sales, online gambling websites, peer-to-peer transactions, as well as through online games and other similar methods. An example of a game that is being used for such a purpose is 'Second Life', which uses a virtual currency, the Linden dollar, which can easily be converted into real currencies.[29] The prepaid storage/ payment cards, different forms of e-money, like ekash, PayPal accounts or payments over mobile phones are also used for easy cyber laundering.

The laundering of funds over the internet and through mobile phones is made particularly easy by the growing use of peer-to-peer transactions, i.e. funds directly being transferred from one individual to another, without the interaction of a third party, such as a financial institution, thus avoiding financial oversight, accountability and potential detection. The invention of mobile banking facilities like "M-PESA"[30] are increasing the vulnerability of misusing the facility of peer-to-peer transactions in the virtual world. The rapid growth of mobile payments, especially in developing countries, like Kenya where M-PESA is booming, makes it particularly easy for terrorists, as payments are handled only by mobile phone companies and are usually conducted directly on peer-to-peer basis, therefore avoiding the prying eyes of financial oversight and law enforcement agencies.[31]

Moreover, since the introduction of digital currencies like "Bitcoins" into the cyber world, the manner in which online transactions take place in the contemporary world has seen a drastic change. "Bitcoin is a peer-to-peer payment system and digital currency introduced as open source software in 2009 by pseudonymous developer *Satoshi Nakamoto*. It is a crypto currency, so-called because it uses cryptography to control the creation and transfer of money."[32] Other similar crypto currencies in use are Ripple, Litecoin, Peercoin, Namecoin, Dogecoin, Primecoin and Mastercoin. The digital currencies can be bought in exchange for real money depending on the day's exchange rate and can be used for online transaction with the advantage of anonymity which can then either be exchanged for real money or can be used to make payments for online purchases. Although these digital currencies are created and transferred using cryptographic methods, they are vulnerable to digital thefts from hackers and being used by online money launderers for their illicit trafficking. Therefore, digital currencies, which combine speed with anonymity, are attractive for terrorists for their illicit fund transfers.

Additionally, credit/debit card frauds, online sale of drugs in the deep web, sale of merchandise and online gambling are other means of fund raising for the terrorist outfits to feed the financial needs of their organisation. Therefore, it can be stated that the cyber world provides safer and speedier options for terrorists to raise funds for their cruel missions than the real world along with the greatest advantage of anonymity.

Data Collection and Information Dissemination
In the information age, where information is equated to wealth, the ability of an individual or an organisation to possess and manipulate sensitive information/data provides an upper hand in society. Therefore, a race

for acquiring information is always on and is competed between various players ranging from governments, individuals, organisations to the non-state actors. This race has become more complex in the 21st century due to the increase in digitalisation of information. Digital data, available in various locations, becomes an easy target for the 'data poachers' due to lack of proper security mechanisms in most cases. In other case, in spite of an existing security mechanism, the attacker/s use modern digital tools for stealing information for selfish needs.

The non-state actors/ terrorists use the internet for the collection of data and information, mainly for two reasons: first being collection of data as there is so much information available electronically 'for free' on the web and the second being dissemination of the information as web gives high level of anonymity. The former is evident from "*Al-Qaeda* training manual", which was confiscated from the apartment of a suspected *Al-Qaeda* member in Manchester, England in May 2000which stated that, "*Using this public source openly and without resorting to illegal means, it is possible to gather at least 80% of information about the enemy.*"[33]

The above statement clearly denotes the motive of the terrorists for their data theft activities in the virtual medium. Also, this is one of the major reasons behind the increase in the number of incidents of hacking and data theft all around the world, especially the ones involving theft of credit/debit cards' data. For instance, "during the arrest of a terrorist suspect *Ali SalehKahlah al-Marri* in Illinois on December 2001, the authorities found his laptop with compiled data of more than 1,000 stolen credit cards details on it along with a host of internet bookmarks pointing to fraud and fake identity-related information websites."[34]

In another incident, it was also discovered that a series of hacks on customers of AT&T was carried out and the attackers were apparently able to steal more than US$2 million by making fake calls to premium call services. Later, the money made from that attack was diverted to a Saudi Arabia based militant group that is also believed to have helped in funding the deadly 26/11, 2008 Mumbai terror attacks in India where the coordinated series of attacks claimed 164 lives.[35] This is an example of the extent of damage that terrorists can inflict using the tactics of identity theft through digital networks.

Furthermore, the '2002 Bali Bombing', which killed 202 people in the tourist city of Kuta of Indonesia, *Imam Samudra,* master mind of the bombing, wrote an autobiography titled "I Fight Terrorists" on his jihadist life during his captivity. In this book he dedicated one chapter titled "Hacking, Why Not" which speaks of data theft and hacking, in which he urges fellow radical *jihadis* to take holy war into cyberspace. He says that the computer networks are vulnerable to hacking, credit-card frauds and money laundering and that the *jihadists* have to exploit them. He also discussed the process of scanning websites vulnerable to hacking and also the basics of online credit card fraud and money laundering. The chapter was also focused on how to find techniques on the internet and how to connect with people in chat rooms to perfect hacking and carding skills.[36] This book is widely popular among terrorists all over the world as it provided them with information on how to become more accomplished hackers.

The terrorists use the various facilities available in the cyber world to disseminate their knowledge to the wider audience. This explains the reason behind the increasing number of websites, blogs and videos in video hosting sites which contain destructive information from making a bomb in the house to hacking a bank account because of the increase in demand for destructive information by the audience. For example, as early as in 1999, it was estimated that there were nearly 30,000 web pages devoted to teaching hacking techniques. These websites allowed the users to download software that were used for hacking and performing other disruptive utilities, as well as providing a forum for discussion on hacking techniques and tips.[37] Clearly, the number of web pages providing much advanced hacking tips, techniques and training is now crossing more than million web pages which in turn signifies the increase in demand for the information.

Moreover, the web acts as a free publishing house for the terrorists to publish their research articles on various issues ranging from international politics to technical issues. For example, the bi-monthly online magazine called "Technical Mujahidin" distributed by 'Al-Fajr Information Center', deals with the topics like information security, ways of protecting computers, editing, sound engineering, the news of the jihadist media, and monitoring the crusader leaders' comments about the impact that the jihadist media have on them, etc. Also, the editor of the magazine gives the following reason for publishing such a magazine:

"We seek to attain the following objectives by publishing this magazine:
- *To remove the fear and panic complex from the hearts of some people who are held back from actively participating in jihad because they think that intelligence services are watching their every move and counting their every breath. When they are better informed of the facts, they will know when to go forward and when to hold back.*
- *To disseminate a sense of security in a scientific way among the members of the jihadist websites as a precaution that we are required to take in a logical, organized, and realistic way with neither exaggeration nor disregard.*
- *To spread technical awareness of everything that might be useful in the jihadist media sphere including visual editing, sound engineering, and other basic media skills.*
- *To publish scientific articles about some modern techniques that can help to develop the work of the brother mujahidin who operate in the field."*[38]

There are also more online magazines similar to this like "Inspire", which contain articles like "How to make a bomb in the kitchen of your mom". In addition to this, the terrorists surf the internet to find information about possible attack targets which includes railway stations, airports, markets, malls, and more sensitive areas like dams, nuclear facilities, government buildings, etc. They look for blue prints of installations, detailed maps for particular locations, existing security information for the infrastructure, etc. They use the expertise of hackers who in turn hack into the servers of various organisations to acquire the desired information by exploiting the vulnerabilities available in the organisation's network facility.

The terrorists also use open source mega data providers like 'Google Earth' for their collection of coordinates, maps and other data about a particular location. The existence of open source availability of digital designs of small arms like rifles, pistols, etc. are exploited by the terrorists to manufacture them on their own. The websites like www.defcad.com provide digital designs of weapon systems in support of open source. Such information provides easy access of arms to those terrorists who otherwise do not possess the ability to purchase arms due to lack of funding.

To the larger audience, i.e. to the normal browser around the world, this information becomes the primary data based on which the surfer develops his/her own idea about that particular organisation. By following this strategy of disseminating manipulated information, the terrorists slowly spread their propaganda by trying to change public opinion, to stimulate public debate, to enhance the support base and finally to de-moralise the government.

Also, being aware of the fact that 'cyber footprint' is the key for detection, the terrorists resort to various covert tactics to override the detection mechanisms and pass their message across the digital medium to their brothers in arms. While technology itself provides a natural cover and anonymity in most cases, in order to be safer they even carry out their communication in more stealthy methods by using encryption of messages to avoid any detection. Though the techniques of terrorist using digital medium of communications are evolving further few most common as well as interesting techniques are as follows:

USB Drives: The USB drives provide an easy source to carry/ transfer large data. Although, USB drives are vulnerable to malwares when plugged into affected systems, they still appear in the list of most used digital means of communication by the terrorists. This is evident from the fact that, "Osama Bin Laden stored his messages in a thumb drive and sent it through his human courier, who in turn travelled long distances and sent the messages saved in the thumb drive via e-mails from a public cyber booth to the fellow *jihadis* around the globe."[39] Also, the use of hardware/software based encryption in USB devices especially in thumb drives are a big advantage for the terrorists.

Use of E-mails and SMS: Even though e-mails and SMSs can be traced and intercepted, the terrorists' practice is that of using coded language and metaphors to hide the content of the message from the prying eyes of intelligence agencies. By following this method, even if the message is intercepted by the intelligence agencies, the terrorists would complete their task while the agencies are busy decoding it or would even get out of the suspicion radar as in the following case. "During the preparation for 9/11 attacks, the operator *Mohamed Atta* and conspirator *Ramzi bin al-Shibh* exchanged e-mails pretending as students, in which they used metaphors like "architecture" for the World Trade Center, "arts" for the Pentagon, "law" for the Capitol and "politics" for the White House."[40] By using these metaphors, they escaped from the radars of the intelligence agencies at the same time succeeded in communicating through digital medium. A similar tactics can be followed in SMS too.

Moreover, another tactic that terrorists follow in using e-mails as the communicating medium is by creating multiple login IDs and passwords. For example, two terrorists, each on the other end of the world, would create some 50 different login IDs with 50 different passwords for every ID. They would use a particular ID for one week or a month or even for one message, depending on their will, importance of message and prior planning. Once all of these login IDs have been exhausted, they would again start the process by creating more login IDs and passwords.

Dead Drops: This is an old technique where spies would drop off physical packages of information or photographs in places like hedges or behind dustbins and later it would be retrieved by someone else who knows the exact location of the dropped item. Similarly, in the digital age, the terrorists use a tactic called the dead drops in the mail services. The person who wants to convey a message creates the message and just leaves it in the drafts instead of clicking the send button. The intended receiver of that message logs in with the same ID and password which was shared before and reads the message from the drafts column and deletes it. By resorting to this technique, both sender and receiver avoid the vulnerability of leaving a cyber-footprint.

Dispose SIM cards: In the present scenario where mobile phones have become basic necessity of life, terrorists also use these devices to share information among them. In spite of the strict regulations followed in sale of SIM cards in many countries, the use of external SIM cards are a big boon for the terrorists as they are cheap, easily available and can be purchased by submitting fake identities and also can be disposed off when the work is over. The terrorists also use stolen SIM cards for their purpose and dispose them off to escape tracking.

Social-Networks, Public Chat Rooms, Forums and Gaming: The public chat rooms and forums are the most secretive places for the terrorists not only for sharing information but also for publicity, propaganda and recruiting. While many chat rooms are in-built with encryption software to provide privacy for its customers, this facility helps the terrorists to share their information in a safe zone. Also, there are numerous pages in the various social-networking sites that are operated by the terrorists to spread their information among the global audience and also to their targeted audience. For example, the twitter account *@alemarahweb* was active since 2011 with more than 6000 tweets and more than 8000 followers. The account claims that it belongs to the official website of Islamic Emirate of Afghanistan, but the language of the tweet denotes it otherwise. Few of the tweets on May 6, 2013 are below:

> *"6 invaders killed in Kandahar as enemy tank hits IEDs: KANDAHAR,*
> *May 06 - On Sunday evening an armored tank o..."*
> *"Fighting kills several puppets in Oruzgan amid Operation Khalid bin*
> *Waleed: ORUZGAN, May 06 – A fierce firefig..."*
> *"Mujahideen overrun 8 enemy posts in Ghour province; dozens killed:*
> *GHOUR,*
> *May 06 – In the morning hours of Su...*[41]

The words invaders, puppets and enemy in the tweet denote the NATO troops more specifically the U.S. troops.

Interestingly, even the online gaming sites are not left by the terrorists for their communications. While they launder funds through some games, they also chat in the cover of playing game while all these online gaming services provide chatting options for their players. The only consoling fact is that in recent years all these social media sites, forums, chat rooms and even the online gaming sites are under scanner by the intelligence agencies around the world with their data mining projects, but it is again an issue involving violation of privacy rights which is a different topic in itself.

Peer-to-peer communication: In order to avoid eavesdropping of the intelligence agencies in their conversations, especially during an operation or while transmitting secret information, the terrorists resort to more secure means of communications that function on peer-to-peer basis like satellite phones, Voice Over Internet Protocol (VOIP) and Video Voice Over Internet Protocol (VVOIP). The satellite phone uses direct uplink and downlink of data using satellites to provide the line of communication, and in the case of VOIPs and VVOIPs "the basic philosophy is converting visual image and audio signals into a digital form of data which is further compressed into units that are known as packets. These packets are in turn introduced into point to point communications by creating what is commonly referred to as a data stream over the internet. The data stream may be used for sharing data back and forth between two points, or involve a point of origin connected to multiple points of termination, with all points using the internet as the platform for communication.[42] This is in contrast to using the traditional technology that involves the circuits of a public switched telephone network that can be tapped easily.

The investigations of 26/11 Mumbai attack took the investigating agencies to Italy and to their surprise, it was revealed that the handlers and the operators of the brutal attack, which took more than 164 innocent lives, were using VOIP technology to get instructions from the handlers during the attack. "It was found that on November 25, on the eve of the attack, a request with the number 88647575 was made from a person called Kharak Singh, in India to the telephone company, Callphonex- a U.S. based company, in order to activate 5 Austrian DID lines of the VOIP account in the name of Mohammed Ashfaq from Pakistan. On the same day, payment for the VOIP account was made in Italy using Western Union money transfer by a Pakistani origin who claimed to be Kharak Singh. During the attacks, the terrorists used the U.S. based number 201-253-1824 to communicate amongst them and the attack commander received real time instructions and information from their handlers using the same number."[43]It was even found that the handlers and attackers had made 150 test calls before the attacks between November 24 and 26 to test the voice clarity, sound audibility, etc. Such is the expertise of the terrorists in using the latest technologies for their communication purposes.

Digital Steganography: Steganography is the art and science of writing hidden messages in such a way that no one apart from the intended recipient knows the existence of the message. While the conventional methods of steganography are being followed since 440 BC, the digital version of it uses three methods which are:

- Masking and Filtering,
- Algorithms and Transformations and
- Least Significant Bit Insertion.

Figure 4.2: A pictorial representation of how a steganograpic message is communicated.

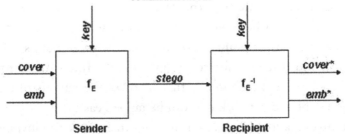

fE:steganographic function "embedding" **fE-1**: steganographic function "extracting"
Cover: cover data in which emb will be hidden **emb**: message to be hidden
key: parameter of fE **stego**: cover data with the hidden message
Source: http://io.acad.athabascau.ca/~grizzlie/Comp607/basics.htm. Accessed on February 27, 2014.

While this technology is being used by various people all around the world to transfer their secret messages, one of the most well-known use of modern day digital steganography by the terrorists was during the planning stages of 9/11 attacks. It is being speculated that Osama Bin Laden and his team of tech savvy *Al-Qaeda* members used steganography technique to discuss their plans in the online medium by sending and receiving mails containing hidden messages. Although this claim was kept aside by the investigating agencies publicly, they have not totally rejected the possibility of such an event in any case.

Apart from such covert means of communications and information gathering, the terrorists also use many other methods for their purpose like plugging into cloud computing, using Remote Access Trojans which collect data and send it back to the handler, use of encryption software like '*Mujahideen* Secrets 2" for encrypting their mails and other digital communications and so on.

Recruitment and mobilisation

> "*They lost their base in Afghanistan, they lost their training camps, they lost a government that allowed them do what they want within a country. Now they're surviving on internet to a large degree. It is really their new base,*"[44]
> — Peter Bergen.

Unlike the statement made by Peter Bergen, it is not only *Al-Qaeda* that used the internet as a virtual terrorist recruitment and training base but most other terrorist organisations around the world also follow the same practice. In fact, the Islamic State terrorist organisation which was once an off-shoot of *Al-Qaeda* in Iraq is a classic example of using cyberspace for recruitment. It is one of the leading terrorist organisations of the world which has managed to recruit thousands of foreign fighters through cyber means. For any organisation new recruits are like fresh blood flowing in their arteries and especially for a terrorist organisation the younger the recruits are easier for its leaders to mould them for their cause. Therefore, in order to catch those young, the terrorists target them online who use internet a lot more than their older counterparts and manipulate their emotions by their various approaches through internet. The terrorists follow a pattern for their recruitment process on the internet by methods mentioned below:

- They employ various tactics like spreading online propaganda through their websites, blogs, forums, chat rooms and social media accounts.
- Sending out repeated clear and simple messages to their targeted audience.
- Using video streaming to convey the message of their leaders, interviews, or to show doctrine photos and video footages of exaggerated plights of a particular community to gather sympathy towards them.
- By using cartoons, games and other multimedia facilities to indoctrinate the minds of children.
- By identifying the prospective recruits and disseminating destructive information through publications, video chatting, etc.

However, it should be noted that modern terrorists do not recruit directly online, rather use the net only to identify, profile and select potential candidates for recruitment. Afraid of having their groups infiltrated by security agencies and counter-terrorism forces, they use the internet only for the early stages of the recruitment process.[45]

After identifying their potential recruits, the terrorists give some sort of pre-terrorist camp training which is like brain washing their recruits through internet by using various methods of communications. While internet is the home to millions of websites and blogs that teach anyone how to build bombs, explosives, small arms etc, the terrorists go a step higher by publishing their own technical and theoretical journals and books to educate and train their potential future cadres across the globe. Few of the most commonly used publications by the terrorists are:

- *The Terrorist's Handbook*, Author: Unknown.
- *The Anarchist Cookbook*, Author: William Powell.
- *The Mujahideen Explosives Handbook*, Abdel-Azia.
- *The Explosives Course*, Abu Khabbab al-Misri.
- *INSPIRE*, Magazine edited by Anwar Al Awlaki.
- *Technical Mujahideen*, Edited by Abu-al-Muthanna al-Najdi.

Apart from these special efforts, they also train their recruits psychologically by chatting with them through text messages, audio or videos to brainwash them and prepare to take up the organisation's missions whenever necessary. The young recruits are also advised to keep themselves physically trained to be able to take up arms at any moment.

As a next step the recruits who are trained and ready for the missions are mobilised using internet. For instance, in 2006, during the violent clashes between Israel and the Hezbollah, an Iranian website posted online a call urging volunteers to join the war against Israel. Later, on July 26 2006, the Iranian news agency *Alborz* announced that volunteers could sign up online for the "Army of the Fighters of Muhammad." According to the report, the recruits would be sent to Lebanon and that their minimum age for enlisting is sixteen and anybody interested can call the phone number: 88938821 in Tehran.[46]

Planning and coordination

"The semester begins in three more weeks. We've obtained 19 confirmations for studies in the faculty of law, the faculty of urban planning, the faculty of fine arts, and the faculty of engineering."[47]

— Mohammad Atta

The above message was the final message sent by the infamous commander of 9/11 terrorist attack, Mohammad Atta, to his other 18 fellow terrorists involved in the attack through a mail that used secret metaphors. This is one of the initial methods by which the terrorists used the cyber arena for their planning and coordination process.

In general any information/data available freely in the society does not cause any conflict by itself but, the way in which it is manipulated by various players of the society can cause serious repercussions. The terrorists use or to put it right, misuse the information available in the public medium for their own needs and cause serious destruction to the society. Apart from misusing the cyber technology for all their other needs like publicity, propaganda, fund raising, psychological operations, etc., the terrorists also misuse this technology for planning, execution and coordination of their evil missions.

One classic example for this would be the use of cyber technology in the planning and coordination of 26/11 Mumbai terror attacks by the *Lashkar-e-Taiba* (LeT) terrorist organisation. During the planning phase, Google Earth imagery was extensively used by the LeT terrorists to conduct virtual reconnaissance of their targets. The reconnaissance was precise to the extent of locating the entrances and exits of the primary target locations. Also, with the help of Google, the attackers marked the geographic coordinates of their target used to program their GPS devices.[48] It is by the use of these co-ordinates the attackers infiltrated the location via sea undetected in the cover of darkness.

The whole attack was coordinated by the handlers in real time with the help of VOIP enabled phones, satellite phones and social media sites. The handlers of the attack kept monitoring live updates from the social networking sites like Facebook and Twitter to know the situation in Mumbai and also analysed movement of security forces in different locations with the help of live relay in TV News Channels. In fact, after having realised that the handlers are using the updates from social networking sites and TV News Media, Indian security forces made a public appeal in social media sites to stop updating anything related to the attack. Also, the media was instructed not to relay live video footages of the attack.

Later during the investigations, it was revealed that the terrorists used the VOIP connection provided by "Callphonex" - a U.S. based company – and had paid US$250 and US$229 using Western Union money transfer in Pakistan and Italy respectively few days before the attack. Further investigations revealed that the terrorists had used unsecured Wi-Fi connection to send e-mails before the attack.[49] This is the expertise level of the modern day terrorists who use cyber technology to its utmost level in planning and coordinating their attacks in a precise manner.

Also, in another terror incident, the Boston Marathon Bombings in 2013, the accused *Dzhokhar Tsarnaevis* is believed to have acquired his knowledge of making cooker bomb from the online magazine INSPIRE. He was also in possession of extremist literature *"Defense of the Muslim*

Lands, the first Obligation after Imam" with him. This is also one of the numerous examples of how terrorists use destructive information available on the internet for planning and execution of their evil act.[50]

As terrorist organisations are becoming more decentralised and more global, and along with the advent of more new technologies in the cyber world, the use of internet for the purposes discussed above are only going to increase in the coming years. Nevertheless, the government agencies around the world are trying their best to track, trace and eliminate the terrorist activities on the internet with their data mining projects like the X-Keyscore project of the U.S (See Chapter 6 for more information). But these data mining projects also have their own disadvantages as they violate the personal freedom and privacy of individuals in the virtual world. Therefore, undoubtedly, the cyber world would be a highly contested battleground of the future where not only the states would compete against each other but they also have to face the more violent unconventional challenge from the non-state actors in the form of terrorists.

Notes

1. http://www.brainyquote.com/quotes/authors/k/kevin_mitnick.html, accessed on March 10, 2015.
2. One of the most famous hacker of his generation, Mitnick has been described by the US Department of Justice as "the most wanted computer criminal in United States history." After a highly publicised pursuit by the FBI, Mitnick was arrested in 1995 and after confessing to several charges as part of a plea-bargain agreement, he served a five year prison sentence. He was released on parole in 2000 and today runs a computer security consultancy. He didn't refer to his hacking activities as 'hacking' and instead called them 'social engineering'.
3. In October 2001, *The New York Times* published an article claiming that *Al-Qaeda* had used steganography to encode messages into images, and then transported these via e-mail and possibly via USENET to prepare and execute the September 11, 2001 terrorist attack.
4. Gabriel Weimann, "www.terror.net How Modern Terrorism Uses the Internet"; *Special Report*, United States Institute of Peace, March 2004.
5. Gabriel Weimann, "Virtual Training Camps: Terrorist Use of the Internet, in Teaching Terror: Strategic and Tactical Learning in the Terrorist World 110, 111 (James J.F. Forest ed.), 2006.
6. John Bumgarner, "Tech-Savvy Terrorists", *APD Forum*, 2012.

7. http://www.worldwidewebsize.com/, accessed on February 20, 2016.
8. "ICT Facts and Figures – The world in 2015", *International Telecommunication Union*, 2015, http://www.itu.int/en/ITU-D/Statistics/Pages/facts/default.aspx, accessed on February 10, 2016.
9. Ibid.
10. Ibid.
11. A copy of the letter translated was released by the Office of the Director of National Intelligence on October 11, 2005. http://www.globalsecurity.org/security/library/report/2005/zawahiri-zarqawi-letter_9jul2005.htm, accessed on January 31, 2014.
12. http://en.wikipedia.org/wiki/Hezbollah, accessed on January 31, 2014.
13. Ibid.
14. Gary R. Bunt, Virtually Islamic: Computer – Mediated Communication and Cyber Islamic Environments 10 (2000).
15. http://archive.adl.org/main_Terrorism/jihad_brigades_80805.htm, accessed on February 1, 2014.
16. http://www.youtube.com/watch?v=omnKITLL0jA&feature=player_embedded#t=0 at Youtube, accessed on Feb 28, 2014. A video in which a woman who claims to be a victim of rape by the U.S. forces in Iraq narrates the incident to Al-Jazeera news media.
17. Timothy Thomas, "Al-Qaeda and the internet", *Parameters, USAWC*, Spring 2003, pp. 112-123.
18. Taken from the video posted at http://www.liveleak.com/view?i=01e_1175818014. The video can also be seen in the following website.
19. Maura Conway, "*Terrorism and the Internet- New media – new threat?*", School of Law and Government, Dublin City University, Ireland.
20. Ibid.
21. IntelCenter, Al-Qaeda videos and 3rd 9–11 anniversary v.1.0., Alexandria, VA: IntelCenter, 2004.
22. "TRAI tracking panic-spreading SMS", *The New Indian Express*, August 17, 2012.
23. Ibid.
24. "Department of Justice Shuts Down Several Financial Networks Exploited by Terrorist Groups", *Attorney General Transcript of the speeches*, November 07, 2001. USA, http://www.justice.gov/archive/ag/speeches/2001/agcrisisremarks11_07.htm, accessed on February 13, 2014.
25. Sean Paul Ashley, "The Future of Terrorist Financing: Fighting Terrorist Financing in the Digital Age", Penn *State Journal for International Affairs*, 2012.
26. Gabriel Weimann, "www.terror.net How Modern Terrorism Uses the Internet"; *Special Report*, United States Institute of Peace, March 2004.
27. Timothy Thomas, Al-Qaeda and the internet, Parameters, USAWC, Spring 2003, pp. 112-123.
28. "Al-Qaeda in Iraq looks for fundraising ideas"; *The Telegraph*, July 16, 2011.
29. Kilian Strauss, "How can we effectively combat the use of the internet for money laundering?" 2012.

30. M-Pesa is a mobile-phone based money transfer and micro-financing service. Currently the most developed mobile payment system in the developing world, M- Pesa allows users with a national ID card or passport to deposit, withdraw, and transfer money easily with a mobile device.

31. Strauss, n. 29.

32. http://en.wikipedia.org/wiki/Bitcoin, accessed on February 14, 2014.

33 "Al-Qaeda Training Manual", Provided courtesy of the Behavioural Analysis Program, Operational Training Unit, Counterintelligence Division, FBI Headquarters.

34. Bod Sullivan, "9/11 report light on ID theft issues, *NBC News*, April 04, 2004, at www.nbcnews.com/id/5594385/ns/us_news-security/t/report-light-id-theft-issues/#.Uxgj4uXchgg, accessed on February 25, 2014.

35. Neal O'Farrell, "Could your identity be funding terrorism?", January 23, 2012, at http://blog.identitytheftcouncil.org/?p=441, accessed on February 26, 2014.

36. Dennis Lormel, "Terrorists and Credit Card Fraud…a Quiet Epidemic", Counter-terrorism Blog, at http://counterterrorismblog.org/2008/02/terrorists_and_credit_card_fra.php, accessed on February 26, 2014.

37. Lt Col Patrick S. Tibbetts, "Terrorist Use of the Internet And Related Information Technologies", Monograph, School of Advanced Military Studies, United States Army command and General Staff College, 2002.

38. "*Technical Mujahidin*", Issue 2.

39. Mark Benjamin, "Bin Laden's Secret Communications Plan: Use a Thumb Drive", Time, May 12, 2011 at http://nation.time.com/2011/05/12/bin-ladens-secret-communications-plan-use-a-thumb-drive/#ixzz2vG9lYpmx, accessed on February 26, 2014.

40. "The Terrorist's Tricks and Counter measures", *Frontline,* January 25, 2005, at http://www.pbs.org/wgbh/pages/frontline/shows/front/special/techsidebar.html, accessed on February 26, 2014.

41. https://twitter.com/alemarahweb, accessed on February 27, 2014.

42. "What is VVoIP (Video and Voice over IP)?", at http://www.wisegeek.com/what-is-vvoip-video-and-voice-over-ip.htm, accessed on February 27, 2014.

43. Vaiju Naravane, "Italian police explain how VOIP was used on 26/11", *The Hindu*, November 23, 2009, at http://www.thehindu.com/news/national/italian-police-explain-how-voip-was-used-on-2611/article53189.ece, accessed on February 27, 2014.

44. Gordan Corera, "A web wise terror network", *BBC*, Wednesday, October 6, 2004. URL: http://news.bbc.co.uk/2/hi/in_depth/3716908.stm, accessed on February 4, 2014.

45. Gabriel Weimann, "Using the Internet for Terrorist Recruitment and Mobilisation", chapter in ed. Ganor, Boaz, Hypermedia Seduction for Terrorist Recruiting, (IOS Press, 2006), pp. 47-58.

46. Ibid.

47. Major J P I A G Charvat, "Cyber Terrorism: A New Dimension in Battle space", *NATO Cooperative Cyber Defence Centre of Excellence.*

48. "John Bumgarner, "Tech-savvy terrorists", *Asia Pacific Defence Forum*, November 4, 2011.
49. Sanjay Poduval, "Contours of Security in Cyberspace", *Maritime Affairs*, Vol. 08, No.02, Winter 2012, pp. 73-94.
50. "Feds: Boston Marathon suspect had bomb-making instructions, jihad literature available online", *Fox News*, June 28, 2013, at http://www.foxnews.com/us/2013/06/28/feds-boston-marathon-suspect-had-bomb-making-instructions-jihad-literature/, accessed on February 28, 2014.

5

DRAGON'S FIRE IN THE VIRTUAL WORLD

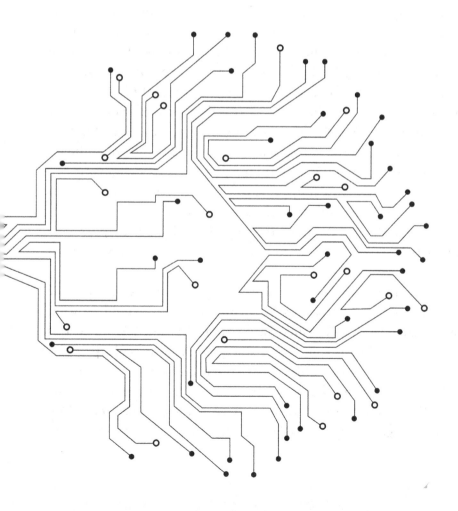

While the three previous chapters discussed the different kinds of threats posed by the non-state actors and the threat in-built in the cyber domain, this and the following chapters would discuss in detail the various kinds of covert threats that states pose against each other in the cyber domain. When a country is overtly using cyber means to attack another country it is known as cyber warfare which is not a usual occurrence. On the other hand, countries opt for more covert methods to attack each other especially in the case of big powers like China, the US, Russia, etc., where in spite of their overt active friendly diplomatic participation in the real world, they enjoy the liberty to simultaneously fight against each other covertly through networks.

Cyber space, widely considered as the fifth domain of warfare, is a conflict ridden domain where actual war is a rare case scenario but other forms of conflicts are taking place almost daily between the challenging players. In fact, this is a more competitive domain than the domains of conventional warfare where different parties compete with one another with latest cyber technologies with the intention to prove their superiority to lead the race in technology and to use it as a force multiplier. In fact, cyber is the only domain where even one individual with appropriate knowledge and evil intentions can cause a huge adverse impact. Therefore, in order to enhance their capabilities and also to move ahead in this highly competitive virtual domain, individuals and more importantly states strive hard covertly to exhibit their capabilities when the need arises from time to time.

As mentioned earlier, since warfare is a rare case scenario in the cyber domain, the question which could come up would be what are the other kind of conflicts in this domain? The answer to this question in simple words is that since the cyber domain provides access to players from individuals to nation states, the conflicts could be in the form of cyber thefts, hacking, cyber espionage, data collection through ex-filtration, cyber sabotage, cyber terrorism, cyber propaganda, cyber warfare and so on. Among all the major players in the world, one country which is well known to be involved in all the above mentioned forms of cyber conflicts not only in the military sector but also in the civilian sector, is the Peoples Republic of China. Therefore, with a view to have a broader perspective of global cyber security, it is necessary to understand the modus operandi and other methodologies being used by different groups from China, both in military and civilian sector during cyber conflicts creating potential terror in the cyber domain.

Cyber Environment in China

The Asian giant is not only the largest populated country in the world but also has the largest number of internet users with more than 710 million people subscribed to use internet at the end of June 2016. The penetration of internet among the total population of China is estimated to be 51.7 percent. The number of people using internet in their mobile phones is 656 million and the mobile netizens accounted for 92.5 percent of the total netizen population.[1] In other words mobile phones are the driving force for the growth of internet in China. Internet is utilised by common public in China mainly for the following purposes:

* Personal and business communications,
* Entertainment by watching and downloading videos, listening and downloading music,
* Social networking,
* Online shopping and
* Gaming.

With more and more new applications being introduced in mobile phones, creation of new websites for shopping, gaming and social networking along with increase in the number of videos and music files being uploaded in the internet the number of users of internet in China is growing at an alarming pace.

But at the same time, according to the information available recently China is one of the few countries which have imposed the 'strictest form of censorship on internet'[2] and is also one of the five countries along with Bahrain, Iran, Vietnam and Syria which conducts intrusive surveillance on the users of internet in its own territory.[3] Moreover, China is the leading exporter of censorship technologies to other countries such as Saudi Arabia, Iran, North Korea etc., which also impose a high level of censorship on internet in their country. There are also several Government Departments and Bodies in China, which engage in monitoring and censoring activities of the internet. The details of Government Departments/Bodies which are involved in monitoring the internet are as follows:

- The Internet Affairs Bureau and the Centre for the Study of Public Opinion of the State Council Information Office.
- The Internet Bureau and the Information and Public Opinion Bureau of the Publicity Department (formerly the Propaganda Department).
- The Ministry of Industry and Information Technology (MIIT).
- The Internet Information Security Supervision of the Ministry of Public Security.
- The Internet Illegal Information Reporting Centre under the Ministry of Industry and Information Technology.
- China Internet Network Information Centre.
- Office of the Centre Leading Group for Cyberspace Affairs (CAC).

It is well known that everything in China is related to the Communist Party of China and internet is no exception. Internet in China is controlled by several bodies which operate in the interest of the Party. The framework of these controlling bodies, which monitor and manipulate internet in China is given below:

Figure 5.1: Bodies which control and regulate Internet in China

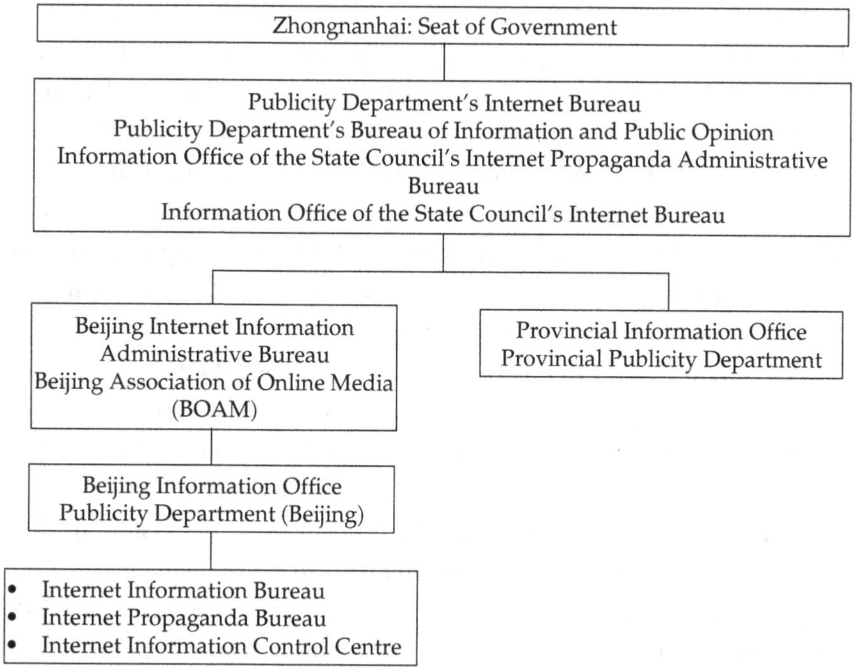

Zhongnanhai: Seat of Government

Publicity Department's Internet Bureau Publicity Department's Bureau of Information and Public Opinion Information Office of the State Council's Internet Propaganda Administrative Bureau Information Office of the State Council's Internet Bureau

Beijing Internet Information Administrative Bureau Beijing Association of Online Media (BOAM)	Provincial Information Office Provincial Publicity Department

Beijing Information Office Publicity Department (Beijing)

• Internet Information Bureau • Internet Propaganda Bureau • Internet Information Control Centre

Source: "Era of Digital Mercenaries", http://surveillance.rsf.org/en/, accessed on July 2, 2014.

The above mentioned government agencies in China that filter and monitor internet content in the country utilises certain tools and methods which operates under the name "Golden Shield Project" (金盾工程).It is also known as "The Great Firewall of China" in the west. This project which was initiated in 1998 became operational in November 2003. It mainly filters the access to foreign websites in China. China succeeds in analysing and manipulating internet traffic band controls the Internet gateways for Internet traffic between China and the rest of the world. China also uses a combination of firewalls and proxy servers at these gateways. The basic rules which China applies while monitoring and controlling the internet are:

- do not jeopardise social stability,
- do not organise and
- do not threaten the Party.[4]

These three rules were made as a result of 'Tiananmen Square Protest of 1989' to ensure that no such incidents happen again. When the cyber domain became popular, same set of rules were applied to maintain order in this domain too. Therefore, these three rules form the foundation of all the rules that were formulated in order to govern the internet and cyberspace in China. Any online content which directly or indirectly violates these rules will face censorship. Whenever there is a violation of any of these rules, the golden shield activates its censorship methods on that particular IP address, which is requesting the information on the officially banned keywords or websites. The methods followed under Golden Shield Project to censor information are as follows:

DNS poisoning: Normally whenever a user requests for connection to a website, the usual process is that the computer contacts its DNS (Domain Naming System) server asking for the IP address of that particular website and when obtained, connects the user's system to that IP address to give access to the website. But, in China whenever a user requests for a connection with a website, the system contacts its DNS Server and server checks from the list of banned websites. If the user had requested for any of the banned websites, the server poisons its DNS caches with wrong addresses for the website which either take them to a different website or will show an error on the user's computer.

Blocking access to IPs: In order to prevent people from accessing the banned websites by using direct IPs or by using some private DNS servers, which are not poisoned, the tools in Golden Shield may block access to the IP addresses of certain banned websites.

Analysing and filtering URLs: The firewalls in the servers scan URLs for certain sensitive keywords like 'http://en.wikipedia.org/wiki/Tiananmen_Square_protests_of_1989'. When it is found, the firewall blocks the webpages associated with these URLs.

Inspecting and filtering packets: A technique called "Deep Packet Inspection" is used to examine the unencrypted packets, looking for politically controversial keywords. Whenever a user requests through a search engine to look for information on such sensitive keywords, the packets associated with the search are examined and blocked.

Resetting connections: Whenever a particular website or some web pages are blocked by the great firewall the communication between the user's computer and the computer at the destination is reset automatically by the firewall. This is happening because the firewall sends a "reset packet" to both the user's computer and the desired destination computer lying that the connection was reset and therefore it cannot connect during that time. Every time there is a reset, the user loses his connectivity temporarily for 90 seconds.[5]

Blocking VPNs: During the 18th Communist Party Congress in November 2012 the Chinese Cyber Security authorities enhanced the abilities of the great firewall by expanding its capacity to block VPNs (Virtual Private Networks). These VPNs were previously used by the users to escape the great firewall. After the enhancement of the firewall's ability, the encrypted VPN traffic is also monitored and killed when being used.[6]

Apart from the above measures to impose censorship, Chinese officials also conduct monitoring of internet and surveillance programme effectively by employing more than two million "Internet Opinion Analysts" across the country to monitor and analyse public opinion on Chinese social media. Specially designed software is used by these Internet opinion analysts, who are mostly government employees to rummage around through various blogs, micro-blog posts and social networks and dissect public opinion on local issues by identifying accusations of corruption and poor governance. The extracted information are then analysed and reports are forwarded to the local leadership from country to province daily via text messages.[7] Given the huge numbers, it is a logical assumption that all these Internet Opinion Analysts may not be exclusively recruited for this purpose, but they are assigned with this additional job apart from their regular business.

Moreover, in certain cases where a netizen is found to be vocal against the Chinese politics or the Party or any of its leaders or in general violates the basic rules of China's censorship and monitoring, then the officials keep special watch on the particular user's online activity. The police will also tap all his/her phone lines, read his/her mails and other social media posts and also monitor his/her other online activity. Thus, the targeted user loses his/her privacy in the cyber space and is forced to live a transparent life.[8] Also there are regular instances of arrests of users who are found to be violating the strict cyber censorship rules. Those who are found to be vocal against the state or the party, especially in the Autonomous Xinjiang province where on the pretext of curbing the spread of Jihadi ideas authorities arrest people who share their dissatisfaction in the online social media.[9]

Chinese Cyber Terror

While the cyber environment inside China is in a state of curfew with strict censorships and surveillance, the Cyber capabilities developed by the government is made use of without any restrictions while flexing its virtual muscles beyond its borders. In other words, China's cyber warfare capabilities are a real asset for the country but a real threat for other countries in the world. According to a US report on China's Military and Security Developments, cyber warfare serves three key purposes for China. They are:

- Data collection through ex-filtration.
- To restrict an adversary's actions or slow response time by employing cyber technologies and targeting network based logistics, communications and commercial services, and
- To serve as a force multiplier combined with kinetic attacks during times of crisis or conflict.[10]

Till now, China has not overtly declared any cyber war against any of its adversaries but is conducting a number of cyber operations covertly against various countries in the world. Most of its cyber operations deal with data ex-filtration, espionage and industrial espionage and theft of sensitive information. While many countries across the globe have suffered as a result of the threat from China's covert cyber operations, two important targets of China are US and India.

The Prime Targets: India and US

Though India's policy of development is non aggressive and peaceful coexistence, the Asian giant, China never allows India to be a passive neighbour as it views India as a potential competitor. While the conventional aggressive strategies adopted by China would reveal China's true intentions, it also engages India through covert cyber operations both on government and private sector. Hence, with the amount of its covert cyber operations, it can be stated that China assumes the role of a cyber bullying neighbour by threatening, attacking and gathering sensitive information discreetly from India's premier institutions.

For instance, in 2012, computers in the campus of India's Eastern Naval Command were infected with Chinese malwares. The virus which infected the systems through an USB drive which was accidently inserted into one of the systems and this system was not connected to the internet. The infected USB drive collected all the data and when the same drive was inserted into another system which had internet access, the data was diverted to a particular IP address located in China.[11] A logical reasoning for this attack could be that, the Eastern Naval Command is home to India's indigenously built Nuclear Powered Submarine, INS Arihant, where it is undergoing sea trials and made it a lucrative target for the attack. Though the IP address to which all data were sent was traced to China, benefit of doubt was given to it as it is very hard to find 'Smoking Gun' evidence in any sophisticated cyber attack.

It was reported that in the year 2013 the computers in the Defence Research and Development Organisation (DRDO), India's premier defence research organisation, had been compromised by the Chinese and a large number of electronic files were stolen and diverted to a server located in Guangdong Province in China. This included files on the proceedings of the Cabinet Committee on Security (CCS), country's highest decision making body on defence and security affairs. The Indian authorities came to know about this attack accidently, while NTRO (National Technical Research Organisation) was investigating another case.[12] With these and more such attacks everyday on Indian computers by the Chinese covert cyber operators, India has become a persistent target of cyber espionage and other kinds of cyber attacks by the Chinese government and facing a serious threat to its cyber security.

Apart from India another country which is being constantly targeted by China for its covert cyber operations is the US. In fact, the magnitude of cyber attacks on the US is much larger in scale than the attacks on India. The specific targets of the Chinese cyber attacks are the technological research and development centres both in the government and private sector. The US accuses China of cyber espionage, technology theft, intelligence gathering, ex-filtration of information, research on Department of Defence (DoD) operations and the creation of dormant presence in DoD networks for future operations in various government and private agencies.[13]

The Chinese strategy is to look for vulnerabilities and weak points in the network of others and conduct its advanced persistent attack through those vulnerable areas. For instance, in November 2006, the Chinese hackers virtually intruded into US Naval War College's (NWC) network and started looking for specific data which forced the college to shut down its e-mail and other computer systems for several weeks. Later, the cyber forensic analysis on the attack showed that the Chinese were looking for the War Games which were being developed in NWC. Also it was found that since NWC's network was connected to internet and not to Navy Marine Corps intranet, it became a vulnerable target.[14] Thus, the Chinese hackers keep analysing the network of their targets and are always on the lookout for vulnerable spots to begin their attack.

Besides, Chinese hackers are also constantly in the hunt for high level technical data to support their country's research and development projects mainly for defence and security related development programmes. While defence related research projects require lots of time, manpower and money to develop technological expertise, stealing similar technology from some other country is profitable for China and they are in possession of the same in the shortest time possible with comparatively less effort. Therefore, in recent years unofficial cyber theft has become a part of the research and development methods adopted by China in connection with their defence related development programmes. This is evident from the high level of covert cyber theft operations organised by China against the US in the recent past.

In September 2003, a computer-network security expert, Shawn Carpenter, working for the Sandia National Laboratories of the US was the first to uncover a high profile, sophisticated and well organised covert cyber espionage operation which was later traced to China.[15] Although initially it was considered as a regular cyber attack on the US networks, it was later realised that it was one of the biggest, organised covert series of cyber operation on the US. Secret investigations on this series of attacks was dubbed as 'Titan Rain' which started in 2004 and by 2005 it was found that the attackers have already compromised the computer networks in NASA, Lockheed Martin, World Bank, Redstone Arsenal Military base, and many other important military and other technological development centres across the US. Huge quantum of documents related to solar panelling and fuel tanks for the Mars Reconnaissance Orbiter belonging to NASA, a large number of files related to Army Aviation and Missile Development belonging to Redstone Arsenal, specifications related to aviation-mission-planning system for the Army helicopters, the flight-planning software - Falconview 3.2, used by the army and Air Force, are among the few sensitive data in the big list of stolen information from the US computer networks.[16]

A cyber forensic investigation on these attacks carried out by FBI after taking a few independent cyber network security experts into confidence, traced the attack initially to a few zombie servers in South Korea, Hong Kong and Taiwan. Further deep cyber tracking led the trail of the attack to the southern Chinese province Guangdong where three main Chinese routers were found to have been used for establishing a first connection from a local network to the internet to carry out these attacks.[17] It was speculated that all these attacks were carried out with lightning speed and it would take only 10-30 minutes for the attackers to compromise the computers and steal all the information from it. The attackers were so well organised and their attacks so sophisticated that they always made a quite escape, wiping out their cyber footprints and at the same time leaving behind an almost undetectable beacon which would allow them to re-enter the network at will whenever they wished to.

The US alleges that the Chinese spies are stealing American technology in order to enable them to compete with US without delay otherwise it will incur more time and energy if they opt to conduct research on their own. In response to these American allegations, Chinese totally deny all charges against them pertaining to cyber espionage and technological thefts from the US and call all the claims of the US as "totally groundless, irresponsible and unworthy of refute". They have also refused to cooperate with the US authorities on any investigations especially regarding 'Titan Rain'.

Although there is no "smoking gun" evidence neither with India nor with the US, to prove that all the cyber attacks and other covert espionage operations were conducted by China against them, the cyber forensic investigators of both these countries are convinced that these attacks originated from China and also the attackers have a strong backing from the Chinese government or in other words Chinese state sponsors cyber terror attacks on their network. The claims made by the US and Indian authorities proved to be true as a result of the exposure of the existence of a secret unit in the People's Liberation Army (PLA) of China called Unit 61398.

Unit 61398[18]

As US was facing a series of cyber attacks since 2003, investigations were being carried out on a few detected major attacks with the help of private cyber security companies across the country in order to unmask the real culprits behind the attacks. As part of one such investigative operation, the Information Security Company 'Mandiant'[19] came to assist US in 2006. Since then, the cyber security experts of 'Mandiant' started monitoring and tracking one particular group of attackers who were conducting advanced threat on the US networks. This group of attackers were given the name "Advanced Persistent Threat 1 (APT1)". It was noticed that APT1 was one of the most prolific cyber espionage groups in terms of sheer quantity of information that they had stolen from their broad range of victims at least since 2006. As the number of attacks and the quantity of information being stolen were steadily increasing from time to time, the experts in 'Mandiant' felt that it is necessary to identify the real attackers. A more stringent cyber investigation by 'Mandiant' traced the operations of APT 1 to four large networks in Shanghai, out of which two were found to be allocated directly to the Pudong New Area in the same city.[20]

Figure 5.2: Location of Unit 61398

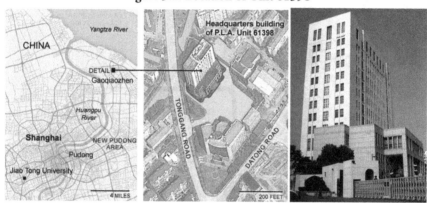

Source: David E. Sanger, David Barboza and Nicole Perlroth, "Chinese Army Unit is Seen as Tied to Hacking against U.S.", *The New York Times*, February 18, 2013, http://www.nytimes.com/2013/02/19/technology/chinas-army-is-seen-as-tied-to-hacking-against-us.html, accessed on August 28, 2014.

While investigating these four large networks especially the two networks in the Pudong New Area, a major breakthrough was achieved in this case. It was found that the two networks in the Pudong New Area was emerging from a 12 storied high rise building situated on Datong Road in Gaoqiaozhen which houses a part of the Unit 61398 of PLA. The Unit 61398 is part of PLA's cyber command fully institutionalised within the Communist Party of China (CPC) and is supported with resources for its operations from China's state owned enterprises. In fact, Unit 61398 is the 2nd Bureau under the 3rd Department in the PLA General Staff Department (GSD), which comes directly under the control of Communist Party of China's Central Military Commission.[21]

Figure 5.3: Unit 61398's position in PLA

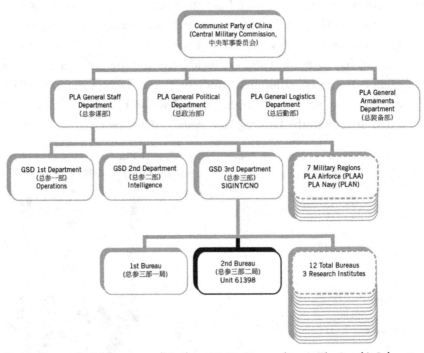

Source: James C. Mulvenon and Andrew N. D. Yang, editors, *The People's Liberation Army as Organization: Reference Volume v1.0*, Santa Monica, CA: RAND Corporation, 2002.

Based on the magnitude of the attack operations carried out by the group APT1, it was earlier speculated that the size of the group would be in hundreds where people work in a group. But later, after identifying the source and the fact that APT1 is nothing but Unit 61398 of PLA, the calculations about the size of the unit has multiplied to thousands of individuals who are trained in computer security, computer networking operations especially in English language as most of their targets are primarily English speaking countries. It is also likely that, such a large group of operators would definitely need substantial number of support staff with expertise in various fields like linguists, open source researchers, malware authors, industry experts, IT staff to acquire and maintain the computer equipments, financial staff, facility and logistics managers etc. During the investigations it was also found that China's state-owned Information Technology Enterprise 'China Telecom' has built dedicated special fiber optic communication lines to the Unit's building in Datong Road to support the operations of Unit 61398 under the cover of 'national defence construction'.[22]

In May 2014, the Federal Bureau of Investigation (FBI) of the US filed charges of cyber espionage against five individuals belonging to the PLA alleging that they are part of Unit 61398 and have massive involvement in the cyber espionage operations against the US for the past few years. The US even asked China to extradite these five Chinese nationals to the US in order to face trials. But China as always has denied all the allegations against it regarding state sponsored cyber espionage and cyber theft and stated that the allegations against them are irresponsible and unprofessional. Also in this case they denied the request for extraditing the five Chinese nationals.[23]

The Case of OPM Hack

In June 2015, the US allegedly accused China for breaching the huge data of the digital records belonging to the United States Office of Personnel Management (OPM). It was initially identified by OPM agency that the background investigation records of current, former, and prospective Federal employees and contractors had been stolen through hacking. Investigations made in June 2015 revealed that the personnel data of 21.5 million current and former Federal government employees had been stolen which includes information such as full name, date of birth, home address and Social Security Numbers etc. Further investigations revealed a bigger breach of 5.6 million fingerprints from the OPM database.[24] This posed a grave threat to the US federal government employees as their personal information along with their fingerprints was available to unknown people. China, however, denied any involvement in any such hacking incidents against the US and claimed the allegation to be irresponsible. Hong Lei, a Foreign Ministry spokesman of China stated that:

"Cyber attacks are generally anonymous and conducted across borders, and their origins are hard to trace,… Not to carry out deep investigation and keep using words such as 'possible' is irresponsible and unscientific."[25]

This breach in data in the US is considered as the largest data breach in the country's history and America has setup an interagency investigation group to analyse the post data breach scenario regarding the possible ways in which the breached data could be used against the country.[26] In September 2015, when Chinese President Xi Jingping visited the US on a state visit, both the US and China discussed extensively on the OPM hack and the Heads of States of both countries agreed that neither side will indulge in commercial espionage against each other. Apart from this, a week or two before Xi Jingping's state visit to the US in 2015, there was a visible change in the attitude in China towards the US regarding this particular case as China arrested a handful of Chinese hackers in its own territory on the request of the US. A week before Xi's arrival, the Chinese President sent his special envoy Meng Jianzhu, a member of the political bureau of the Communist Party Central Committee, to Washington to negotiate a deal.[27] Meng Jianzhu negotiated with Secretary of State John F. Kerry, Homeland Security Secretary Jeh Johnson and National Security Adviser Susan E. Rice and formulated an agreement which to an extent saved China from the US sanctions against it. Therefore, it would not be an exaggeration to state that the OPM hack incident brought both China and the US very close to a cyber-diplomatic standoff.

Chinese Hackers Groups

After observing the various kinds of covert threats posed by China in the cyber domain to different countries, especially India and the US, the study would be covering the Chinese Hackers Groups who are in most cases nurtured by the state thereby becoming State sponsored hackers groups.

Honker Union

Honker (红客) Union, which means Red Hackers Union, is a large group of voluntary hackers with patriotic and nationalistic feelings towards China. The name 'Honker' initially emerged in May 1999, when the United States bombed the Chinese Embassy in Belgrade, Yugoslavia.[28] Angered by this attack, furious young hackers of China formed this union and discussed various hacking skills and techniques in different blogs, forums, and chatrooms and formed a big network of hackers in China as a preparation for future cyber wars. Later in 2001, when a US spy plane and a Chinese fighter jet collided over the South China Sea, a diplomatic spat ensued between the US and China, which also ignited a hacker war between the patriotic hackers of the two countries. United in a group, Honker Union, the Chinese patriotic hackers started their operations on May 1, 2001 and attacked the government websites of the US and they even managed to shut down the website of White House for a brief period. The publicity they gained in China through this attack attracted around 80,000 individual hackers to join this group in the next few months which made 'Honker Union' the largest hacking group of the world.[29]

Apart from this attack, the Honker Union is also suspected of being involved in another high profile cyber attack on Japan during 2012 in response to the dispute of Senkaku Islands, which the Chinese claim sovereignty, naming it as Diaoyu Islands. At least 19 Japanese websites, including those of the Ministry of government, courts and a hospital came under cyber attack. This was followed by a huge number of messages posted by 4000 people boasting about the attack by China in one of China's leading chat site 'YY Chat'.[30]

While China claims that it discourages all forms of cyber attacks even if it emerges from its own territory, the fact that such huge number of hackers of this group 'Honker Union' were able to conduct their operations without facing any legal hurdles from Chinese authorities creates doubts about the covert support that Honkers Union might be enjoying from the CPC and PLA. It is likely that the PLA would have recruited members of this hackers group into their cyber army like the Unit 61398 to enhance their capabilities.

NCPH

In 2005, the PLA observed an attack on the Japanese websites and they were able to trace the attack which led them to a Sichuan University student named Tan Dailin. Instead of punishing him, the PLA offered an invitation to Dailin to participate in a PLA sponsored hacking competition. Dailin was victorious and he underwent a rigorous training programme for one month, along with other regional winners, where they were involved in developing new cyber invasion methods and building different hacking exploits. Later he was chosen for Sichuan regional team to compete against the other regional teams from Yunnan, Guizhou, Tibet and Chongqing Military districts. His team won the competition and he got a cash award of 20,000 RMB.[31]

Figure 5.4: Wicked Rose (Tan Dailin)

Source: Ken Dunham & Jim Melnick, "Wicked Rose and the NCPH Hacking Group", *An iDefence Research Report*, 2007.

Thinking of making a future as a hacker, Tan Dailin dropped from his studies on April 30, 2006 and later formed a hackers group under his leadership with the pseudonym "Wicked Rose". The group which he formed was called Network Crack Programme Hacker (NCPH). This group had four core members in 2006 namely: '*Wicked Rose*' – the Ring Leader, KuNgBim, Ronag, and Charles. They began their work by building sophisticated rootkits and by exploiting the zero-day vulnerabilities in MS Office. Through this process the group was able to exploit a number of targets and also managed to extract thousands of documents for their clients. For all these operations the group was regularly funded by unknown source, which is assumed by the US authorities to be the PLA. The popular rootkit payloads authored by

Wicked Rose are GinWui.A and GinWui.B. These two rootkits were the mostly used rootkit payloads by this group in many of their attacks. In 2007, they came up with another rootkit payload called RipGof.B which is an enhanced version of their previous GinWui tool. All their zero-day vulnerability tools exploited the vulnerabilities existed in the Microsoft Office software.[32] Through their successful campaigns 'Wicked Rose' and NCPH rose to fame among the hackers community in China and their payment also increased five-fold from their unknown sponsor.[33]

Figure 5.5: NCPH hackers at work in the "ncph studio" (Left to right) "Wicked Rose," KuNgBiM, Charles and Rodag

Source: Ken Dunham & Jim Melnick, "Wicked Rose and the NCPH Hacking Group", *An iDefence Research Report,* 2007.

But things did not go well for long for NCPH and especially 'Wicked Rose'. In 2009, for some unknown reasons, 'Wicked Rose' started conducting DDoS attacks on fellow Chinese hackers like *Hackbase, HackerXFiles* and *3800hk*. Annoyed by this, the hacker organisations turned over all evidence against 'Wicked Rose' to the Public Security

Department which made him to face a jail term of seven and half years and his website was also shut down by the authorities.[34]

Hidden Lynx

Hidden Lynx is one of the most elite groups of hackers in the world who are active almost from 2009 and offer their hackers service for hire. It is being speculated that the group has 50 to 100 people and they are more sophisticated than the group APT1 or Unit 61398. It is stated that this group operates with two pronged strategy namely 'Team Naid' and 'Team Moudoor'. Team Naid distributes a Trojan named, 'Trojan.Naid' for more limited attacks against high value targets and the Team Moudoor distributes a Trojan named, 'Backdoor.Moudoor', a version of "Ghost RAT" malware, for large-scale operations across industries. The members of this group are experts in exploiting Zero-day vulnerabilities and they also have the ability to redesign and customise the exploits quickly. The involvement of this group was recognised in different operations like 'Bit9 Incident', 'VOHO Campaign' and 'Operation Aurora'.[35]

The group operates on a diverse set of targets cutting across all the sectors from Government, Education, Finance, Information Technology, Health care, Defence, etc. Due to the fact that the group's activities are not focused on one particular sector it may be inferred that they are being hired by their clients for specific missions. The list of countries which had become victims of this group is led by USA, followed by Taiwan, China, Hong Kong, Japan, Canada, Germany, Russia, Korea, Australia, Ukraine, UK, France, Singapore and India. Symantec, a leading antivirus manufacturing company has identified that the attack infrastructure and tools used during their various campaigns by this group originates from network infrastructure from China.[36]

Conclusion

Although the general cyber environment of China is strictly controlled, monitored, censored and kept under surveillance round the clock and throughout the year, all these restrictions are only for the general public. At the same time, the government owned and backed cyber armies, and other patriotic hacker groups in China have got a free hand on their operations which help in meeting China's national interest. Though China denies any allegations about its involvement with any hacking incident in the public forum, it gives very strong support and backing with necessary resources to its hacking groups for conducting various cyber attacks, to gather information through espionage and to carry out intellectual property thefts from various countries. Through such covert information gathering and intelligence property thefts China is not only enriching its intelligence on its rivals but it is also filling the technical gap in its Research and Development programmes with the appropriate stolen technical information thereby speeding the whole process. From the method of operations of various hackers groups in China, a pattern is visible, i.e. the government hackers groups like Unit 61398 are used for conducting espionage and intellectual property theft operations and the other voluntary patriotic hackers groups like Honker Union are used to conduct DDOS style of cyber attack and operations to spread malware.

The numbers of hackers both in the military and in voluntary groups in China are increasing day by day which is a big threat to the cyber security of the world. It is believed that there are more than 20 units similar to Unit 61398 in the command chain of PLA which is a worrying factor. Apart from this, the existence of other voluntary patriotic hackers groups like Honker Union, who are enhancing their strength and skills, makes the situation worse. The fact that everything in China is some way connected to the CPC makes it easy for the Party to effectively coordinate and operate them under one command. But it may also be noted that all these groups might turn into rogue groups like in the case of 'Wicked Rose', and backfire at CPC if anything goes wrong in the future which will not only create a chaotic situation for CPC but for China as a country.

Notes

1. "38th Statistical Report on Internet Development in China", China Internet Network Information Centre, July 2016, https://cnnic.com.cn/IDR/ReportDownloads/201611/P020161114573409551742.pdf, accessed on December 21, 2016.

2. "Top 10 Countries that Censor the Internet", Listverse, in http://listverse.com/2010/10/02/top-10-countries-that-censor-the-internet/, accessed on July 2, 2014.
3. "Era of Digital Mercenaries", The Enemies of Internet, in http://surveillance.rsf.org/en/, accessed on July 2, 2014.
4. "How does China censor the internet?", *The Economist*, April 21, 2013, in http://www.economist.com/blogs/economist-explains/2013/04/economist-explains-how-china-censors-internet, accessed on July 2, 2014.
5. "HTG Explains: How the Great Firewall of China Works", *How To Geek*, in http://www.howtogeek.com/162092/htg-explains-how-the-great-firewall-of-china-works/, accessed on July 5, 2014.
6. "The Internet in China", *The Enemies of Internet*, in http://surveillance.rsf.org/en/china/, accessed on July 5, 2014.
7. "Two million 'internet opinion analysts' employed to monitor China's vast online population", *South China Morning Post*, October 3, 2013, in http://www.scmp.com/news/china-insider/article/1323529/two-million-employed-monitor-chinese-public-opinion, accessed on July 6, 2014.
8. "The Transparent Chinese", *The New York Times*, November 17, 2013, in http://www.nytimes.com/2013/11/18/opinion/xuecun-the-transparent-chinese.html?_r=1&, accessed on July 6, 2014.
9. "Uighur Muslims in China Arrested For 'Online Jihad'", *International Business Times*, October 28, 2013, in http://au.ibtimes.com/articles/517429/20131028/china-internet-jihad-online-xinjiang-province-muslim.htm#.U7pmzMbgtgj, accessed on July 6, 2014.
10. "Military and Security Developments Involving the People's Republic of China", *Annual Report* to Congress, 2011, USA.
11. "Indian Navy investigates cyber attack on military PCs", *BBC*, July 4, 2012, in http://www.bbc.com/news/technology-18703508, accessed on July 7, 2014.
12. N. C. Bipindra, "Chinese 'hack' DRDO computers; Antony seeks report", *The New Indian Express*, March 14, 2013, in http://www.newindianexpress.com/nation/article1500336.ece, accessed on July 7, 2014.
13. Rogin, Josh, "Cyber Officials: Cyber hackers attack 'anything and everything'", *FCW.com*, Feb 13, 2007.
14. Ibid.
15. Thornburgh, Nathan, "Inside the Chinese Hack Attack", August 25, 2005, in http://content.time.com/time/nation/article/0,8599,1098371,00.html, accessed on July 8, 2014.
16. Thornburgh, Nathan, "The invasion of the Chinese Cyberspies", *TIME*, September 5, 2005.
17. Ibid.
18. Unit 61398 is a Military Unit Cover Designator (MUCD) of a certain unit in the PLA. Generally in Chinese military five digit MUCDs are given to any unit to provide basic anonymity and for standard reference that facilitates communications and operations.

19. Mandiant was an American cybersecurity firm. It rose to prominence in February 2013 when it released a report directly implicating China in cyber espionage. On December 30, 2013, Mandiant was acquired by FireEye in a stock and cash deal worth in excess of US$1 billion.

20. "APT1: Exposing One of China's Cyber Espionage Units", Mandiant, February 2013.

21. Ibid.

22. "Unit 61398: Chinese cyberspies", *CBC News*, February 20, 2013, in http://www.cbc.ca/news/world/unit-61398-chinese-cyberspies-1.1367960, accessed on July 10, 2014.

23. Sanchez, Raf, "China hacking charges: the Chinese army's Unit 61398", *Telegraph*, May 19, 2014, in http://www.telegraph.co.uk/news/worldnews/asia/china/10842093/China-hacking-charges-the-Chinese-armys-Unit-61398.html, accessed on July 11, 2014.

24. "Cyber Security Resource: Cyber Security Incidents", *Office of Personnel Management*, Federal Government of the United States of America, https://www.opm.gov/cybersecurity/cybersecurity-incidents/, accessed on November 27, 2015.

25. Swati Khandelwal, "Is China Behind the Massive Data Theft of 4 Million US Officials?", *The Hacker News*, June 06, 2015, http://thehackernews.com/2015/06/china-data-theft.html, accessed on November 27, 2015.

26. "Statement by OPM Press Secretary Sam Schumach on Background Investigations Incident", *Office of Personnel Management*, Federal Government of the United States of America, https://www.opm.gov/news/releases/2015/09/cyber-statement-923/, accessed on November 27, 2015.

27. Ellen Nakashima and Adam Goldman, "In a first, Chinese hackers are arrested at the behest of the U.S. government", *The Washington Post*, October 09, 2015, https://www.washingtonpost.com/world/national-security/in-a-first-chinese-hackers-are-arrested-at-the-behest-of-the-us-government/2015/10/09/0a7b0e46-6778-11e5-8325-a42b5a459b1e_story.html, accessed on November 27, 2015.

28. http://en.wikipedia.org/wiki/Honker_Union#cite_ref-wan_1-4, accessed on July 12, 2014.

29. "From hackers to entrepreneurs: The Sino-US cyberwar veterans going straight", *South China Morning Post*, August 21, 2013, in http://www.scmp.com/news/china/article/1298200/hackers-entrepreneurs-sino-us-cyberwar-veterans-going-straight, accessed on July 12, 2014.

30. "Chinese cyber attacks hit Japan over islands dispute", *The Globe and Mail*, September 19, 2012, in http://www.theglobeandmail.com/news/world/chinese-cyber-attacks-hit-japan-over-islands-dispute/article4553048/, accessed on July 12, 2014.

31. Testimony of Alan Paller of the SANS Institute before the U.S. Senate Committee on Homeland Security and Government Affairs, "Cyber Security: Developing a National Strategy", April 28, 2009, http://www.hsgac.senate.gov//imo/media/doc/042809Paller.pdf?attempt=2, accessed on August 23, 2014.

32. Ken Dunham and Jim Melnick, "Wicked Rose and the NCPH Hacking Group", *An iDefence Research Report,* 2007.
33. Ibid.
34. "Withered Rose…law done come and got him", http://www.thedarkvisitor. com/2009/04/withered-roselaw-done-come-and-got-him/, accessed on July 15, 2014.
35. Doherty, Stephen, et.nl, "Hidden Lynx – Professional Hackers for Hire", *Symantec,* Version1.0, September 17, 2013.
36. Ibid.

6

EAGLE'S CLAW ON CYBERSPACE

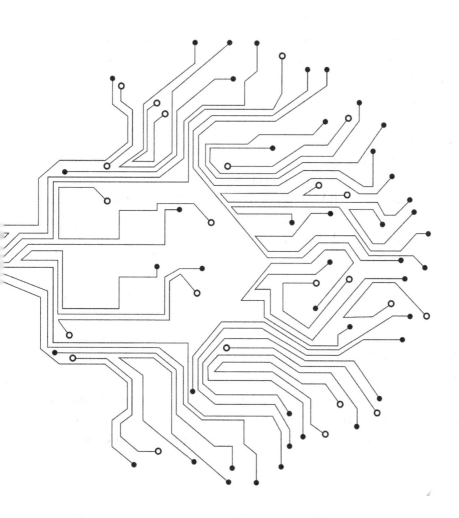

In the previous chapter the covert cyber operations being conducted by China and various kinds of hacking operations which in most cases are sponsored by state, were discussed in detail. However, People's Republic of China is not the only country with such covert capabilities in cyber space. In fact, almost all significant powers in the world like Russia, United Kingdom, Germany, Israel, France, Australia, Canada, India, etc., have the capacity to undertake such covert cyber operations with varying levels of capability. The capabilities of Chinese in this area were highlighted due to its frequent utilisation and also with a view to understand the level of their technological sophistication. It is a well known fact that there is one more country in the world which has achieved higher level of technological sophistication and which frequently make use of their covert cyber capabilities around the world. It is none other than the United States of America, the country claiming to be the super power of the world. This chapter is devoted exclusively to the study of the covert cyber capabilities of the US and its different kinds of covert operations and programmes undertaken against different targets.

Background

Though declared as the global common by the world, it is an undeniable fact that internet technology was conceived, developed, and nurtured in the US during the second half of the 20th century. In other words, the US is the cradle of cyber technology, especially internet which is currently the back bone of the global communication network. In fact, internet is still indirectly governed by US laws which are discreetly amended at times in furtherance of its national interests. Therefore, by default, US has an edge over the rest of the world in the field of cyber with advanced technological skills, institutional mechanisms, policy initiatives, skilled workforce and advanced implementation strategies. Such vital factors play an important role in making the US a leading vibrant player in the complex domain of cyber space.

However, being the widely acclaimed super power of the world, the US has more accountabilities and responsibilities than any other country in securing and streamlining the conduct of activities in cyber space. Moreover, being the global hub for internet traffic because of the location of a large number of cyber infrastructure, the responsibility of US increases manifold. The fact that there are more internet service providers in US than any other country, along with the location of Internet Corporation for Assigned Names and Numbers (ICANN), a privately owned internet regulatory organisation guided by the laws of the US, make the responsibility of that country very much higher. In other words, it can be said that in the present scenario the governance of the cyber world, functioning of internet is primarily dependent on the laws, policies, infrastructure and security agencies of the US, though claimed otherwise.

In this context, it is imperative for the US to have a robust security mechanism in order to safeguard cyber space from various threats across the domain. The defensive and offensive capabilities of the US should be effective and efficient not only to protect its national interests in cyber space but also to defend the global communication network. The defensive capabilities of the US are claimed to be the best in the world, but it is an unproven fact as the country has not faced any real threat of an all out cyber war as yet. Nevertheless, the effectiveness of their offensive capabilities in the cyber realm has been tested at various instances in the recent past and the level of its capabilities is again going up progressively. An in depth study of the US offensive capabilities in cyber space will reveal a few startling facts not about their overt cyber capabilities but regarding its covert cyber capabilities as well.

While several countries of the world have a certain level of overt cyber capabilities, these by themselves do not pose any threat to others as these capabilities would be employed only during the time of conflict. On the other hand, the concept of covert cyber capabilities itself pose a serious threat to other players in the world as it is an invisible weapon which can sabotage the ability of the target without his knowledge. Therefore, the revelations about the covert cyber capabilities of the US gathered through various sources since mid-2013 has created serious turbulence in the global cyber world which has led to a tectonic shift on all aspects from governance, regulations, ownership, legality, safety and security. It is this shift that will determine the fate of the internet and the future of cyber space.

In their efforts to remain as the only superpower of the world in a multi-polar environment, covert cyber capabilities of the US play an important role by virtually penetrating any inaccessible corners of the world which otherwise would not have been possible through traditional means in the real world to keep the authorities updated on matters of national interest. This chapter deals with these various covert cyber capabilities of the US which has taken the cyber community of the world surprised. We will also concentrate on the different covert cyber operations of the US which have more precise targeting capability and consequently more serious impact.

Existing Legal Enablers

Post 9/11, US was forced to enhance its intelligence gathering capability which led to new policy initiatives, legal measures, intelligence collection methods and programmes which would enable the intelligence agencies of the country to support the country's security measures adequately. Under the premise of 'Global War on Terror', the US had amended its laws several times and introduced new policies especially for information gathering from all possible sources. Its intelligence agencies, both domestic and external, were provided more funds which resulted in the establishment of more new methods for collection of information by these agencies. A detailed description of the different methods using cyber technology adopted by the US intelligence agencies are explained in this chapter.

The operations of US intelligence agencies outside the country are regulated by the 'Foreign Intelligence Surveillance Act 1978' (FISA) which is a Federal Law which prescribes the procedures for the physical and electronic surveillance and collection of "foreign intelligence information" on "foreign powers" and "agents of foreign powers" (which may include American citizens and permanent residents suspected of espionage or terrorism). This law was amended several times after 9/11 which includes the 'Terrorist Surveillance Act of 2006', 'Protect

America Act of 2007' and 'Foreign Intelligence Surveillance Act of 1978 Amendments Act of 2008'. FISA prohibits unauthorised surveillance on any target, and requires the intelligence agencies to get approval from a three Judge Court setup under the Foreign Intelligence Surveillance Act to conduct surveillance on its foreign targets.

'The USA Patriot Act' came into force with the approval of the then President George W Bush on October 26, 2001 with the objective of "uniting and strengthening America by providing appropriate tools required to intercept and obstruct under the Terrorism Act of 2001'.[1] Under this law, the President assumed broader powers to authorise operations in support of Global War on Terror. Using these powers, Bush ordered the US intelligence services to carry out surveillance without warrant, thereby bypassing FISA which were previously restricting the powers of intelligence agencies from conducting their operations. The contradictions in the Federal Law favoured the intelligence agencies of the US and they were able to continue and even enhance their operations both in the physical and digital world.

Apart from this, on a few occasions, the intelligence services like FBI, CIA and NSA also managed to get authorised warrants for their surveillance through secret rulings from FISA courts and were used by the intelligence services to conduct widespread surveillance mostly in the digital medium. For instance, through a secret ruling from a FISA court, NSA gained authority to collect telephone call records including the metadata of millions of US customers using 'Verizone' service provider. This ruling also stated that "*no person shall disclose to any other person that the FBI or NSA has sought or obtained tangible things under this order...*".[2]

Thus, the FISA was smartly used to favour the intelligence agencies including the Patriot Act which grants more authority to the intelligence agencies and were efficiently used by these agencies for much bigger programmes. One such covert programme especially in the digital world is the infamous NSA Prism programme. More details about this programme and various other covert programmes in the cyber realm by the US are given in another part of this chapter.

In April 2016, the U.S. Supreme Court approved a change in Rule 41 of the 'Federal Rules of Criminal Procedure' that would let the US judges to issue warrants for using remote access to electronic devices outside their jurisdiction. Under the amended rule it would make it easier for the FBI to hack any computer or network, literally anywhere in the world.[3] The amendments to rule 41 came into effect on December 01, 2016. However, the change invited a lot of criticism and opposition from the technical giants and American civil liberties groups. The amendment has added more powers to the legal backing of the US agencies in conducting covert cyber operations which would be a big blow to global cyber community in terms of privacy and cyber freedom.

US Covert Cyber Capabilities

This part deals with the various covert cyber programmes of the US like Prism, X-Keyscore, Quantum, and ANT which came to light as these activities were disclosed to the world through known and unknown whistleblowers.

NSA Prism

Prism is a covert cyber surveillance programme of NSA which was the first programme to be exposed and attracted the attention of the whole world almost immediately. This is in fact, the most popular or rather infamous programme that was exposed by Edward Snowden in mid 2013. The exposed documents include a presentation which was a training material about the programme used by the agency. It was first exposed by *The Guardian* and *The Washington Post* on June 6, 2013.

It was revealed through these documents that the intelligence agencies of the US were obtaining information directly from the main servers of nine leading U.S. internet service providing companies and they were providing the information such as audio extracts and video chats, photographs, e-mails, documents, and connection logs to them. This information was used by the intelligence agencies to track their foreign targets in the digital medium. The nine companies enlisted as partners in this covert programme are **Microsoft, Yahoo, Google, Facebook, PalTalk, AOL, Skype, YouTube** and **Apple.**[4]

Apart from NSA, the information collected through this covert programme was also shared with Government Communications Headquarters (GCHQ), the intelligence agency of UK, bypassing its laws. In fact, Prism programme was made possible in the US due to the contradictory laws which were discussed earlier. The government agencies issued legal notifications to all the nine companies which were approved by FISA courts which ordered the provision of the required information to the intelligence agencies. NSA got a back door entry into the servers of these internet companies through this programme which enabled them to get access to majority of the world internet traffic. This is evident from one of the slides revealed titled "U.S as world's Telecommunication Backbone".[5]

The presentation which came to light also spells out the dates on which each of these companies were enlisted to this programme. The dates on which these companies were enlisted in this programme are as follows:

- Microsoft – September 11, 2007.
- Yahoo – March 12, 2008.
- Google – January 14, 2009.
- Facebook – June 03, 2009.
- PalTalk – December 07, 2009.
- YouTube – September 24, 2010.
- Skype – February 06, 2011.
- AOL – March 31, 2011.
- Apple – October 2012.

It was also revealed that the US government spends nearly US$20 million of public money only for this programme to steal digital information of the whole world every year.[6]

After the revelation about this programme, all the internet companies accused of being associated with this, denied their involvement and cooperation with the US government agencies and the spokes person of the companies also came up with separate statements of denial. A spokesperson from Google stated that:

"Google cares deeply about the security of our users' data,... We disclose user data to government in accordance with the law, and we review all such requests carefully. From time to time, people allege that we have created a government 'back door' into our systems, but Google does not have a 'back door' for the government to access private user data."[7]

The chief Security Officer of Facebook stated that:

"We do not provide any government organisation with direct access to Facebook servers,...When Facebook is asked for data or information about specific individuals, we carefully scrutinise any such request for compliance with all applicable laws, and provide information only to the extent required by law."[8]

Apple, the company which also joined the programme in 2012, came up with a statement from their Spokesperson Steve Dowling that:

"We have never heard of Prism," said Steve Dowling, a spokesman for Apple. "We do not provide any government agency with direct access to our servers, and any government agency requesting customer data must get a court order."[9]

A careful observation of the statements made by the spokespersons of various companies associated with Prism programme indicates that their statements revolve around legal measures and that the companies are trying to cover up their immoral activities behind the contradictory and manipulated laws of the US.

The Prism programme along with another covert programme called the 'Upstream' are the two different mechanisms adopted for collection of information under the operations called "FAA702 Operations". It provided the maximum quantum of information for the NSA. The programme 'Upstream' is another covert cyber operation of the NSA undertaken in association with many other agencies of allied countries of the US to tap the submarine cables that carry the internet traffic across the world. By tapping the submarine cables at the entry and exit points, the intelligence agencies are extracting information using various filters. It is revealed that Upstream programme is an important source of information which is used to produce the President's daily brief.

The information collected from Upstream and Prism and from various other sources are raw information which needs further processing in order to enable the agency to extract the required data. For this purpose, the NSA had created a covert data processing programme called XKeyscore.

X-Keyscore

According to NSA, X-Keyscore is a part of the agency's lawful foreign signals intelligence collection system. NSA also claims that only a limited number of personnel in the agency can get access to X-Keyscore in order to complete their assigned tasks. Moreover, there are multiple technical, manual and supervisory checks and balances within the system in X-Keyscore to prevent deliberate misuse by anybody along with full audit on every search made by an NSA analyst to ensure that they are proper and within the law. The agency argues that such a programme allows them to collect information that enables them to perform their missions to defend the nation successfully and to protect US and allied troops abroad.[10]

While that seems to be a legitimate claim by the NSA, the real purpose of X-Keyscore was revealed when Edward Snowden exposed it through *The Sydney Morning Herald* newspaper and *O Globo* newspaper in July 2013. The exposed document also includes a power point presentation with 32 slides meant for explaining the functions of the XKeyscore programme to its new trainees. This exposed classified power point document, which was supposed to be declassified on August 1, 2032, reveals a number of shocking details about the programme. An entry in the Special Source Operations (SSO) directorate located inside the NSA dated September 21, 2012 showed that X-Keyscore is operational.[11] It was also revealed that a large portion of the information collected through the internet by NSA comes from its allies across the globe. Based on the exposed slides and documents, it can be assumed that countries like Australia, Canada, Great Britain and New Zealand have played an active role in this programme as contributors and partners in sharing information under this programme. According to Edward Snowden, Germany also has access to X-Keyscore which he revealed in a TV interview.

X-Keyscore Location and Function

According to the exposed slides, X-Keyscore is a Software tool which acts as a Digital Network Intelligence (DNI) Exploitation System/ Analytical Framework that performs strong (e.g. e-mail) and soft (e.g. content) selection of data and metadata and provides real time target activity surveillance. The programme stores all the data in the collection site indexed by metadata and can even provide a series of viewers for common data types. This programme has a very small but focused team which works closely with the analysts and the support staffs are integrated with developers. The actions of the whole team in the programme are based on requirements of the mission. The programme is based on more than 700 servers situated in approximately 150 sites around the world and the network is a massively distributed Linux cluster.[12]

Figure 6.1: Location of X-Keyscore sites.

Source: NSA X-Keyscore exposed slides

In this programme virtually anything can be stored by indexing the data with a metadata. This programme has the capability to analyse data at two levels, shallow and deep. While the shallow method would help to look into more data for identification of possible intelligence, a deep method with strong selection pointer is used to gather intelligence. Extraction of information from the X-Keyscore is based on "Strong Selection" pointer. When there are strong selection pointers, the results are precise otherwise huge volume of data would be extracted which has to be browsed again and again in order to get the required information. This shows that the analysts have to be smart and innovative in order to extract the required information from the humongous volumes of collected data.

During a TV interview, when asked about the usefulness of X-Keyscore to its users, Snowden replied that:

"You could read anyone's email in the world. Anybody you've got email address for, any website you can watch traffic to and from it, any computer that an individual sits at you can watch it, any laptop that you're tracking you can follow it as it moves from place to place throughout the world. It's a one stop shop for access to the NSA's information. And what's more you can tag individuals using 'XKeyscore'. Let's say I saw you once and I thought what you were doing was interesting or you just have access that's interesting to me, let's say you work at a major German corporation and I want access to that network, I can track your username on a website on a form somewhere, I can track your real name, I can track associations with your friends and I can build what's called a fingerprint which is network activity unique to you which means anywhere you go in the world anywhere you try to sort of hide your online presence hide your identity, the NSA can find you and anyone who's allowed to use this or who the NSA shares their software with can do the same thing..."[13]

This statement of Snowden clearly points out that anybody can become a target of NSA and the NSA can track that person anywhere in the world with the help of X-Keyscore and an intelligent and innovative analyst can do it without moving from their location. The data for analysis is pooled in from all sources including allied countries, data collected through other surveillance programmes, other departments of NSA, and also data acquired through aerial surveillance using drones.

In short, X-Keyscore is used during the processing and analysis phase of intelligence in NSA, gathered through various covert sources using which the agency claims to have captured over 300 terrorists. But a few reports points out that X-Keyscore brands any user of the Tor network as an 'extremist' and the user is listed in the NSA's target list.[14] This raises the question whether the terrorists arrested through X-Keyscore analysis were actually involved in terrorist activities or are they just frequent visitors of Tor networks, deep web and other encrypted methods in the cyber space and also whether their activities in the physical world could justify branding them as terrorists. Although finding answers to such questions would be an impossible task, the fact remains that, X-Keyscore is the first step in digital intelligence in the internet world and more such software will be operated in the cyber space as this domain is a pandora's box of intelligence according to the intelligence agencies around the world.

Tailored Access Operations (TAO)

The TAO department in NSA is responsible for developing and employing technologies for endpoint operations. Endpoint operations involves the process of actively subverting systems that create, store or manage information like computers, peripherals and telephone switches, in order to directly retrieve data of intelligence value or achieve other operational ends. According to another document which was brought before the public titled "Expanding Endpoint Operations", which was written by an unknown Colonel of US Army as early as September 17, 2004, TAO department was expanding endpoint operations in terms of numbers and diversity of targets and building a more scalable and robust endpoint operations infrastructure. The expansion of process included the acquisition of a new endpoint access Remote Operations Centre (ROC) which would enable dramatically to expand the operations of the

TAO department and its services would be available for both its internal and external customers. While the internal customers are NSA, Central Intelligence Agency (CIA) and Joint Special Operations Command (JSOC), the list of external customers include various intelligence agencies of countries like Australia, Canada, Great Britain and New Zealand.[15]

One part of TAO department of NSA is believed to be operating from a base in Texas, which was earlier a Sony Chip Company and later converted as NSA's location for operations in 2005.

Figure 6.2: The location of NSA's TAO department.

Source: Google Earth.

According to a document on Texas Cryptology Centre, available in public, the breakup of the employees in TAO department housed in the Texas based centre as on March 11, 2008 is as follows:

Table 6.1: Sector-wise employees' breakup of TAO based in Texas

Sector	Number	Breakup
Civilians.	30	Includes 1 AIA, 1 Intern.
Military.	30	US Air Force 10. US Army 8. US Navy 10. US Marine Corps 2.
Total 60		

Civilian.	Unknown.	7 Selected. 9 Nominees. Unknown No. of External Hires – 03 CJO'd, 7 preliminary.
Military.	Unknown.	Unknown No. Chief, etc. 5 x USA Great Skills Billets. 2 (additional) FIOCers not included (R&T).
Contractor	1	TAO/ ANT Contract.

Source: "Secret Documents: The special department TAO NSA introduces itself", *DerSpiegel*, December 30, 2013, inhttp://www.spiegel.de/fotostrecke/nsa-dokumente-die-abteilung-tao-der-nsa-fotostrecke-105355-3.html, accessed on April 6, 2014.

Until 2008, TAO operations were conducted on targets in countries including Cuba, Venezuela, Iraq, Afghanistan, Mexico and Colombia. There were various kinds of operations conducted by TAO department involving different types of malwares/spywares and using different tactics for penetration of network and installation of these spywares in the target's system. This includes spyware operations like Olympus Tickets, SHARPFOCUS (SF2), PARCHDUSK (PD) and FOXACID Messages. Initially e-mails were used to spam the target with FOXACID messages, later NSA Quantum method was used which was to be followed by inserting the malware.[16] The operations of TAO are based on its motto *"Your data is our data, your equipment is our equipment – any time, any place, by any legal means".*[17] This statement exhibits the overall intention of these clandestine organisations and covert cyber missions of the US and their arrogance due to their possession of superior technology.

NSA Quantum

One of the covert programs of NSA's Tailored Access Operations (TAO) department, targeting computer of individuals is Quantum which is meant to implant specially built Trojans and this will enable surveillance on web based accounts of the user in various platforms. The details about Quantum programme was revealed in the German Weekly *Der Spiegel* on December 30, 2013. This programme works on a concept known as "man-on-the-side capability". The Quantum method of implant is possible on the target if the chosen target has a selector that is vulnerable to Quantum technique and active for the last 14 days and if detected by the single-sign on site which has Quantum capabilities. When a target satisfies all these conditions, it is possible to detect the communication between the target's computer and the server in real time and send the Trojan piggy backing the requested content and implant the host.[18]

The documents released on Quantum disclose the involvement of one of America's largest management consulting firm Booz Allen Hamilton in the programme along with TAO department of NSA. As the company's name appears in the document along with the TAO department, it could be presumed that Quantum was developed by a team comprising personnel from both NSA's TAO department and Booz Allen Hamilton Company. The documents further reveal that apart from the US, the interests of Australia, Canada, Great Britain and New Zealand were also served by Quantum. In fact, it is to be understood from the document that there is a partnership agreement between the GCHQ of the UK, and the Research and Technology analysts of TAO department of NSA, US for utilisation of GCHQ resources to enhance additional capabilities to their QuantumTheory.[19]

Functioning

The Quantum programme involves several nodes for its functioning. They are the target, Internet router, Web application server, SSO site and the NSA's TAO Foxacid Server.

Figure 6.3: Various nodes involved in the functioning of Quantum

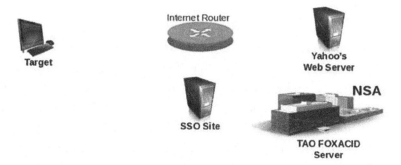

Source: "(TS) NSA Quantum Tasking Techniques for the R & T Analyst, *Der Spiegel*, December 30, 2013

The Foxacid server is an exploit server that is operated by NSA's TAO department for the Quantum programme to install the Trojans into the target. The method of functioning of Quantum is clearly explained in the exposed document and this revelation underlines the sophistication of technology being used and the quantum of effort it requires for applying this covert method of bugging. It is also mentioned that Quantum was effective and successful against Yahoo, Facebook accounts operating with Static IP Addresses. The process of functioning of Quantum as mentioned in the documents is as follows:

- Target logs into his/ her yahoo account.
- SSO site connected with the internet router sees the Quantum tasked Yahoo selector's packet and forwards it to the TAO's Foxacid Server.
- Foxacid server injects a Foxacid URL into the packet and sends it back to the target's computer.
- Simultaneously, the Yahoo server receives the packet from the target's computer through internet router requesting email content.
- Before the Yahoo packet reaches the target's computer, the Foxacid packet intervenes and beats it back to the end point.
- Though the target's Yahoo page is loaded, the Foxacid URL also loads in the background which redirects to the Foxacid exploit server in NSA's TAO.
- Now based on the exploitability of the browser, the Foxacid server deploys a stage1 implant back to the target thus implanting the target with Trojan.

It is reported in the documents that Quantum is capable of targeting a wide range of realms like IPv4_public, alibabaForumUser, doubleclickID, rocketmail, hi5Uid, hotmailCID, linkedin, mail, mailruMrcu, msnMailToken64, qq, facebook, simbarUuid, twitter, yahoo, yahooBcookie, ymail, youtube and watcherID.

It is stated that the Quantum can be used for tasks in two different ways. The R and T analysts, who can be inferred to be the Research and Technology analysts, can submit QUANTUMTHEORY tasking upon from a stage1 implant called VALIDATOR which would be implanted on the target. In another case, TOPI analysts, the expansion for Topi is not known, can submit QUANTUMNATION tasking upon from a stage0 implant called SEASONEDMOTH (SMOTH) is implanted on the target. SMOTHs die within a period of 30 days of deployment unless it is requested to extend its life. Validator is a small Trojan implant used as a backdoor access service against personal computers of targets in national interest, including but not limited to terrorist targets.[20]

Therefore, it is clear from NSA's Quantum that anybody in this world can become a target for Validator or any other espionage and surveillance tool of NSA if the person is perceived to be important in the national interest of the US. Moreover, the NSA has the technological expertise to identify its target in this crowded virtual space and it can also pursue its covert methods of espionage by camouflaging its virtual communications within the trusted communications system between the user and the web applications server. It is well known that the US is having a free hand in tapping the internet router and is able to watch the communications between the user and the web applications servers because of the fact that most of the cyber infrastructure is available well within its legal and control jurisdictions. A feasible solution to end the US monopoly can be achieved in this matter only when an effective Internet Governance model is implemented with the involvement and participation from a truly global community and not the US and West promoted model of governance.

NSA ANT Catalogue

In December 2013, *Der Spiegel,* the German weekly news magazine, reported about the existence of another sophisticated programme developed by NSA consisting of a digital toolbox called the "NSA ANT (Advanced/ Access Network Technology) Catalogue". This article exposing the development of the programme was co-authored by Jacob Appelbaum, Judith Horchert and Christian Stöcker. Unlike the Prism programme which was exposed by Edward Snowden to *The Washington Post* and *The Guardian*, the exposure/whistleblower of this project is unknown. But the exposed catalogue reveals the magnitude and variety of digital tools being used by the US intelligence agency to spy on its targets. The operations of ANT division in the TAO department of NSA cover a wide range of activities from penetration of network, monitoring mobile phones, computers, to diverting, modifying and even deleting data. The web of network created by the implants of these sophisticated tools is so big that it has succeeded in establishing a covert network for NSA that operates parallel to the internet.

The leaked NSA ANT Catalogue is a 50 page document created in 2008. Its list appears like a mail-order catalogue of digital tools, from which the employees of NSA can order technologies from the ANT division for using it against its targets. The Advanced/ Access Network Technology (ANT) division is part of NSA's Tailored Access Operations (TAO) Department and they are specialised in covert data-mining and data-skimming operations especially on specific difficult targets. ANT tools are like elite forces which are moved in only when TAO's usual hacking and data-skimming methods are not sufficient to gather the required information from their target systems.[21] While the ANT division develops both hardware and software required for these digital tools, the catalogue of these tools not only defines the operations of the tools but also gives the price for every tool which ranges from free to US$250,000.[22]

Every tool that has been developed by ANT has its own special purpose and their operating devices cover almost all areas of the digital world from monitors, cables, USBs, routers, servers, mobile phones and chips both in hardware and software. The functioning of the digital tools of NSA ANT Catalogue differentiating them according to their operating platform are explained below:

Keyboards

SURLYSPAWN

Figure 6.4: Surlyspawn

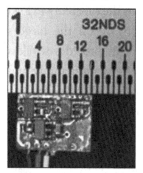

Source: Product Data –
NSA ANT Catalogue,
USA

"SURLYSPAWN" is a hardware implant costing US$30 designed to notify keystrokes of the targeted user's keyboard without requiring any supporting software on the targeted system. The retro-reflector is compatible with both USB and PS/2 keyboards while the laptop keyboard variant was still under development in 2009.

This hardware board taps the data line from the keyboard to the processor and generates a square shaped wave oscillating at a preset frequency. The wave frequency is shifted from higher or lower depending on the level of the data-line signal or in other words, the square wave becomes frequency shift keyed (FSK). When the unit is illuminated by a CW signal from nearby radar operated by an agent, the illuminating signal is amplitude-modulated (AM) with this square wave. The radar receives the signal re-radiated and demodulates the signal, which is then processed to recover the keystrokes.[23]

USBs

Since USBs are the most widely used connecting device available, NSA has created implants to exploit this facility and to spy upon the targets. This form of disguised USB bug can be any kind of USB extension plug that is silently inserted into the different ports of the computer. They work by sending and receiving signals to short distances or by creating channels for other implants to work or by sending signals over long distances. These implants allow both the computer and the network it is connected to, to be monitored as well as send and receive signals both to the computer and to the hijacked network.

COTTONMOUTH-I

Figure 6.5: Cottonmouth-1

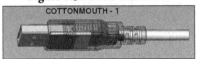

Source: Product Data – NSA ANT Catalogue, USA.

Cottonmouth-1 (CM-I) is a USB hardware implant that provides a wireless bridge into the target's network and has the capability to load exploiting software on the target's PCs. This implant provides wireless bridging, software persistence capability, 'in-field' re-programmability and covert communications with a host software implant over the USB. The radio frequency link through this implant enables command to resort to data infiltration and extraction. It also communicates with Data Network Technologies (DNT) software, Straitbizarre through a covert channel implemented on the USB and passes the commands and data to the hardware and software implants using this channel.[24]

This implant is capable of concealing other components like Trinity, switches and Howlermonkey within the USB Series-A cable connector. This implant also has the ability to contact other Cottonmouth devices using a wireless protocol known as Speculation. There are practically no details on the working of this protocol. The use of the term Straitbizarre gives the impression regarding development of an unknown software technology which has not been exposed and therefore can be treated as a high end technology belonging to another or same family of digital espionage tools.

COTTONMOUTH-II

Figure 6.6: Cottonmouth-II

Source: Product Data – NSA ANT Catalogue, USA.

Cottonmouth -II (CM-II) is also a USB hardware h implant which provides a covert link over USB into the target's network. It is intended to operate within a long haul relay subsystem, which could also be located within the target's devices.

CM-II provides software persistence capability, 'in-field' re-programmability and covert communications with host software implant over the USB. Like CM-I, CM-II also communicates with DNT software, Straitbizarre through a covert channel implemented on the USB and transfers commands and data between the hardware and software using this channel. It has the ability for long haul relay through CM-II and provides wireless bridge into the target's network. According to the exposed documents, CM-II costs around US$200K for 50 units.[25]

COTTONMOUTH-III

Most of the operations of Cottonmouth-III (CM-III) are similar to that of Cottonmouth -I but it is an improved version of CM-I as it conceals the digital components such as Trinity, switches, and Howlermonkey radio frequency transceiver within a RJ45 Dual Stacked USB connector unlike CM-I which conceals it in a USB Series-A Cable Connector. Apart from this CM-III provides a short range inter-chassis link to other CM devices and it can also provide inter-chassis radio frequency link to a long haul relay subsystem. CM-III costs US$1,248K for 50 units.[26]

FIREWALK

Firewalk is a bi-directional network implant which is provided within a dual stacked RJ4/ USB connector. It is capable of collection of data from Gigabit Ethernet network traffic and injection of Ethernet packets onto the same target network. According to the document, Firewalk can bypass any firewall or wireless protection in order to exploit the targeted network. It works in sync with Howlermonkey, another digital tool for communications. Firewalk costs US$537 for 50 units.[27]

VGA Cables

RAGEMASTER

Figure 6.7: Ragemaster

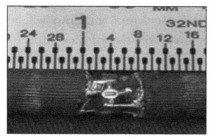

Product Data – Source: SA ANT Catalogue, USA.

The hardware implant designed for the use in VGA cable is called Ragemaster costing US$30 per unit. It provides a target for Radio Frequency (RF) flooding and allows for easier collection of the VAGRANT (unknown technology) video signal. This implant is neatly concealed in a standard computer Video Graphics Array (VGA) cable between the video card and video monitor. It is usually installed in the ferrite on the video cable tapping the red video line between the video card within the desktop unit and the computer monitor. The document available suggests that a radar unit is used to illuminate the Ragemaster, which in turn modulates the red video line information. The re-radiated information from the red line is picked up at the radar, demodulated and passed on to the processing units. The processer recreates the horizontal and vertical cross sections of the targeted monitor, thus allowing the NSA personal to see the visuals displayed on the targeted monitor.[28]

The technologies used for processing the re-radiated information are named in the available document of the NSA as LFS-2, Nightwatch, Gotham and Viewplate (as a future technology). There is no information available about these technologies except Nightwatch. Therefore, it can be assumed that these technologies are part of other secret tools belonging to the same or another family of digital tools of espionage developed by NSA.

CPU

GINSU

Ginsu is a software application that enables persistence for the CNE software implant KONGUR, which in turn works on the PCI bus hardware implant B, implanted on the target system. During operations, if the software implant Kongur, which supports the functions of Bulldozer hardware implant on the PCI bus, is removed from the system due to any upgrade in the operating system or due to reinstallation, the Ginsu will be triggered on the next reboot of the system to restore the software implant. This technique can operate on any desktop PC system that functions on Microsoft Windows 9x, 2000, 2003, XP or Vista based operating system and has at least one PCI connecter for enabling Bulldozer implant. This implant comes free of cost.[29]

IRATEMONK

Iratemonk is another software application that provides persistence by implanting the hard drive firmware on the targeted desktop or laptop in order to gain execution through Master Boot Record (MBR) substitution. This technique works on many brands of hard drives like Western Digital, Seagate, Maxtor and Samsung, but can boot only from systems which does not have 'RAID' hardware.

The agency uses its technique of 'Interdiction' for the implants like Unitedrake or Straitbazzare in conjunction with Slickervicar to upload the hard drive firmware to the machine in order to implant Iratemonk to the system. Once implanted, Iratemonk's frequency is configurable and starts functioning whenever the target system is put on. This implant technology is again free of cost.[30]

SWAP

"Swap is also a software application that enables periodic execution before the Operating System loads by exploiting the motherboard BIOS and the hard drive's Host Protected Area. Windows, Linux, FreeBSD or Solaris based single or multi-processor systems support this technique. Swap and its payload are implanted on the targeted machine through remote access or interdiction. ARKSTREAM is used to re-flash the Bios and TWISTEDKILT to write the Host Protected Area on the hard drive of the targeted system to implant Swap. This tool is available free of cost."[31]

WISTFULTOLL

Wistfulltool is a plug-in software for UNITEDRAKE and STRAITBIZZARE implants and is used for extracting and forwarding forensic information from the target system using Windows Management Instrumentation (WMI) calls and Registry extractions. Systems based on Microsoft Windows 2000, 2003, and XP operating systems support this plug-in. The plug-in is executed through remote access or interdiction, either as a UNITEDRAKE or STRAITBIZZARE plug-in or as a standalone executable system and the extracted information is sent back to NSA through the hardware implants. If the plug-in is executed via a USB thumb drive then the extracted information is stored in the same thumb drive. This is a free of cost tool.[32]

SOMBERKNAVE

Figure 6.8: Somberknave

Source: NSA Exploit of the Day", February 05, 2014, in http://www.the-ethical-hacker. com/2014/02/somberknave-nsa-exploit-of-the-day/, accessed on June 03, 2014.

"Somberknave is a Windows XP software implant that provides covert internet connectivity for isolated systems. This software implant routes TCP traffic from a designated process to a secondary network via an unused embedded 802.11 network device. A wireless target computer is connected via 802.11 interface through OLYMPUS or Validator with the help of Somberknav. But if the 802.11 interface is already in use by the target computer, Somberknave will not attempt to transmit."[33]

During operation, Validator initiates a call and Somberknave triggers from the specified incident and tries to associate with an access point. Once the connection is successful, data is transmitted over the 802.11 interface to the ROC. Receiving the instructions, Validator downloads Olympus and disassociates itself and gives up the control of 802.11. Now Olympus will be able to communicate with the ROC via Somberknave, as long as the access point is available. The cost of one unit of this software implant is US$50k.

HOWLERMONKEY

Figure6.9: Howlermonkey

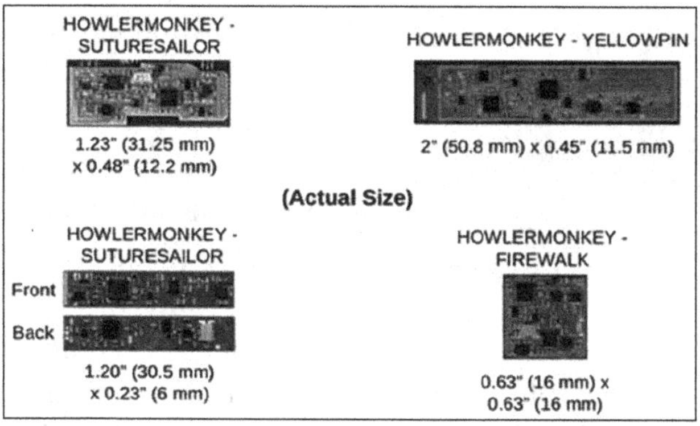

Source: http://www.telefoniert-nach-hause.de/index.php/NSA/HOWLERMONKEY, accessed on June 04, 2014.

Howlermonkey is a custom built Short to Medium Range Radio Frequency Transceiver hardware implant that is used in conjunction with a digital core to make a complete implant. The Printed Circuit Board (PCB) layouts of the Howlermonkey implants are tailored according to individual implant space requirements and differ in form factor. These PCBs are designed to be compatible with CONJECTURE/SPECULATION networks and STRIKEZONE devices that run on Howlermonkey hardware. The cost of 40 units of Howlermonkey is US$750 each and when the number of units demanded is 25 units or lesser, then the cost increases toUS$1000 each.[34]

JUNIORMINT

Juniormint is a hardware implant which comes in two forms; a digital core packaged in a mini PCB which can be used in a conventional concealment and also a miniaturised Flip Chip Module which can be used in implants with size constraining concealments. TAO's standard implant architecture model is used to make Juniormint and this architecture is claimed to provide a robust, reconfigurable, standard digital platform which can result in dramatic performance. The cost of this implant is unavailable and will be stated on placing the order based on the sophistication of the required implant.[35]

MAESTRO- II

Figure 6.10: Maestro -II

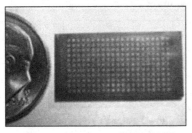

Source: Product Data – NSA ANT Catalogue, USA.

Maestro – II is a hardware implant of miniaturised digital core packaged in a Multi-Chip Module (MCM) which can be used in size constraining concealments. This implant contains an ARM7 microcontroller, FPGA, Flash and SDRAM memories. Maestro – II is also made using the TAO standard architecture for a robust, reconfigurable, standard digital platform that can result in a dramatic performance. The unit cost of this implant is US$3-4k.[36] The suffix 'II' in the name of this tool denotes that there could have been an earlier version to this tool.

TRINITY

Figure 6.11: Trinity

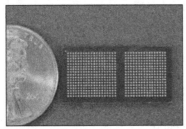

Source: Product Data – NSA ANT Catalogue, USA

Trinity is also a hardware implant of miniaturised digital core packaged in a Multi-Chip Module (MCM) which can be used in size constraining concealments. The function of Trinity is similar to that of Maestro – II and the unit cost of this implant is US$625k for 100 units.[37]

W-LAN

The NSA ANT has developed tools for tapping the W-LAN for detecting the wireless networks from a considerable distance and it can be used to either tap into the network or to map the various networks in a particular jurisdiction.

NIGHTSTAND

Figure 6.12: Nightstand

Source: Product Data – NSA ANT Catalogue, USA.

Nightstand is used in operations where cable connectivity to the target's system is impossible and hence this can be used to exploit the active wireless LAN of the target and inject payload like a malware. This tool is used for exploitation of Windows Operating System and has a history of successful battle in field operations. Nightstand is a standalone tool running on x86 Laptop loaded with Linux Fedora Core 3 Operating System.[38]

This tool has the ability to exploit targets running on Win2k, WinXP, WinXPSP1 and WINXPSP2 operating systems and using Internet Explorer versions 5.0 to 6.0. This tool also has the capability to target multiple clients or multiple targets simultaneously. This tool has a successful operational range of 8 miles or 13 Kms while the unit cost varies from platform to platform.[39] Should the target use the latest version of Windows Operating System or a different operating system like Linux and use updated version of internet explorer or any other browser, then the user has the opportunity to escape from this tool.

SPARROW II

Figure 6.13: Sparrow II

Source: Product Data – NSA ANT Catalogue, USA.

Sparrow II is one of the most sophisticated tools in the NSA ANT Catalogue. It is used in airborne operations especially on board of UAVs. This tool is embedded with the software tool called BLINDDATE (another software tool which is not listed in the exposed NSA ANT catalogue). It is also integrated with Mini PCI slots for added functions like GPS and multiple Wireless Network Interface Cards. This tool collects the WLAN networks from the specified location and maps them. This tool also gives the option for connecting more PCI devices to it for the purpose of wireless command and control or to install second or third 802.11 card. The unit price of this tool is US$6K.[40]

Router

A Router is a computer network device that is used to forward data packets between various networks thus forming interlink of networks.[41] The NSA ANT department has managed to develop tools to exploit these router devices and according to the exposed catalogue the tools can exploit routers of two manufacturers: Huawei and Juniper.

HEADWATER

Huawei is the second most popularly used networking device in the world after CISCO. The fact that Huawei is a Chinese brand makes it vulnerable to attacks from the US as both China and USA are in a virtual technological race. Therefore, the NSA ANT department has developed the tool Headwater exclusively for exploiting the routers manufactured by Huawei. It is a Persistent Backdoor (PBD) software implant which enables covert functions to be remotely executed within the router via an internet connection. The software tool will be installed in the router's boot ROM and will get activated after a system reboot. After activation, the PBD software captures and examines all IP packets passing through the router. This tool is also adapted in joint operations between NSA and CIA again to exploit Huawei Network equipments under the cover name TURBOPANDA.[42]

SCHOOLMONTANA

Juniper is an American network equipments manufacturing company which manufactures five families of routers: T-series, M-series, E-series, MX-series, and J-series and other networking devices. The NSA ANT tool Schoolmontana is designed to exploit the J-Series routers of the Juniper devices. This tool provides persistence for Digital Network Technologies (DNT) implants. When this tool is deployed, it modifies the target system's BIOS and adds the necessary software to it which can be executed remotely by the handler.[43]

SIERRAMONTANA

Sierramontana exploits the M-Series of Juniper router devices and deploys a DNT implant into the target's BIOS. After the implant, once the system is rebooted, the implant provides kernel modifications to support the execution of implant remotely by the handler.[44]

STUCCOMONTANA

The Stuccomontana tool developed by NSA ANT provides persistence for DNT implants on the Juniper T-Series routers and its functions are similar to that of its contemporaries, Schoolmontana and Sierramontana.[45]

Server

DEITYBOUNCE

Deitybounce is a software application which exploits the motherboard BIOS and utilises the System Management Mode (SMM) in order to periodically execute itself while the operating system loads. The limitation of this tool, however, is it can exploit only Dell PowerEdge Servers which use particular BIOS versions namely A02, A05, A06, 1.1.0, 1.2.0 and 1.3.7. Deitybounce can be installed in the target system either by interdiction or by using a technique called ARKSTREAM. Arkstream is a virtual technology to reflash the software into the target system. Once installed, Deitybounce's execution is configurable and it becomes active when the target system power is on.[46]

GODSURGE

Godsurge is a software application persistence tool, again directed against the Dell PowerEdge servers to exploit the JTAG debugging interface of the server's processors. This software application runs on the hardware implant called Fluxbabbit, which is again an espionage tool of ANT whose technologies have not been exposed.[47]

Figure 6.14: Fluxbabbitt

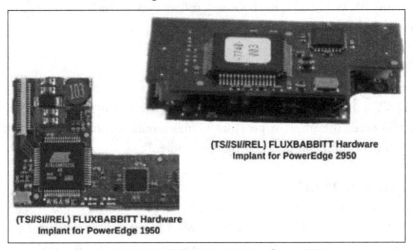

(TS//SI//REL) FLUXBABBITT Hardware Implant for PowerEdge 2950

(TS//SI//REL) FLUXBABBITT Hardware Implant for PowerEdge 1950

Source: Product Data – GODSURGE", NSA ANT Catalogue, USA.

In order to enable Godsurge to conduct its task, the target system has to be fitted perfectly with JTAG scan chain and the hardware implant Fluxbabbit through interdiction. Fluxbabbit has to be pre-programmed with Godsurge application code, the payload and the implant installer. Once the target system powers on, Godsurge will appear and its frequency of execution is configurable. The cost of Fluxbabbit hardware implant and installation of Godsurge in it together is estimated to be US$500.[48]

IRONCHEF

Ironchef enables persistence in access to communicate with the hardware implant like Unitedrake and Straitbizzarre which provides two way Radio Frequency (RF) communications. This technique is supported by HP Proliant 380DL G5 model server. Interdiction is the technique used to install Ironchef, the software implant and the hardware implant in the target system. Even if the software implant is removed from the machine, Ironchef can be used to access the machine, determine why the software was removed and also to reinstall the software from a nearby listening post to the target system.[49]

Firewalls

JETPLOW

Jetplow is a software persistent application for the BANANAGLEE software implant that is used to exploit Cisco PIX Series and ASA Firewalls. It also has the potential to act as a back door persistent. Jetplow gives persistence to Bananaglee software implant to modify the Cisco firewall's operating system (OS) during the booting stage. Even if Bananaglee software did not find support during booting the operating system, Jetplow provides a back door capability through which the OS can be modified and even Bananaglee can be installed later through the back door. Jetplow can also be remotely installed provided Bananaglee already exists at the target.[50]

HALLUXWATER

Halluxwater is a persistent back door implant designed especially for Huawei Eudemon firewall to function as a boot ROM upgrade. Halluxwater gives covert access to the NSA operator to read and write memory, execute an address or a packet using a Turbopanda insertion tool. This implant has the capability to survive boot ROM upgrades and even OS upgrades.[51]

FEEDTROUGH

Feedtrough is a persistence providing technique for two software implants, namely DNT's Bananaglee and CSE's Zestyleak. Feedthrough works only against Juniper Netscreen Firewalls. When the firewall is booted, the first step taken is to direct the code to check if the OS is in the list of Feedthrough database. If it exists, then a chain of events ensures the installation of either Bananaglee or Zestyleak software or in some cases both the implants. The limitation of Feedthrough is that it can work only when the OS is listed in its database. According to the exposed document, Feedthrough has been deployed in many platforms.[52]

GOURMETTROUGH

Gourmettrough is a software persistent implant for certain Juniper firewalls. It gives persistence to Bananaglee software during reboot and

OS upgrades. According to the document available, Gourmettrough has also been deployed in many target platforms.[53]

SOUFFLETROUGH

Souffletrough is a BIOS persistence implant for Juniper firewalls specified to SSG 500 and SSG 300 series. It also has the capability to provide back door persistence. This implant modifies the Juniper firewall's OS during booting by persisting the Bananaglee software implant. Souffletrough is remotely upgradable and it can take advantage of Intel's System Management Mode (SMM) for enhanced reliability and covertness. The document available also reveals that the deployment of this implant was going on and there was huge stock available ready for deployment.[54]

Audio and Visual Radars

CTX4000

Figure 6.15: CTX4000

Source: Product Data – NSA ANT Catalogue, USA.

CTX4000 was used as a portable continuous wave radar unit which would illuminate the target system from which off net data can be retrieved. This tool has the capacity to collect signals which otherwise is extremely difficult to obtain and process. It works in a frequency range of 1 to 2 GHz and on a bandwidth upto 45 MHz. This tool was primarily used in VAGRANT and DROPMIRE collection devices which can only be presumed to be useful in some clandestine information gathering operations. This tool was operational till August 2008 after which it was replaced with another tool called Photoanglo.[55]

PHOTOANGLO

Photoanglo is a radar tool which was developed as the replacement for CTX4000 and it was jointly developed by NSA and Government

Communications Headquarters (GCHQ) of UK. Unlike CTX4000, this tool is smaller in size where it can fit inside a small briefcase and it has a frequency range of 1 to 4 GHz and functions at a bandwidth of 450 MHz. The un-modulated continuous wave (CW) signal generated from the radar unit is amplified and sent to a radio frequency connector which is transmitted through an antenna. When the signal is retransmitted from the target system, the receiver antenna captures the signal and it is amplified, filtered and mixed with transmit antenna. The resulting RF signal is connected to processing systems like NIGHTWATCH, LFS-2 or VIEWPLATE using an external Bayonet Neill–Concelman (BNC) connector for visual intelligence.[56]

NIGHTWATCH

Figure 6.16: Nightwatch

Source: Product Data - NSA ANT Catalogue, USA.

Nightwatch is a specially designed portable computer protected in a case and used for video reconstruction for surveillance. The video output from collecting tools like CTX4000, Photoanglow or any other general purpose receiver is connected to the Nightwatch. The user can adjust the horizontal and vertical sync of the output video of the target's screen. When the sync matches the desired readable quality, 'Sync Lock' is activated which enables the user to view all that is displayed on the target's computer screen. The user also has an option to forward all the frames from Nightwatch to NSAW for further intelligence gathering by expert analysts. Like CTX4000, this tool was also on the verge of being obsolete in 2008 and according to the available documents a new tool called VIEWPLATE was slated to replace Nightwatch.[57]

LOUDAUTO

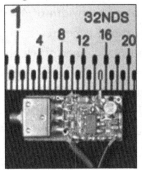

Figure 6.17: Loudauto

Source: Product Data - NSA ANT Catalogue, USA.

LOUDAUTO is the conventional audio bugging tool which is used to gather audio from the target space to a remote location. This tool picks up the room audio and it can pick up speech at a standard volume from a distance of 20 feet. The tool is powered by a replaceable battery and it uses very minimal battery charge for its operations. The audio picked up by the microphone in this tool is converted into analog signal which is used to pulse position modulate (PPM) a square wave signal at a pre-set frequency. The square wave is then used to turn a FET (field effect transistor) on and off. When the FET is illuminated, the signal is amplitude modulated and it is retransmitted and then finally processed to recover the room audio. This tool is also part of Angryneighbor family. The cost of one unit of this tool is US$30.[58]

TAWDRYYARD

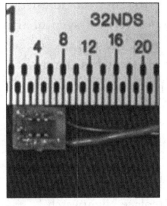

Figure 6.18: Tawdryyard

Source: Product Data - NSA ANT Catalogue, USA.

Tawdryyard is a simple detection radar unit used to detect the deployed Ragemaster tool of NSA ANT with a radius of 50 meters. The tool work with the simple radar functioning model and it is part of the Angryneighbor family of retro-reflectors. The cost of one unit of this tool is US$30.[59]

Mobile Devices

DROPOUTJEEP

Dropoutjeep is a software implant for Apple iphone operation system (models available during 2005-2009) which uses an undisclosed framework called CHIMNEYPOOL to provide specific signal intelligence. This implant can be used to remotely push or pull files from the mobile device including SMS, contacts, voicemails, geographic location, room audio through hot mic, camera visuals, mobile tower location, etc. Through SMS or GPRS connectivity, the command, control and exfilteration of data from the implanted device can be achieved covertly and in encrypted format.[60] Although this implant was in the development phase during 2007, it is believed that the ANT department would have succeeded in developing this technology later.

TOTEGHOSTLY 2.0

Toteghostly 2.0 is software based implant but meant for the Microsoft Windows operating system based mobile devices, to provide specific signal intelligence. Its functions are similar to Dropoutjeep, except the fact that this implant operates on windows based mobile devices and also was under development in 2007.[61]

GOPHERSET

Gopherset is a software implant for GSM (Global System for Mobile Communications) based SIM (Subscriber identification Module) cards. This implant is used to extract phonebook, SMS and the call log information from the target device and sends it to a user-defined phone number via SMS. Exploiting the SIM Toolkit interface (the interface issues commands and makes requests to the device) GOPHERSET retrieves the information from the target. This implant is loaded to the target's SIM card either using a USB smartcard reader or via using wireless methods.[62]

MONKEYCALENDER

Monkeycalender is a software implant for GSM (Global System for Mobile Communications) SIM (Subscriber identification Module) cards. This implant retrieves the geographic location information from the target's handset and sends it to the user defined phone number via SMS. The functioning and installation process of this implant is similar to that of Gopherset.[63]

TOTECHASER

Totechaser is a specially built software implant for Thuraya 2520 handset. This implant exploits the Windows CE operating system of the device. Thuraya 2520 is an advanced smart phone that functions as a 3-in-1 integrated handset with satellite, GSM (Tri-band), and GPS connectivity.[64] This implant is used to extract information like GPS and GSM geo-location, call log, contact list and other user information from the phone. The implant uses SMS messaging for command, control and data exfiltration path both in satellite mode and GSM mode without alerting the target. The Totechaser system consists of the modified handsets and a collection system.[65]

PICASSO

Picasso is the technology for modifying handsets which are used to collect data stored in the device, information on location and even audio in a room. Command and Data exfiltration is done from a laptop and via regular phone via SMS without alerting the target. The data exfilterated through these modified handsets includes call log, recently registered networks, Geo-location codes, room audio using hot mic, recent successful PINs entered into the phone during the power-on cycle, phone number when the phone is turned on in case new SIM has been used. Apart from these the controller can also block calls to deny service to the device. The device models which are used for this purpose are Eastcom 760c+, Samsung E600, X450 and Samsung C140 and the cost for making one unit with this technology is approximately US$2500.[66]

CROSSBEAM

Crosbeam, according to the documents available is a GSM module that mates a modified commercial cellular product with a WAGONBED controller board. This tool is capable of collecting and compressing voice data. It can also receive GSM voice, record voice data and transmit the received information via connected modules or 4 different GSM data modes (GPRS, Circuit Switched Data, Voice over Data and DTMF) back to a secure facility. The cost of one unit of this tool is US$4K.[67]

GENESIS

Genesis is a technology that is used as a covert signal intelligence transceiver through a modified commercial GSM handset. A commercial GSM handset is modified to include Software Defined Radio (SDR) and additional system memory. This SDR allows the user to covertly perform network surveys, record Radio Frequency spectrum or perform handset location functions in hostile environments. This modified handset has a concealed SDR, external antenna port, 16GB internal memory, multiple internal antennas, spectrum analyser capability and integrated Ethernet facilities. The cost of one unit of such modified handset is US$15K.[68]

Mobile Networks

WATERWITCH

Figure 6.19: Waterwitch

Source: Product Data – NSA ANT Catalogue, USA.

Waterwitch is a hand held detection tool used for geo-location of targeted handsets in the field. This is a tactical tool used by operators in the field to locate the targeted handsets. This tool has an external antenna for target detection and an internal antenna for communication with active interrogator and also the device uses E-ink technology in its display for low light emissions. The tool possesses multiple technology capability based on SDR platform.[69]

CANDYGRAM

Candygram is not a single tool but a setup of devices that mimics the GSM cell phone tower of a target network. When the target handset enters the area of range of Candygram base station, the system sends out an SMS to the user through an external network. This system operates on the frequency of 900, 1800 and 1900 MHz. Following are the scenarios in which Candygram can be deployed:

• for asset validation,

- for target tracking and identification and
- for identifying hostile surveillance units with GSM handsets.

Figure 6.20: Candygram operational concept

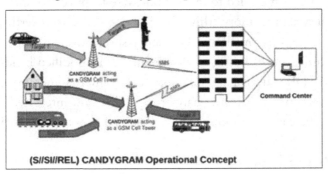

source: Product Data – NSA ANT Catalogue, USA.

The technology has unique features like automatic network configuration, capable of configuring 200 phone numbers in its target deck, remote restart and data erasure.[70]

CYCLONE Hx9

Figure 6.21: Cyclone Hx9

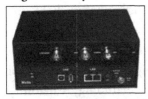

Source: Product Data – NSA ANT Catalogue, USA.

Cyclone Hx9 is a Network-In-a-Box (NIB) system which uses the existing Typhon Graphical User Interface and supports the full Typhon feature base and applications. This tool is a base station router, when employed provides network for field operations. This tool has a range of more than 32 Km and it can handle voice and high-speed data transfer.[71]

EBSR

Figure 6.22: EBSR

Source: Product Data – NSA ANT Catalogue, USA.

EBSR is a low power tri-band active GSM base station interrogator with internal 802.11/GPS/handset capability. This device is used in the operations on the networks. This has two models namely LxT and LxU with voice and high-speed Data capability and also SMS capability.[72]

ENTOURAGE

Entourage is a direction finding software application operating on the device called HOLLOWPOINT. This system as a whole is capable of providing line for transmission of GSM/UMTS/CDMA200/FRS signals. This software application works in conjunction with another base station router called Nebula to achieve Find/Fix/Finish capabilities of the Galaxy programme.[73]

NEBULA

Figure 6.23: Nebula

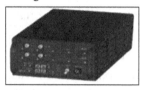

Nebula is a base station router and a Network-In-a-Box system. The cost of one unit of this device is US$250K. This device supports GSM, UMTS, CDMA2000 applications at the ranges of 900, 2100 and 1900 MHz respectively.[74]

Source: Product Data – NSA ANT Catalogue, USA.

TYPHON HX

Figure 6.24: TyphonHX

Source: Product Data – NSA ANT Catalogue, USA.

Typhon HX is a base station router and Network-In-a-Box (NIB) system supporting GSM bands 850/900/1800/1900 MHz and associated full GSM signalling and call control. This equipment is used in tactical operations to find, fix and finish targeted handset users. Using this equipment it is possible for the operators to geo-locate the handset and the user.[75]

Analysis on NSA ANT Catalogue

A study and understanding of the functions and operational capabilities of the 50 NSA ANT tools helped us to arrive at the following inferences:
- These tools are meant for special operations which are highly covert in nature for the purpose of gathering information, sabotage, espionage and surveillance.

- The functionality of the tools can be mainly associated with military operations but not necessarily be confined to military only, as few tools like Cottonmouth can also be used for non-military civilian operations.
- Few tools belong to a family of tools called ANGRYNEIGHBOR, which gives the impression that there are more families of tools either under operation or development.
- All the documents disclosed related to NSA ANT catalogue were pertaining to the year 2007. It is, therefore, likely that these tools have become obsolete and new versions of tools and models would have replaced in the later stage.
- There are passing references to many new technologies but the utilisation of which do not appear in any of the exposed documents. This means that there are several undisclosed tools developed by ANT department whose capabilities are not known.
- The fact that the details of these tools are being revealed to the world indicates that there would have been a compulsion for the agency to either abandon these tools on the whole or switch to more covert methods of espionage and surveillance.
- If it is a question of abandoning, the agency would have abandoned several units of these tools which were operational in the field somewhere across the globe. Identifying those tools and examining them if any by agencies of other countries which could lay hands on them might uncover more precisely the capabilities of these tools.
- In many instances, both hardware and software are implanted on devices manufactured by most widely used brands like Samsung, Cisco, Juniper, Dell, etc. As a result of this disclosure there is distrust about these brands which in turn create more hassles for the procurement body of any country in terms of rigorous audit during procurement of any such devices, especially for national security purposes.
- Countries like India which are mainly dependent on import for their defence equipments are most vulnerable to these US cyber tools.
- It is also revealed from the documents that the NSA implants a few of their tools by a method called interdiction, in which the agency would

intervene during the supply chain process and place their implant on the devices before it gets delivered to the intended recipient. This emphasises the need for enhancing safety for any supply-chain process, especially for defence equipments, irrespective of their size or function.

- The fact that many implants can be installed, controlled, operated and executed remotely emphasises the need for enhanced network security and also acts as a pointer to the need for disintegrating and isolating a few sensitive and important networks from other national grids.

- It also emphasises the need to develop indigenous capabilities for manufacture of hardware in countries like India which at present are dependent on imports and it cannot afford to become easy targets to such covert cyber tools.

What Lies Ahead?

Having studied a few covert cyber capabilities of US and also of China in the previous chapter one question that might linger in everyone's mind would be what is the real purpose in undertaking all these covert programmes that the US and other countries are conducting in the cyber world? Is it really only for the sake of their national security or do they have much bigger ambitions? If yes, what are they?

The answer is obviously yes. By taking a futuristic outlook into the cyber space beyond capabilities, and vulnerabilities and by mapping the indicators on this issue it is evident that there is a bigger picture of a game played by many players to achieve 'Supremacy'. The US refers to this supremacy in the cyber domain as 'Global Network Supremacy'.[76] As we live in the age of information, the ability to control and manipulate any available information gives a player an upper hand in this game. Since cyber world is holding an enormous quantum of information, and has the ability to virtually connect anything and everybody, this medium is utilised well by all players for their covert operations with a view to achieve supremacy to the maximum extent possible. Hence, cyber domain has become the battleground of the future. The different players involved in these activities are none other than those who operate in the cyber world, ranging from individuals to countries. Although the cyber world is progressively influencing the lives of the people in the real world, there is still a lot more to be part of virtual world as majority of the world is still not connected to internet. Till this is achieved and even after that, the covert cyber capabilities will be used as sabotaging tools in the cyber space to stop another player, in most cases a country, from enhancing their capabilities both in the virtual and the real world and to keep them engaged in tackling the threats of sabotage. At present, the use of covert capabilities helps the players to know about the hidden plans of another by silently intruding into their networks, which helps them not only to orchestrate their immediate move but also to frame long term policies and strategies.

An appropriate example to understand the amount of danger a successful covert cyber operation can cause would be the series of events which unfolded in Iran in the recent past that changed the fate of the country's ambitious nuclear programme. Iran had started its ambitious nuclear programme with aid from US in 1950s under the then 'Atoms for Peace' policy of the US. As years passed due to change of regime, the country, which was once an ally of the US became a foe and faced economic sanctions. The rift between the two countries also affected Iran's nuclear programme with which the country had struggled for long until recently. However, with help from Russia and other countries and through the nuclear black market, Iran sustained and enhanced its nuclear programme. Later in 2005, when Mahmoud Ahmadinejad became the President of Iran, the nuclear programme gained momentum and Iran began its work towards enrichment of weapons grade uranium. Due to the failure in talks between the US and Iran, in December 2006, there were sanctions from United Nations which was initiated by the US on Iran to curb its nuclear programme. However, these sanctions were not successful in achieving its objective and Iran managed to move further in its nuclear programme.[77]

However, in 2008, the centrifuges in Natanz Nuclear facility in Iran began to face unprecedented crashes. These breakdowns, which seemed to be like independent and random accidents, continued till Spring 2010 and the engineers in the facility were clueless about the reason for those crashes. In Spring 2010, the situation in Natanz facility began to deteriorate further when the centrifuges in the facility started to function in a haphasard manner which was followed by more frequent and high intensity breakdowns thus affecting the whole nuclear programme of Iran. During this period, the engineers struggled to decipher the reasons behind the disruptions in Natanz nuclear facility. It was later discovered by Symantec, a cyber security products manufacturing company, that, the malfunction was due to a highly sophisticated computer worm that affected the controller systems or Supervisory Control and Data Acquisition (SCADA) systems in the facility.[78] This computer worm was named as Stuxnet, thus becoming the first computer programme to be used as a cyber weapon. Consequently, technical papers started coming out related to its functioning.

Later, Stuxnet started getting media attention and slowly media reports emerged about the origin of this computer worm. It was generally reported across all media that Stuxnet was the result of joint effort by US and Israeli intelligence agencies - NSA and Unit 8200 respectively. It was reported that way back in 2006 after the negotiations between Iran and the West floundered, the US under the Bush administration started a covert cyber programme codenamed Olympic Games in order to sabotage Iran's nuclear programme. The engineers at NSA and Israeli Unit 8200 initially wrote a 'beacon' programme that could map the functioning of Natanz facility and introduced it into the facility possibly with the aid of an unsuspecting insider. The 'beacon' programme collected and transmitted information related to the facility's computer configurations and more such sensitive information to the agencies. Using the collected data, the engineers wrote another complex 'worm' programme with the ability to disrupt the facility and thus, introduced this programme into the computers of the facility through various unknown methods. The worm programme took control of many centrifuges in the facility which made them run either too fast or too slow and at times the centrifuges even exploded, thereby the worm succeeded in disrupting the nuclear programme of Iran. Surprisingly, in Summer 2010, the worm programme due to some programming error, copied itself into the laptop of an Iranian scientist who worked in the facility. When the scientist connected his laptop to internet the worm spread itself to other parts of the world through internet and this is when the world community took notice of such a malicious programme. It was later revealed by the cyber research community that the Stuxnet programme that had spread through internet, was only one version of the various programmes written under the Olympic Games project and many such variants were utilised on the facility in order to disrupt and sabotage Iran's nuclear programme. The Stuxnet had made use of some 'Zero-day' vulnerability in the Siemens Step7 software which was widely used in the facility to cause disruption. It was also reported that when Barrack Obama became President of the US in 2009, his predecessor, President Bush successfully persuaded him to continue the Olympic Games project by highlighting its importance.[79]

In 2013, Symantec came up with a research paper exclusively on Stuxnet, describing its evolution and its different variants. This report indicated that Stuxnet 0.5 was the oldest known stuxnet version which was in the process of development as early as 2005 and it was in wild since November 2007. Stuxnet 0.5 was less aggressive than its later versions especially the Stuxnet 1.x.[80] Some highlights and its relevance about different versions of Stuxnet are given in the appendix 1.

The figure given below refers to the uranium enrichment production at Natanz to key milestones of Stuxnet development. Interestingly, the highlighting dates in Stuxnet's lifecycle coincide with the dips in feed or quantum of production and lower levels of production given the same or greater feed amounts (shown as gaps between the two lines).

Figure 6.25: Low enriched Uranium Production and milestones in Stuxnet coincidences

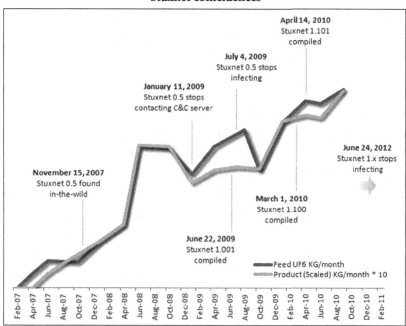

Source: Geoff Mcdonald, Liam O Murchu, Stephen Doherty & Eric Chien. "Stuxnet 0.5 – The Missing Link", Symantec, version 1.0, February 26, 2013.

Although the operational success of different variants of Stuxnet worm remains unclear, it has succeeded in achieving various other objectives. These are:

- First, this computer programme has succeeded in making cyber weapon a reality.

- Second, different variants of Stuxnet together succeeded in delaying Iran's nuclear programme by one and a half to two years time.

- Third, the whole Stuxnet episode that disrupted Iran's nuclear programme has instilled fear about prospective danger of cyber weapons in the mindset/ psyche of the world community.

- Fourth and most important, the Stuxnet episode might have been one of the arms twisting coercive diplomatic strategy which changed the mindset of Iranian political circle to again go to the diplomatic table and discuss its nuclear programme with the West which resulted in the famous US-Iran Nuclear deal.

The Iranian nuclear episode is a clear example of what covert cyber operations using cyber tools are capable of in causing disturbances to a state's national security or even in creating change and disturb the balance of power in international politics.

Conclusion

In the context of global cyber security, the mere existence of these covert cyber capabilities poses a serious threat due to its sheer nature–ability to undertake covert activity. While it is claimed by US and other countries that these covert cyber capabilities are used to conduct network operations like tracking, detecting and identifying prospective terrorists and anti-social elements and their activities in the cyber world, the possibility of these invisible and 'capability-disabling' weapons being pointed or targeted against any individual or a particular group of people or even against a state cannot be denied. Such capability poses grave danger to cyber freedom and virtual existence for any individual in the domain as well as a serious threat to national security of the targeted nation.

This fear acts as a compelling factor for common users to lean towards more secretive and clandestine means of operations in the cyber domain such as using TOR networks for everyday browsing in order to hide their location and identity, fearing the wrath of being targeted. Also, many states desire to acquire covert cyber capabilities so as to participate in the ongoing game for 'Supremacy' and also to develop the ability to fight against their perspective perpetrators. If this situation continues, the deep web would go deeper and the cyber 'under' world would expand more rapidly which would only increase the complexities that already exist in this highly technical realm and eventually would also do so in the physical world. With the current trend it could be stated that development and operation of covert cyber capabilities not only in the US but across the globe is here to stay and the cyber weapons such as Stuxnet are the weapons of the future.

Notes

1. Public Law 107–56, United States of America, 2001.
2. "Verizone forced to hand over telephone data, full court ruling", *The Guardian*,

June 6, 2013, in http://www.theguardian.com/world/interactive/2013/jun/06/verizon-telephone-data-court-order, accessed on March 3, 2014.

3. Swati Khandelwal, "U.S. Supreme Court allows the FBI to Hack any Computer in the World", *The Hacker News*, April 28, 2016, http://thehackernews.com/2016/04/fbihackingpower.Html, accessed on May 20, 2016.

4. "NSA Prism program taps in to user data of Apple, Google and others", *The Guardian*, June 7, 2013, in http://www.theguardian.com/world/2013/jun/06/us-tech-giants-nsa-data, accessed on April 3, 2014.

5. "NSA slides explain the Prism data collection program", *The Washington Post*, June 6, 2013, in http://www.washingtonpost.com/wp-srv/special/politics/prism-collection-documents/, accessed on April 3, 2014.

6. Ibid.

7. "U.S., British intelligence mining data from nine U.S. Internet companies in broad secret program", *The Washington Post*, June 7, 2013, in http://www.washingtonpost.com/investigations/us-intelligence-mining-data-from-nine-us-internet-companies-in-broad-secret-program/2013/06/06/3a0c0da8-cebf-11e2-8845-d970ccb04497_story.html, accessed on April 4, 2014.

8. Ibid.

9. Ibid.

10. "XKeyscore: NSA tool collects 'nearly everything a user does on the internet'", *The Guardian*, July 31, 2013, in http://www.theguardian.com/world/2013/jul/31/nsa-top-secret-program-online-data, accessed on April 4, 2014.

11. "How the NSA is still harvesting your online data", *The Guardian*", June 27, 2014, in http://www.theguardian.com/world/2013/jun/27/nsa-online-metadata-collection, accessed on April 4, 2014.

12. "NSA X-Keyscore", Exposed document in http://www.documentcloud.org/documents/743244-xkeyscore-slidedeck.html, accessed on August 4, 2013.

13. Edward Snowden, Personal interview by Norddeutscher Rundfunk, January 26, 2014.

14. "XKeyscore Exposed: How NSA tracks all German TOR Users as 'extremists'", *RT*, July 03, 2013, in http://rt.com/news/170208-nsa-spies-tor-users/, accessed on April 5, 2014.

15. "Expanding Endpoint Operations", *SIDtoday*, NSANet, September 17, 2004, https://www.eff.org/files/2015/01/23/20150117-speigel-document_about_the_expansion_of_the_remote_operations_center_roc_on_endpoint_operations.pdf, accessed on April 6, 2014.

16. "Secret Documents: The special department TAO NSA introduces itself", *Der Spiegel*, December 30, 2013, in http://www.spiegel.de/fotostrecke/nsa-dokumente-die-abteilung-tao-der-nsa-fotostrecke-105355-3.html, accessed on April 6, 2014.

17. "The ROC: NSA's Epicentre for Computer Network Operations", *SIDtoday*, NSANet, September 6, 2006, https://www.eff.org/files/2015/01/23/20150117-speigel-document_explaining_the_role_of_the_remote_operations_center_roc.pdf, accessed on May 30, 2014.

18. "(TS) NSA Quantum Tasking Techniques for the R & T Analyst", *Der Spiegel*, December 30, 2013.

19. Ibid.

20. Ibid.

21. Appelbaum, Jacob and et al., "Die Klempner aus San Antonio", *Der Spiegel*, January 2014.

22. "Inside TAO: Documents Reveal Top NSA Hacking Unit", *Spiegel Online International*, December 29, 2013, at http://www.spiegel.de/international/world/the-nsa-uses-powerful-toolbox-in-effort-to-spy-on-global-networks-a-940969.html, accessed on April 6, 2014.

23. "Product Data – SURLYSPAWN", NSA ANT Catalogue, USA, https://nsa.gov1.info/dni/nsa-ant-catalog/, accessed on May 1, 2014.

24. "Product Data – COTTONMOUTH - I", NSA ANT Catalogue, USA, https://nsa.gov1.info/dni/nsa-ant-catalog/, May 1, 2014.

25. "Product Data – COTTONMOUTH- II", NSA ANT Catalogue, USA, https://nsa.gov1.info/dni/nsa-ant-catalog/, accessed on May 2, 2014.

26. "Product Data – COTTONMOUTH- III", NSA ANT Catalogue, USA, https://nsa.gov1.info/dni/nsa-ant-catalog/, accessed on May 2, 2014.

27. "Product Data – FIREWALK", NSA ANT Catalogue, USA, https://nsa.gov1.info/dni/nsa-ant-catalog/, accessed on May 3, 2014.

28. "Product Data – RAGEMASTER", NSA ANT Catalogue, USA, https://nsa.gov1.info/dni/nsa-ant-catalog/, accessed on May 3, 2014.

29. "Product Data – GINSU", NSA ANT Catalogue, USA, https://nsa.gov1.info/dni/nsa-ant-catalog/, accessed on May 3, 2014.

30. "Product Data – IRATEMONK", NSA ANT Catalogue, USA, https://nsa.gov1.info/dni/nsa-ant-catalog/, accessed on May 4, 2014.

31. SWAP: NSA Exploit of the Day, February 6, 2014, in https://www.schneier.com/blog/archives/2014/02/swap_nsa_exploi.html, accessed on June 3, 2014.

32. "Product Data – WISTFULTOLL", NSA ANT Catalogue, USA, https://nsa.gov1.info/dni/nsa-ant-catalog/, accessed on May 4, 2014.

33. "SOMBERKNAVE: NSA Exploit of the Day", February 5, 2014, in http://www.the-ethical-hacker.com/2014/02/somberknave-nsa-exploit-of-the-day/, accessed on June 3, 2014

34. http://www.telefoniert-nach-hause.de/index.php/NSA/HOWLERMONKEY, accessed on June 4, 2014.

35 "Product Data – JUNIORMINT", NSA ANT Catalogue, USA, https://nsa.gov1.info/dni/nsa-ant-catalog/, accessed on May 5, 2014.

36. "Product Data – MAESTRO-II", NSA ANT Catalogue, USA, https://nsa.gov1.info/dni/nsa-ant-catalog/, accessed on May 6, 2014.

37. "Product Data – TRINITY", NSA ANT Catalogue, USA, https://nsa.gov1.info/ni/nsa-ant-catalog/, accessed on May 7, 2014.

38. Jacob Appelbaum , "NSA ANT W-Lan", 30C3, December 30, 2013, https://cryptome.org/2013/12/nsa-ant-w-lan.pdf, accessed on May 8, 2014.

39. "Product Data – NIGHTSTAND", NSA ANT Catalogue, USA, https://nsa.gov1. info/dni/nsa-ant-catalog/, accessed on May 9, 2014.
40. "Product Data – SPARROW II", NSA ANT Catalogue, USA, https://nsa.gov1. info/dni/nsa-ant-catalog/, accessed on May 7, 2014.
41. http://en.wikipedia.org/wiki/Router_(computing), accessed on August 2, 2014.
42. "Product Data – HEADWATER", NSA ANT Catalogue, USA, https://nsa.gov1. info/dni/nsa-ant-catalog/, accessed on May 8, 2014.
43. "Product Data – SCHOOLMONTANA", NSA ANT Catalogue, USA, https:// nsa.gov1.info/dni/nsa-ant-catalog/, accessed on May 9, 2014.
44. "Product Data – SIERRAMONTNA", NSA ANT Catalogue, USA, https://nsa. gov1.info/dni/nsa-ant-catalog/, accessed on May 9, 2014.
45. "Product Data – STUCCOMONTANA", NSA ANT Catalogue, USA, https:// nsa.gov1.info/dni/nsa-ant-catalog/, accessed on May 10, 2014.
46. "Product Data – DEITYBOUNCE", NSA ANT Catalogue, USA, https://nsa. gov1.info/dni/nsa-ant-catalog/, accessed on May 10, 2014.
47. "Product Data – GODSURGE", NSA ANT Catalogue, USA, https://nsa.gov1. info/dni/nsa-ant-catalog/, accessed on May 11, 2014.
48. Ibid.
49. "Product Data – IRONCHEF", NSA ANT Catalogue, USA, https://nsa.gov1. info/dni/nsa-ant-catalog/, accessed on May 12, 2014.
50. "Product Data – JETPLOW", NSA ANT Catalogue, USA, https://nsa.gov1.info/ dni/nsa-ant-catalog/, accessed on May 12, 2014.
51. "Product Data – HALLUXWATER", NSA ANT Catalogue, USA, https://nsa. gov1.info/dni/nsa-ant-catalog/, accessed on May 12, 2014.
52. "Product Data – FEEDTROUGH", NSA ANT Catalogue, USA, https://nsa.gov1. info/dni/nsa-ant-catalog/, accessed on May 13, 2014.
53. "Product Data – GOURMETTROUGH", NSA ANT Catalogue, USA, https:// nsa.gov1.info/dni/nsa-ant-catalog/, accessed on May 13, 2014.
54. "Product Data – SOUFFLETROUGH", NSA ANT Catalogue, USA, https://nsa. gov1.info/dni/nsa-ant-catalog/, accessed on May 14, 2014.
55. "Product Data – CTX4000", NSA ANT Catalogue, USA, https://nsa.gov1.info/ dni/nsa-ant-catalog/, accessed on May 14, 2014.
56. "Product Data - PHOTOANGLO", NSA ANT Catalogue, USA, https://nsa.gov1. info/dni/nsa-ant-catalog/, accessed on May 14, 2014.
57. "Product Data - NIGHTWATCH", NSA ANT Catalogue, USA, https://nsa.gov1. info/dni/nsa-ant-catalog/, accessed on May 15, 2014.
58. "Product Data - LOUDAUTO", NSA ANT Catalogue, USA, https://nsa.gov1. info/dni/nsa-ant-catalog/, accessed on May 16, 2014.
59. "Product Data - TAWDRYYARD", NSA ANT Catalogue, USA, https://nsa.gov1. info/dni/nsa-ant-catalog/, accessed on May 17, 2014.
60. "Product Data – DROPOUTJEEP" NSA ANT Catalogue, USA, https://nsa.gov1. info/dni/nsa-ant-catalog/, accessed on May 17, 2014.
61. "Product Data – TOTEGHOSTLY 2.0", NSA ANT Catalogue, USA, https://nsa.

gov1.info/dni/nsa-ant-catalog/, accessed on May 18, 2014.

62. "Product Data – GOPHERSET", NSA ANT Catalogue, USA, https://nsa.gov1. info/dni/nsa-ant-catalog/, accessed on May 19, 2014.

63. "Product Data – MONKEYCALENDAR", NSA ANT Catalogue, USA, https:// nsa.gov1.info/dni/nsa-ant-catalog/, accessed on May 19, 2014.

64. "Thuraya SG-2520 Brochure", Thuraya Products.

65. "Product Data – TOTECHASER", NSA ANT Catalogue, USA, https://nsa.gov1. info/dni/nsa-ant-catalog/, accessed on May 20, 2014.

66. "Product Data – PICASSO", NSA ANT Catalogue, USA, https://nsa.gov1.info/ dni/nsa-ant-catalog/, accessed on May 20, 2014.

67. "Product Data – CROSSBEAM", NSA ANT Catalogue, USA, https://nsa.gov1. info/dni/nsa-ant-catalog/, accessed on May 21, 2014.

68. "Product Data – GENESIS", NSA ANT Catalogue, USA, https://nsa.gov1.info/ dni/nsa-ant-catalog/, accessed on May 22, 2014.

69. "Product Data – WATERWITCH", NSA ANT Catalogue, USA, https://nsa.gov1. info/dni/nsa-ant-catalog/, accessed on May 22, 2014.

70. "Product Data – CANDYGRAM", NSA ANT Catalogue, USA, https://nsa.gov1. info/dni/nsa-ant-catalog/, accessed on May 22, 2014.

71. "Product Data – CYCLONE Hx9", NSA ANT Catalogue, USA, https://nsa.gov1. info/dni/nsa-ant-catalog/, accessed on May 23, 2014.

72. "Product Data – EBSR", NSA ANT Catalogue, USA, https://nsa.gov1.info/dni/ nsa-ant-catalog/, accessed on May 23, 2014.

73. "Product Data – ENTOURAGE", NSA ANT Catalogue, USA, https://nsa.gov1. info/dni/nsa-ant-catalog/, accessed on May 24, 2014.

74. "Product Data – NEBULA", NSA ANT Catalogue, USA, https://nsa.gov1.info/ dni/nsa-ant-catalog/, accessed on May 25, 2014.

75. "Product Data – TYPHON HX", NSA ANT Catalogue, USA, https://nsa.gov1. info/dni/nsa-ant-catalog/, accessed on May 26, 2014.

76. "The ROC: NSA's Epicentre for Computer Network Operations", *SIDtoday*, NSANet, September 6, 2006, https://www.eff.org/files/2015/01/23/20150117-speigel-document_explaining_the_role_of_the_remote_operations_center_roc.pdf, accessed on May 30, 2014.

77. "Timeline on Iran's Nuclear Programme", *New York Times*, Nov 24, 2014, in http://www.nytimes.com/interactive/2014/11/20/world/middleeast/Iran-nuclear-timeline.html?_r=2#/#time243_7215, accessed on December 10, 2014.

78. "How a secret cyber war program worked", *New York Times*, June 01, 2012, in http://www.nytimes.com/interactive/2012/06/01/world/middleeast/how-a-secret-cyberwar-program-worked.html?ref=middleeast, accessed on December 11, 2014.

79. Ibid.

80. Geoff Mcdonald, Liam O Murchu, Stephen Doherty and Eric Chien. "Stuxnet 0.5 – The Missing Link", Symantec, version 1.0, February 26, 2013.

CYBER INDIA:
A REALITY CHECK

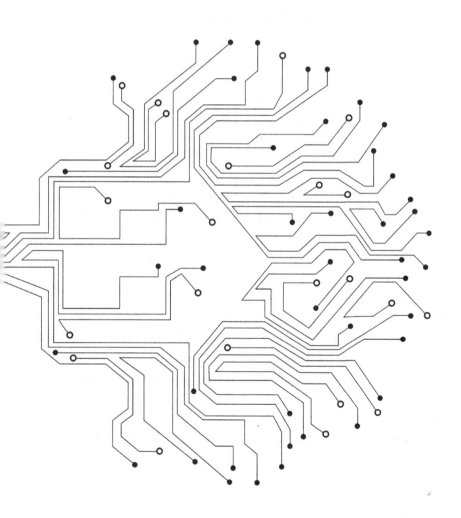

Against the background of facing a wide range of terrors in the cyber world as explained in the previous five chapters, the question in everybody's mind would be - "How safe is the cyber resources of my country?". However, it is unrealistic to try to analyse the security of cyber resources of every country. Since this book is written from an Indian perspective this chapter would try to address the question of "How safe is India's cyber resources?". The chapter would start with tracing the history of computers in India, also analyse the existing cyber environment of the country and project the real picture of cyber India.

It is widely known that cyberspace is composed of data and the smallest unit of any data existing in this domain is a binary digit which can be either zero (0) or one (1). These binary digits are like the sub-atomic particles which form the basic building blocks of this virtual world. The invention of one of the binary digit, zero (0), is widely credited to Indians. India, a huge landmass located in the South Asian region, home to one of the largest population in the world, has immensely contributed to the advancement of world civilisation. It will not be an exaggeration to say that in the foreseeable future too India would definitely continue its contribution towards the advancement of the cyber world. However, the question here is what kind of contribution India would be making to the world, which would be more virtual than ever before with highly intertwined networks connecting every corner of the globe and almost all activities would be heavily depended on these complex networks. Clearly, the reference here is to the cyber world which is undoubtedly expanding at a fast pace across the globe and spreading its tentacles to every corner of the world.

India is no exception and the country with a high proportion of younger generation is increasingly getting familiar to the innovations of technology and more importantly to the cyber world. According to statistics, India has the largest number of internet subscribers and mobile phone users in the South Asian region as a result of its massive population. Moreover, according to recent reports, India has the second largest number of internet users in the world only after China.[1] The dependence on computers and mobile phones for day to day activities in India irrespective of age, educational qualification, financial and social status is rapidly increasing. Along with the advent of smart phones and mobile based applications using internet, its feasibility and access to such devices for communication, has further increased the usage and dependence on this high-end technology among the people. The dependence on mobile phones is so high across the world that it would not be an exaggeration to say that mobile phones are the most widely used gadgets among its peers. On the business front, India is one of the leading exporters of Information Technology (IT) products and has a large IT industry worth hundreds of billions of dollars in the country. The Information and Communication Technology (ICT) sector of India is considered as one of the crown jewel of the country as it contributes immensely to the economy, provides large scale employment, generates huge profits for IT based companies and more importantly enables easy communication for the people. With millions of individuals employed in this sector, where the average age is not more than 35,[2] this sector has become one of the lifelines not only for the country's economy but also for the future generations of the country. While the above mentioned factors are the merits of the cyber environment for India and its development, there are certain demerits which we have to face in respect of cyber environment and need proper evaluation.

Owing to the extensive usage and dependence on cyberspace in the country, India is one of the most targeted countries in the world for cyber attacks. The kind of threats to India's cyber security includes theft of data, malwares, hacking of sensitive networks, defacement of websites, identity thefts, online financial frauds, email spoofing, social engineering scams, Denial of Service (DoS) and Distributed Denial of Service (DDoS) attacks, unauthorised access to critical infrastructure of the country, online surveillance and digital espionage. For instance, in 2014 alone, CERT-IN has handled 130,338 incidents caused by various cyber threats related to cyber security of the country; highest number of incidents handled by the agency in a year till 2016.[3] While many web defacements emanates from unfriendly countries like Pakistan (Chapter 2 - case study), unauthorised intrusion into sensitive Indian networks are emanating from countries like China, USA, Pakistan and a few other countries. The fact that India was identified as the fifth most snooped country by the USA through its digital surveillance programme Prism (Chapter 6), revealed in mid-2013 by Edward Snowden, has brought to light the vulnerable condition existing in the country's cyber security framework and its related technologies. Various fatal malwares like Stuxnet, Duqu, Flame, etc., which have the capability to impose vital damage to the critical infrastructure of the country have also been identified from different Indian networks. Moreover, the existing vulnerabilities in the cyber space being exploited by violent non-state actors and various anti-social elements (refer Chapter 4), also pose a series of threats in this domain for the country.

With this background, it is clear that the cyber environment in India is not all that rosy and the time has come to weigh the merits and demerits of India's cyber environment and its cyber security in a dispassionate manner with a view to understand the reality, which might help in bringing awareness and realisation on the subject matter. A realistic assessment is therefore required to explore about the loopholes and the ways to address them.

Nevertheless, before looking into the current cyber environment of the country it would be wise to revisit the path taken by the county in the field of computers in the past.

History of Computers in India

Ab Initio

Way back in 1950s, as a very young nation, India was introduced to the world of computers by the scientific community of the country. The Indian Statistical Institute (ISI) in Kolkata, which was headed by Prasanta Chandra Mahalanobis and Tata Institute of Fundamental Research (TIFR) in Mumbai headed by Homi Jehangir Bhabha, were the two pioneering institutions which utilised computers for their respective works. Realising the importance of computers in solving complex arithmetic problems, Mahalanobis formed a small computer group at the ISI and placed an order to procure a computer from the British Tabulating Machines (BTM). Accepting to sell a computer to the ISI in 1954, the BTM assembled a computer HEC-2M (Hollerith Electronic Computer Model 2M) which was designed by A.D. Booth, one of the pioneering computer designers of the world, in its workshop and delivered it to India in July 1955. This computer was installed and maintained by Indian scientists on the basis of the notes collected by the scientists while they had visited the company in England, when the machine was being assembled. Thus the country had its first digital computer without much fanfare in 1955.[4]

Figure 7.1: A.D. Booth, one of the early pioneers of small computers, the proud designer of India's first digital computer HEC-2M which was bought by Indian Statistical Institute in 1955.

Source: Simon H. Lavington, "Early British Computers", Manchester University Press, 1980, p 62.

Around the same time, TIFR had started designing the "pilot" computer of the country. After initial research, the team started building the country's first indigenous digital computer in 1957, based on the details of the design of the Illinois Automatic computer (ILLIAC) of the University of Illinois. The project was successfully completed in

1959 and the machine was commissioned in 1960. When TIFR moved to a new building in 1962, the computer was installed at that location and it was named as Tata Institute of Fundamental Research Automatic Calculator (TIFRAC) by none other than the then Prime Minister of the country, Jawaharlal Nehru.[5]

Figure 7.2: TIFRAC Computer at TIFR (Left) and 'TIFRAC' Naming Ceremony (Right).

Source: "R.Narasimhan", Tata Institute of Fundamental Research, Mumbai, http://www.tifr.res.in/~endowment/prof-r-narasimhan.htm, accessed on February 12, 2015.

While TIFR was working on the country's first indigenous computer design, scientists in ISI felt the need for another computer to meet its growing demand in the institution. In spite of problems in funding to the institution due to the crawling economy of the country at that time, Mahalanobis negotiated with the erstwhile Soviet Union, the USSR, to supply an URAL-1 computer for the institution in 1958 with funding assistance from United Nations Trade Assistance Programme. Thus, in 1958, Indian Statistical Institute was the first institution in India which had two working computers and thus became the de-facto 'National Computer Centre' of the country. This computer facility of the institution was utilised by universities, atomic energy establishment and defence research laboratories along with the hosting institution, ISI.[6]

Figure 7.3: A model of URAL-1 computer on display.

Source: "URAL (Computer)" Wikipedia Online Encyclopedia, https://en.wikipedia. org/wiki/Ural_(computer), accessed on February 12, 2015.

Although TIFR successfully built the country's first indigenous digital computer, its decision to manufacture more indigenous computers was changed while it was on the lookout for their second machine. During interactions with experts in the US and after some personal research, the then head of TIFR, R.Narasimhan, realised that the foreign companies are far more advanced in the field of computer design and therefore he felt that it is better to buy the computers from manufacturers than to build the same locally. Thus, a computer called CDC 3600 was purchased from the Control Data Corporation (CDC), USA in 1963 for a sum of US$ 1.5 million with financial aid from United States Agency for International Development (USAID).[7] Although the circumstances at that time made procurement more attractive for India rather than go for indigenous development, had India kept the momentum in designing and building indigenous computers in India rather than procuring it from a foreign company, the capability of the country in Research and Development in the field of computers and the ability to manufacture indigenously designed hardware might have been in a much advanced state as of now.

Figure 7.4: A similar model of CDC 3600 computer was purchased by TIFR.

Source: http://www.computer-history.info/Page4.dir/pages/CDC.3600.dir/, accessed on February 12, 2015.

Later in 1963, one educational institution in India procured its first computer along with a FORTRAN compiler. The US based company, International Business Machine (IBM), installed the computer IBM 1620 in August 1963 in the Indian Institute of Technology (IIT), Kanpur. This computer was also purchased with financial aid from USAID.[8]

Figure 7.5: IBM 1620 in IIT Kanpur in 1964.

Source: "Pictures from IIT-Kanpur from 1963-1965", http://infolab.stanford.edu/pub/gio/personal/1965India/IrvR/, accessed on February 12, 2015.

The installation of IBM 1620 computer in IIT Kanpur provided a window of opportunity for the academic and scientific community of the country to familiarise with the latest advancements in the computing industry. Intensive courses on programming were conducted once a year; a practice which started in 1963 lasted till 1975, and every year around 60 participants from different fields like engineers, faculty members of various universities and scientists would participate and took advantage from their hands on experience on this high-tech machine.[9] This way computing knowledge started spreading slowly to different parts of the country and it slowly started expanding to the commercial sector as well as is evident from the table below:

Table 7.1: No. of computers installed between the periods of 1961-1974.

Year	No. of computers installed at various places across the country
1961	2
1962	1
1963	2
1964	8
1965	12
1966	16
1967	22
1968	20
1969	21
1970	11
1971	33
1972	14
1973	16
1974	11
1971-1974*	28
Total	217

*Exact year of installations not known but installed during this period.
Source: "History", National Informatics Centre, http://as.ori.nic.in/neworiweb/history. aspx, accessed on February 13, 2015.

As the procurement of computers in India was growing, the Directorate General of Technical Development and the Department of Defence Supplies, the two government bodies, were given the responsibility of laying down the policy and control the field relating to procurement of computers. Foreign companies were permitted to manufacture and sell computers in the country provided no foreign exchange is to be spent for the purchase keeping in view the critical shortage in foreign exchange in the country. Among several foreign companies that tried to enter the Indian market, IBM emerged as the leader and by 1970 its 'IBM 1401' was the most popular computer model in the country and more than 80 were installed nationwide. IBM's computers were installed and operating in IIT-Kanpur, Delhi University, Roorkee University, Ahmadabad Textile Industries Research Association, Defence Laboratories, Physical Research Laboratories at Ahmadabad, and also in many other places.[10]

The Emergence of DoE

Although India developed the then latest device of the world in the field of electronics in the form of computers in its territory by early 1960s, the country was not having indigenous capability and expertise in the field of electronics and communications. Moreover, a surprise Chinese incursion in 1962 from the north, which eventually led to the Sino-Indian war brought to light the reality about the country's capabilities and vulnerabilities not only in the defence sector but also in other sectors as well. It is only after the Chinese aggression that the country's leadership woke up to the reality that China is not India's friend/ brother. With the myth broken, Indian leadership understood that India at that time was vulnerable from two directions, Pakistan from the West and China from the North, and it can no longer afford to stay as an underdeveloped country and as an agricultural economy. Keeping in view the threat from two fronts in the future and also to protect the national interest of the country in global politics, the country undertook a series of reforms in all possible sectors. Under the aegis of this long term process, along with other developmental activities the Government of India set up a committee on electronics to study the electronics sector in India in depth and prepare a plan of action for its development. The committee was headed by Homi Bhabha and the report of the Committee was submitted in 1966.[11]

Two of the most important recommendations of this Committee which need to be highlighted were:

- to establish a Department of Electronics (DoE) under the Central Government to promote electronics and computer industry,
- to constitute Electronics Commission (EC) with sufficient finance and wide executive powers in order to take quick decisions to promote electronics.[12]

The report also stated that achieving self-sufficiency in systems engineering and fabrication is of fundamental importance from the point of view of the defence and security of the country.

The Bhabha Committee also constituted a subcommittee on computers which was chaired by R. Narasimhan and this committee was responsible for estimating the volumes of computers required by the country for the next ten years. This subcommittee recommended the import of one very large computer and 3 to 5 medium large computers for meeting the national requirements. The medium large computers were meant to be used as Regional Computer Centres (RCCs). The subcommittee also stated that the country would need approximately 500 small computers every year for the next 10 years and that these small computers have to be manufactured in the country by using local components. [13]

The report of the Bhabha Committee was discussed extensively among a large group of audience including educational institutions, companies, departments of the government, R and D Laboratories and defence forces during the next few years. In fact the said report was also the subject matter of discussion in one high profile National Electronics Conference held at TIFR, Mumbai, in 1970. Dr. Vikram Sarabhai, who chaired the conference opined in his concluding remarks that:

"I think that this field (of computers) is far more fundamental, of wider significance than any other field of electronics. It is an all pervasive way of thinking, looking at problems and analysing, and it is of particular relevance to our developing country where resources are scarce, where we want to optimise to produce the best results from minimum resources"....I do believe that major international companies have a contribution to make in India, on honourable commercially rewarding terms, on ground rules which are acceptable to India. I do not think that this could be at the cost of a major national effort, which we must put out without further delay."[14]

The Bhabha Committee report and the subsequent high level discussions among the various stakeholders resulted in a positive action from the centre as the Government of India established the Department of Electronics and the Electronic Commission in 1970 and it also started a computer division in the Electronics Corporation of India Ltd. (ECIL). The Department of Electronics (DoE) was setup with the primary objective of promoting the development of electronics and computer industry in the country and the department actively funded various projects of the public sector company ECIL.

The DoE was instrumental in establishing and funding various organisations, centres and projects which played a crucial role in modifying the communication and information technology sector of the country in the future. A few initiatives of the DoE taken during 1970s are as follows:

- *Setting up of NCSDCT:* In 1972, the DoE established the National Centre for Software Development and Computing Techniques (NCSDCT) in TIFR, Mumbai with a combined grant of Rs.2.85 million from DoE and US$ 2 million from the UNDP. Later in 1983, NCSDCT was separated from TIFR and renamed it as the National Centre for Software Technology (NCST), which has trained a large number of scientists in advanced software and it was instrumental in bringing internet to India.[15] In 2004, NCST was merged with Centre for Development of Advanced Computing (C-DAC) and since then it functions as part of C-DAC.[16]

- *Establishment of NIC:* In 1975, DoE established the most important institution, from the point of view of India, the National Informatics Centre (NIC) with the combined grant of Rs. 31.72 million from DoE and US$ 4.4 million from UNDP. One of the main task assigned to NIC was providing assistance to the governments in the e-governance projects of the central and the state governments of the country.[17] The NIC is still functioning as an organisation under the Department of Electronics and Information Technology (DeitY) under the Ministry of Communications and Information Technology.

- *Funding Army Radio Engineering Network (AREN)[18]:* The DoE initiated a multi institutional project called AREN involving the TIFR, the Electronics and Radar Development Establishment and the signal engineers of the Army. The AREN is responsible for providing mobile communication links from forward areas via several automatic electronic switches up to the Army Head Quarters.[19] The AREN is still operational and is being used by the Indian Army. Installation of an upgraded system called Tactical Communication System (TCS), as a replacement to this, which could be used for a longer period of time is under consideration.[20]

- *Promoting Software Export:* During early 1970s, DoE was forced to enforce strict regulations for import of computers as the political leadership was keen on indigenous development. Another reason was the shortage of foreign exchange required for imports. However, subsequently realising and recognising the potential of software industry in the future, DoE encouraged software export from the country by relaxing its computer import policy. Companies were allowed to import computers exclusively meant for software development and export.[21] The Tata Consultancy Services (TCS) under the leadership of F.C. Kohli took the maximum advantage of this liberalisation of policy of the DoE by importing 'Burroughs B6700' computer for the purpose of developing software and exporting it. They also successfully converted software to suit computers of other manufacturers so as to be able to run on Burroughs computers and exported the same.[22]

- The DoE also funded projects for the establishment of Regional Computer Centres (RCC) in various university campuses with mainframe computers which were used by industries and educational institutions.

- The DoE also established the Computer Maintenance Corporation (CMC) in 1976 spending of Rs. 53 million, which played a crucial role in maintaining the imported computers in the country especially after the withdrawal of IBM from the country.

- The computer division established in ECIL, which was also funded by DoE, manufactured and sold computers of different models. During the period from 1971 to 1978, the ECIL computer division was able to sell 98 machines to different customers although majority of them were government institutions who had to buy machines manufactured by ECIL due to the policy restrictions of the government.[23] ECIL also manufactured and deployed 75 computers of 'TDC 316' model for a national defence project called Air Defence Ground Environment Systems (ADGES) of the Indian Air Force (IAF). Due to the sensitivity of the project, Indian designed and fabricated machines were needed by the IAF and TDC 316 model machines were employed in the project. 25 systems were deployed in this regard each having 3 TDC 316 machines and they were deployed along the borders of the country to detect intrusion of non-friendly aircrafts.[24] The ECIL manufactured computers were also used in several national projects, which were important from the point of view of national security such as data acquisition systems for the Department of Atomic Energy, monitoring launch of satellites, telemetry etc., for the Department of Space, testing of engines for gas turbines and launch of vehicles for the Department of Defence etc.

Hiccups in the Path towards Computarisation in 1970s

In late 1960s, with a rapid expansion of computer infrastructure across the county and with the growing government support, the country was moving fast towards the world of computers. However, a report prepared by a committee set up by Ministry of Labour in 1969 created hurdles in the path pertaining to computerisation. The 'Dandekar Committee on automation,' which was named after the chairman of the committee, V.M.Dandekar, recommended strict controls on introducing computers in industries and government departments in 1972. The committee strongly felt that India facing large scale unemployment (at that time), the use of computers and other sophisticated machines for labour saving application may not be desirable or may be detrimental.[25]

Apart from the apprehension of loss of jobs due to the introduction of computers, the rise in oil prices in 1973 quadrupled around the world due to decisions taken by Organisation of Petroleum Exporting Countries (OPEC) and as a result, India required more foreign exchange to meet the country's oil demands. Therefore, the country had to drastically cut all its foreign exchange expenditure to reduce the deficit. This resulted in imposing strict clearance procedures for import of computers. In most cases there was a long delay of one to three years in obtaining clearance to import computers and this delay hurt many industries, scientific research laboratories and universities along with companies which wanted to import computers for software export.[26]

Apart from this, the 1971 Indo-Pak war which resulted in the creation of Bangladesh by the division of Pakistan, a US ally, followed by peaceful nuclear test by India in 1974 (Pokhran-I or Smiling Buddha), created an air of uneasiness in the relationship between India and the US. These events which culminated in imposition of a series of embargos against India by the US affected imports of electronics and computer systems, which are considered as duel use technologies. Thus, for some time India lost the lead as one of its biggest exporter of electronic equipments using highly advanced technology, which included high end computers and sophisticated software used in science and technology.

Another major drawback or an issue which was not taken care of in the process of computerisation of the country was the lack of concentrated effort to develop a semiconductor industry in the country though it was recognised as an urgent requirement by the computer community of the country. In spite of this realisation, and recommendations of a committee setup in 1971 under the directions of M.G.K Menon, the then Secretary of DoE, regarding the development of semiconductor industry in India, no substantial steps were taken in this direction.[27] As a result the country is still facing this deficiency in technology and is left way behind the rest of the world as many countries have moved ahead with a competent indigenous integrated chips manufacturing industry. Also, this could be attributed as one of the main reasons for India to still be an import dependent nation for computer hardware in spite of having a leading software manufacturing industry.

The acute shortage in foreign exchange which the country faced during 1960s and 1970s forced the government to bring a Foreign Exchange Regulation Act (FERA) in 1973 thereby ordering the foreign companies in India except those considered essential to dilute their equity base to 40 percent and have partnership with an Indian company. However, IBM which was one of the major foreign companies in India in the computer sector refused to comply with this policy of the government as the company maintained that it was against their policy. After several rounds of unsuccessful negotiations with the Indian government, IBM decided to withdraw its operations from India in 1978 as both parties were stubborn with regard to their respective policies and could not find a common ground.[28]

During the period when it was in India, IBM had made a huge impact in the computer sector of the country as IBM computers had been installed in many establishments including Indian Railways, the Planning Commission, many textiles and petrochemicals companies, and numerous educational research laboratories. It could be stated that introduction computers by companies like IBM, had helped in the development of capabilities of computer users in Indian soil. After exit of IBM from the country the maintenance of IBM computers was taken over by the Computer Maintenance Corporation (CMC), an agency setup by DoE in 1976 to maintain imported computers.

1980s and beyond

Although IBM left the country it did not prove to be detrimental for the nation as the country by then has acquired enough knowledge in the field of computers. This experience and knowledge helped the country to prove that it is a computerised nation during the 1982 Asian Games under the leadership of Rajiv Gandhi, who was in charge and had the overall responsibility of the conduct of the games. Being a technical savvy and an amateur electronics buff, Rajiv Gandhi decided to utilise computers to draw up the schedules of the games, records of events, announcement of results and all other clerical activities related to the games. Computers manufactured in India by DCM computers were used as computer terminals and the entire software system was also developed by Indian engineers in NIC within a short span of six months.[29] The games were a resounding success and India was projected as a computerised country through the lens of global media.

Later when Rajiv Gandhi became the Prime Minister of India more liberalised policies were announced in the field of computers in order to accelerate the country's computerisaton drive. Highlights of the policies which were announced by the then government were:

- Recognition of software development and services as an 'industry'.
- Deputing engineers abroad to develop and maintain software for clients at their sites and profits earned thereby was recognised as "software export".[30]

More incentives were allowed for software exports in the year 1986 such as:

- Computers used to develop software for export could be imported as duty free. However, the importer has to export software and earn 250 percent of the cost of the imported computer within 4 years in order to balance the foreign exchange reserves.
- Software tools needed to develop software for export could be imported as duty free.
- Export earnings of software companies were made tax free for 10 years.
- Software developed in India could be exported using communication systems such as satellites and cable.[31]

The recognition of software development and services as an industry led to many concessions such as obtaining loans from banks on easy terms and duty exemptions for the country's budding software companies. The policy liberalisation of 1984 also had a deeper impact as within 2 years of the announcement of the new policy the growth of computers doubled and the cost went down by almost 50 percent.[32] The growth was due to the liberal import of fully assembled systems. Apart from this, the 1986 software export incentives and policy liberalisations facilitated the entry of many multi-national companies which collaborated with the local companies as minor partners. This collaboration and liberal import policies resulted in the manufacture of inexpensive personal computers (PCs) like the Shiva Personal Computer, an IBM PC clone, manufactured by a start-up Sterling computer for Rs.29,000 in 1987.[33] Thus PCs were made affordable and helped in the spread of computers. Many educational institutions and small companies which could not afford computers earlier were now able to buy a number of computers.

The liberalisation of the import of computers and software enunciated in the policy laid down in 1986 gave the much needed impetus to the software industry of the country boosting the trade from insignificant export earnings in 1978 to US$131 million in 1990.[34] It would not be an exaggeration to state that the country's current status as one of the world leader in IT and ITeS sector was made possible because of the various policy liberalisations and incentives provided during Rajiv Gandhi's government which enabled the then budding software companies like Infosys and others to ably utilise these concessions and eventually become giants and world leaders.

Rajiv Gandhi Government took two more important policy decisions to provide nation-wide connectivity through telecommunication. The first was the establishment of two public sector companies - Mahanagar Telephone Nigam Ltd. (MTNL) and Videsh Sanchar Nigam Ltd. MTNL was formed to provide telephone services in Mumbai and Delhi with a corporatised model of public switch telephone network and VSNL was established in 1986 to improve overseas communication system.[35] Second major decision taken by that government was to develop rural telecommunication through public telephone booths called Public Call Offices (PCOs) with microprocessor based systems for billing telephone calls thereby facilitating last-mile connectivity. Within 5 years, every nook and corner of the country was connected through PCOs and the country witnessed the power of microcomputer.[36]

The computerisation drive of the country spread to various other sectors and computers were progressively being used in the day to day activities of different government departments. The banks were computerised in 1980 after a high-level Reserve Bank committee report recommended such a step. This sudden surge in demand for computers from banking sector gave momentum to private computer manufacturing companies in the country to design and develop minicomputers.

Another most important development was computerisation of the ticket reservation system of the Indian Railways since 1986. It is a well known fact that India has one of the largest railway networks in the world and even in 1984 it handled over 5 million passengers travelling in 600 different long distance trains with around 50,000 reservation requests. Therefore, it was felt that the system of reservation was ripe for computerisation and a proposal was made by CMC to Railways authorities. On accepting the proposal a computerised reservation system was developed and implemented in New Delhi railway station with 50 counters in 1986.[37] This computerised reservation process replaced the then existing practice of meddling with ledgers and standing for hours in long queues. This was seen as a miracle by general public. The entire software used in this process was developed by Indian software engineers without the help of any foreign consultants, which not only boosted the morale but also gave evidence about the skill of indigenous talent in the software sector. The success of the computerised reservation system became a game changer in changing the attitude and outlook in the minds of the general public and white collar workers about the adverse effects of computerisation. Eventually the country started to realise the need for computerisation in every sector possible thus creating a favourable environment for developing a future 'cyber India'.

Additionally, in order to sustain the computerisation of the country, it was realised that structured education in this field is necessary and hence higher education institutions like IITs started offering undergraduate courses and Master's programme in computer science since 1978. In order to further enhance the availability of human resource in this highly technical field the government funded several institutions to start Master of Computer Application (MCA) programme and offer quality computer education to the future computer engineers.[38]

As a result of the various policy liberalisations of the government, the software development and export industry started flourishing and contributed substantially to the country's economy. With the objective of taking advantage of this positive outcome, the government promoted offshore software development and as a long term strategy, established Software Technology Parks (STP). The first STP was established in Bangalore in 1990 and later in many other cities.[39] This again contributed and helped substantially to the growth of IT sector in the country.

By the end of 1980s, the country was showing signs of becoming a software developing hub of the world in the future. This was as a result of the favourable conditions created by the government and the bright response from the industry. Thus it is during the 1980s and especially under Rajiv Gandhi's government the seeds for creating a 'Cyber India' in the future were sown. However, the efforts being made by the government was found to be insufficient as the country did not give adequate importance towards the development of integrated circuit manufacturing industry and other computer hardware which resulted in certain adverse consequences in the future.

India's strong human resources with quality knowledge and skill in software development sector advanced progressively in the 1990s under fortuitous circumstances with the need to fix the Y2K bug, the problems relating to Euro conversion etc., and with the existence of a technical savvy influential Indian diaspora in the USA providing opportunities to Indian software companies. This coupled with the advent of fast satellite communication and later internet, the availability of human resources with good knowledge in English and existing project management expertise allowed the software industry to get remunerative software services contracts from the West, particularly from the US.[40]

Post liberalisation of the economy of the country in early 1990s, the government started allowing Foreign Direct Investment (FDI) in the country which pumped in massive investments from foreign multinational companies especially in the Indian software industry. Many multinational firms like American Express, IBM, etc., setup software development centres either individually or in collaboration with an Indian partner. Apart from this in the telecommunication sector, the National Telecom Policy released in 1994 allowed private companies to enter the business of telecommunication.[41] This shift in policy had far reaching favourable consequences in the future, especially in the mobile phone communication sector.

The software development sector in 1990s provided employment to more than 160,000 software engineers of the country thus opening up a new wave of employment opportunities to the future generations.[42]As a result of successful completion of projects by the Indian software companies, the industry witnessed a steady growth in the business and the growth rate kept increasing year after year (See table 7.2), ultimately elevating the software industry as one of the important contributors for the economy of the country in the 21st century.

Table 7.2: Software export revenue and growth rate from 1987

Year	Exports of software (in US$ million)	Percentage of growth over previous year
1987-1988	52	N/A
1988-1989	67	29
1989-1990	100	49
1990-1991	128	28
1991-1992	164	28
1992-1993	225	37
1993-1994	330	47
1994-1995	450	36
1995-1996	734	63
1996-1997	1,100	49

1997-1998	1,759	60
1998-1999	2,600	48
1999-2000	3,400	31
2000-2001	5,300	56
2001-2002	6,200	17
2002-2003	7,100	15
2003-2004	9,200	30
2004-2005	12,200	33

Source: Subhash Bhatnagar, "India's Software Industry", in *Technology, Adaptation and Exports: How Some Developing Countries Got It Right*, edited by Vandana Chandra, (World Bank, 2006), pp. 95-124.

India's Current Cyber Environment

Although the history of computers in India dates back to 1950s, it is the advent of internet that made this smart machine attractive for wider audience. Internet was introduced in India on August 15, 1995 in Delhi. Since then the user base has grown rapidly and had reached a total of 149.75 million subscribers by March 31, 2016.[43]After computer and internet, the next big thing which drew the attention of the masses in India in the wake of the millennium was mobile phones. The number of mobile phone subscriptions, like the internet users, increased tremendously from the time its services were offered and it had more than 1,033.63 million subscribers as on March 31, 2016.[44] While the government companies lead in the number of the wired line subscribers, the private service providers enjoy domination in the wireless subscription base. 'Bharti', in association with Airtel is currently the leading mobile network service provider (Figure 7.6) and BSNL-the state owned company, is the largest service provider of wired telephone service in the country (Figure 7.7).

Figure7.6: Market share of mobile phone network service providers

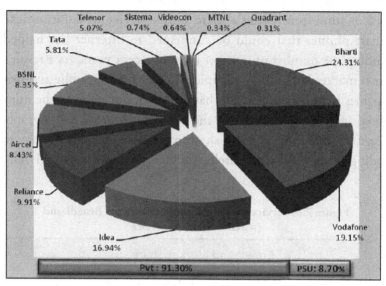

*Source:*Press release on "Highlights on Telecom subscription Data as on March 31, 2016", *Telecom Regulatory authority of India*, Press Release No 34/2016, May 25, 2016.

Figure 7.7: Market share of wired line telephone service providers

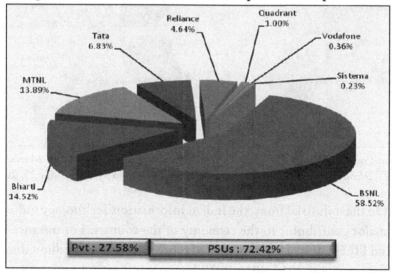

Source: Press release on "Highlights on Telecom subscription Data as on March 31, 2016", *Telecom Regulatory authority of India*, Press Release No 34/2016, May 25, 2016.

The unprecedented level of innovation of mobiles phones over a period of time from being a mere simple device of communication to smart phones that could be connected to internet has helped in expanding the number of internet users in recent years. As a result, the internet market has multiplied rapidly in which both public and private companies have benefitted. This has, however, not reduced the number of wired internet subscribers in the country. Figure 7.8 is a graphical representation of the market share of broadband service providers including both wired and wireless services in India as on March 31, 2016.

Figure 7.8: Service Provider's market share for Broadband (wired + wireless) service

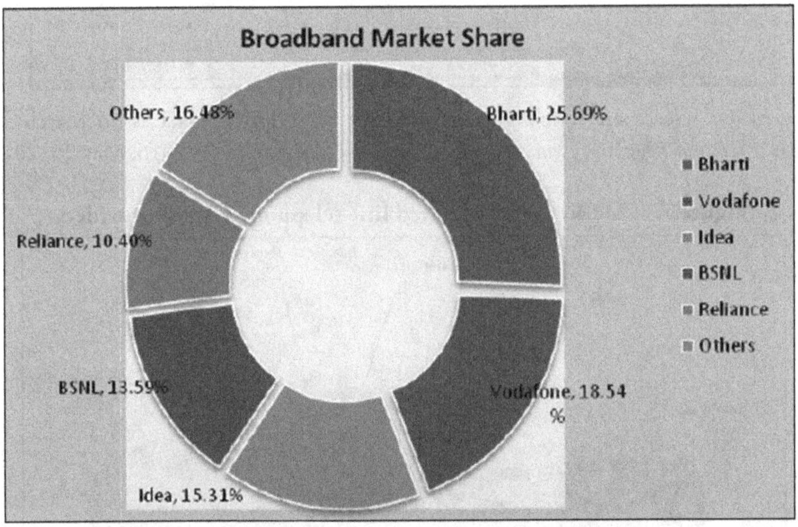

Broadband Market Share

Others, 16.48%
Bharti, 25.69%
Reliance, 10.40%
BSNL, 13.59%
Vodafone, 18.54%
Idea, 15.31%

- Bharti
- Vodafone
- Idea
- BSNL
- Reliance
- Others

Source: Press release on "Highlights on Telecom subscription Data as on March 31, 2016", *Telecom Regulatory authority of India*, Press Release No 34/2016, May 25, 2016.

On the industrial front, the Indian Information Technology industry is a major contributor to the economy of the country. For instance the IT and ITeS industry has contributed more than US$143 billion during the financial year 2015-2016.[45] With a strong base in human resource in software sector with more than two decades of experience at the world level the country has created some of the leading IT companies like Wipro, Tata Consultancy Services, Infosys, Cognizant Technology Solutions, etc., which are the leaders in the IT industry in their own right. Every year the country produces more than one million engineers out of which more than 50 percent look for work in the field of IT. In so far as cyber security is concerned, the number of highly qualified cyber security experts in the country remains low and even that small number is yet to be identified and their level of proficiency has to be enhanced to meet the requirements of the country.

The country is also offering e-government services in a number of areas and its number is growing from time to time. The launch of "Digital India" project, which was unveiled on July 1, 2015, is one of the efforts by the government to make cyber technology more widely available to the people of the country and to ensure the provision of e-Governance services to the beneficiaries. According to one of the official press releases of the government related to Digital India project, *"Digital India has been envisioned as an ambitious umbrella programme to transform India into a digitally empowered society and knowledge economy... All the existing and ongoing e-Governance initiatives have been revamped to align them with the principles of Digital India."*[46] Apart from the government e-services, almost all the banks in the country offer online banking as well as mobile banking services to its customers, which has in a way created a nomadic financial transaction culture in the country in recent years.

Governance of India's Cyber Environment
The Communications and Information Technology sectors of the country are governed at the highest level—Central Government under two Ministries namely – Ministry of Communications and Ministry of Electronics and Information Technology (MeitY).

The ministry of communications functions under two departments namely:
• Department of Telecommunications (DoT).
• Department of Posts (DOP).

DoT, functions with the vision to provide secure, reliable, affordable and high quality telecommunication services anytime, anywhere for an accelerated inclusive socio-economic development.[47] The Department of Posts as the name suggests, is the agency responsible for providing postal services including maintenance of correspondence across the country through Post Offices, which is irrelevant for the subject of discussion.

The Department of Telecommunications is working through a number of units under its administration and each unit has a specific f task to fulfil in the telecommunication sector. The various units of DoT are broadly divided into three categories namely: DoT Units, Rand D Units and Public Sector Units. Table 7.3 lists out the various units under DoT:

Table 7.3: Various Units under Department of Telecommunications under the Ministry of Communication and Information Technology.

DoT Units	R&D Units	PUBLIC SECTOR UNITS
• Telecom Enforcement and Resource Monitoring Cell (TERM Cell) • Controller of Communication Accounts (CCA) units • Wireless Planning and Coordination Wing (WPC) • Telecom Engineering Center • National Telecommunications Institute for Policy Research,Innovation & Training (NTIPRIT) • National Institute of Communication Finance (NICF)	• Center for Development of Telematics (C-DOT) • Telecom Centres of Excellence (TCOEs)	• Bharat Sanchar Nigam Limited (BSNL) • Mahanagar Telecom Nigam Limited(MTNL) • Bharat Broadband Nigam Limited (BBNL) • Telecommunications consusltants India Limited (TCIL) • Indian Telephone Industries Limited (ITI)

Source: Department of communications, Ministry of Communications and Information Technology, http://www.dot.gov.in, accessed on February 15, 2015.

The Ministry of Electronics and Information Technology (MeitY) functions with the mission to promote e-Governance for empowering citizens, promoting the inclusive and sustainable growth of the Electronics, IT & ITeS industries, which enhances India's role in Internet Governance, adopting a multipronged approach that include development of human resources, promoting R&D and innovation, enhancing efficiency through digital services and ensuring a secure cyberspace.[48]

The MeitY is entrusted with the responsibility of governing the electronics and information technology sector of the country. The department operates through various divisions for the purpose of governing the following:

- Electronic System Design and Manufacturing.
- Information Technology/Information Technology enabled Services.
- E-Governance.
- Cyber Laws and E-Security.
- Infrastructure and Governance.
- Human Resource Development/ Knowledge Management.
- Research and Development
- International Cooperation.

The Ministry also supervises the operations of the following organisations which function with specific responsibilities assigned to each one of them separately:

- National Informatics Centre (NIC).
- Standardisation Testing and Quality Certification Directorate (STQC).
- Controller of Certifying Authorities (CCA).
- Cyber Appellate Tribunal (CAT).
- Indian Computer Emergency Response Team (I-CERT).
- Semiconductor Integrated Circuits Layout Design Registry (SICLDR).
- Media Lab Asia.
- National Internet Exchange of India.
- .in Registry.

- Centre for Development of Advanced Computing (C-DAC).
- National Informatics Centre Services Incorporated (NICSI).
- Education & Research Network (ERNET).
- National Institute of Electronics & Information Technology (NIELIT).
- Centre for Materials for Electronics Technology (C-MET).
- Society for Applied Microwave Electronics Engineering and Research (SAMEER).
- Software Technology Parks of India (STPI).

Apart from the various Units, Divisions and Organisations under the two Ministries, there are three other important organisations which play a very important role in the cyber security environment of the country. They are (i) National Technical Research Organisation (NTRO), (ii) National Critical Information Infrastructure Protection Centre (NCIIPC) and Computer Emergency Response Team (CERT-In). CERT-In is the nodal agency for responding to computer security incidents as and when they occur.[49] NTRO is the technical intelligence agency operating under the leadership of the National Security Advisor in the Prime Minister's Office and NCIIPC is the nodal agency under NTRO which works for the protection of Critical Information Infrastructure of the country. In addition to these civilian initiatives taken by the government, the Indian Armed Forces are also setting up a cyber command for the defence of the country in order to deal with the growing threat of cyber warfare and also to provide robust network security for the sensitive defence networks of the country.

India adopted policies and introduced legislations considered necessary in order to regulate, manage and ably secure its ICT environment. Few highlights of the policies and legal mechanisms adopted by India in the ICT sector are as follows:

- With the entry of private sector in to the telecom industry in the country in late 20th century, India framed its Telecom Regulatory Act 1997, to regulate telecom services, including fixation/revision of tariffs for telecom services.

- The ICT sector in India progressed at a fast pace immediately after it was introduced. In order to regulate this growing sector, the Government of India formulated its first Information Technology Act 2000, and amended certain aspects of the law through Information Technology (Amendment) Act 2008. Thus, India was able to address the legal issues associated with this rapidly developing sector well in time.

- On October 15, 2012, the then National Security Advisor of the country Shiv Shankar Menon released a policy document titled 'Recommendations of Joint Working Group on Engagement with Private Sector on Cyber Security' which was a feasibility study undertaken jointly by government and private sector participants for analysing and laying down a roadmap for the public sector to engage with the private sector of the country in the cyber realm especially for the purpose of security.[50]

- The 'National Cyber Security Policy' (NCSP) – 2013 was released on July 2, 2013, with a vision to build a secure and resilient cyber space for citizens, businesses and for government activities and also to integrate the various events and developments taking place in the highly dynamic cyber arena of the country. This policy is an overview of the government's approach and strategy for protection of cyber space in the country.[51]

- On July 19, 2013, the NCIIPC under NTRO released the 'Guidelines for Securing *the* National Critical Information Infrastructures' (NCII) of the country. Having identified 14 critical information infrastructures like Energy, Transportation, Banking/ Finance, Telecommunication, Defence, Space, etc, the NCIIPC guidelines created a broad framework for securing these infrastructures all over the country.[52]

- In September 2013, India achieved another milestone in the field of cyber by becoming an 'Authorising Nation' for IT products from its previous status of being a mere 'consuming nation'. In less academic terms, it can be stated that all those IT products that are certified in India can be authorised to be used in the 26 member countries under Common Criteria Recognition Arrangements (CCRA) without having them retested.[53]

- In the current global cyber environment, one of the biggest buzz words is 'Cloud Computing', which is gaining popularity progressively. In order to address this new development in the cyber domain, and also to utilise and harness the benefits of this next level technology, the MeitY initiated an ambitious and important initiative called 'GI Cloud' or in colloquial terminology- 'Meghraj'. In order to bring out a strategic direction and to implement a roadmap for GI Cloud to gain leverage in the existing or new infrastructure, two reports have been prepared by a special task force and have received the approval of the Minister of Communications and Information Technology. The two reports are: (i) GI Cloud Strategic Direction Paper and (ii) GI Cloud Adoption and Implementation Roadmap. Both these reports have been released in April 2013.[54]

- It is believed that, in the future, smart machines, connected through internet would create an 'Internet of Things' and would revolutionise the way this world interacts. This intertwined network of machines and human beings together would create a complex web of networks that would mostly be automatic in nature with minimal human interference for its activities. This web of network of interconnected machines is known as 'Internet of Things (IoT)' and this is touted to be the future of the world. Under such circumstances, as a first step to enter into the future where machines are allowed to take decisions based on their previous experience, India is in the process of drafting a policy to streamline the activities of the future era of IoT. In fact a 'Draft Policy on Internet of Things' which was prepared in the first half of 2015 is already in the public domain, but is yet to get an official approval from the Ministry. Although, this draft is basic in nature, it is a welcome initiative from the Ministry.

Threats to India's Cyber Environment

Although the above mentioned set up in terms of infrastructural, governmental, legal and policy level initiatives undertaken by the government of the country in streamlining and securing the country's cyber environment could be convincing enough to believe that India has a safe and secured cyber environment. However, it is an undeniable fact that in spite of all these arrangements, the country finds it difficult to prevent a host of threats existing in the cyber domain that constantly threatens its cyber environment.

The cyber threat landscape of the country includes threats like data theft, malwares, hacking, web defacements, identity thefts, online financial frauds, email spoofing, social engineering scams, DOS and DDOS attacks, unauthorised access to critical infrastructure of the country, online surveillance, digital espionage, cyber weapons like Stuxnet, Flameand Duqu, cyber warfare, cyber terrorism, etc. This unending list is proof of the kind of vulnerabilities that Indian networks face in the virtual domain which at times has the potential to create huge chaos in the society and threaten the security and integrity of the nation. For instance, 130,338[55] security incidents were handled by CERT-IN in the year 2014 which saw a steep rise from the previous year as the same agency handled 71,780[56] security incidences in 2013. This trend of increase in the number of cyber security incidents year after year is a constant reminder of India's vulnerable cyber environment. In fact, all the cyber infrastructure of the country ranging from a critical information infrastructure to a small website are vulnerable to the same extent and are persistently victimised through various cyber attacks at different levels by numerous internal as well as external perpetrators.

The first recorded cyber attack on a critical information infrastructure of the country was way back in June 1998 when the server hosting the website owned by 'Bhabha Atomic Research Centre' (BARC) was breached and the website was defaced. Apart from defacing the website, the attackers had also stolen five mega bytes (MB) of email and data from the computer database.[57] Consequently, given the time and target, it is still widely believed that the attack was conducted by Pakistani hackers backed by their notorious intelligence agency, ISI for exhibiting its anger and dissatisfaction towards India for becoming a nuclear weapon powered state in May, 1998. However, the reality is that this attack was perpetuated by a group called 'milw0rm' which consisted of five teenagers who only had developed contacts among them through internet as they belonged to different countries.[58]

One more point to be noted here is that the attackers managed to steal five MB of data. Although the size of stolen data might seem negligible comparing it to the current standards, any amount of data lost from critical infrastructure like BARC, can cause damaging outcomes if used against the country. For instance, data from the Supervisory Control and Data Acquisition (SCADA) systems and other industrial control systems located in a critical infrastructure might not exceed more than a few MBs but it is this crucial data that would enable the enemy to create cyber weapons like Stuxnet, Duqu and Flame which have the potential to totally damage a country's operating ability. Indeed, the infamous Stuxnet cyber weapon which was responsible for damaging Iran's nuclear ambitions (Refer Chapter 6) was also found in Indian networks. It was observed that out of the 10,000 Stuxnet infected Indian computers, 15 were located at critical infrastructure facilities that included Gujarat and Haryana Electricity Boards and an ONGC offshore oil rig. Fortunately, this cyber weapon did not activate itself in any of the Indian networks as it was not customised for that purpose and therefore, the country escaped from facing a similar fate like Iran.

In addition to this, the 2012 attack on India's Eastern Naval Command and the 2013 attack on DRDO (refer Chapter 5), India listed as the fifth most snooped country by the US through their Prism programme (refer Chapter 6), the persistent hacking incidents of Indian public and private networks (refer Chapter 2) and incidents of several web defacements of various Indian websites both public and private including the case of defacement of CBI website in 2010 (refer Chapter 2), all stand witness to the fact that Indian networks and cyber infrastructures are highly vulnerable to cyber intrusions for the purpose of intelligence gathering, stealing of critical information, surveillance, espionage and sabotaging of smooth operations.

Apart from this, the ability to use/ misuse cyber resources by the terrorists and non-state actors to wage war against the Indian state as in the case of 26/11 (refer Chapter 4) is an additional threat to the country. Although, the use of open source cyber resources and the resources in the deep and dark web (refer Chapter 3) by non-state actors need not specifically threaten the cyber infrastructure of India alone, as the threat is global in nature, yet it has to be taken into consideration in view of the fact that vulnerable and poorly governed cyber environment have led to such conditions.

It is a well established fact that countries around the world conduct various surveillance and espionage programmes in the cyber world through internet for information gathering and for using it to their advantage. Among all the countries, China and the US are the most notorious ones in terms of cyber espionage and online massive surveillance (refer chapter 5 and 6 respectively). The existence of UNIT 61398 in the Chinese PLA, and the existence of the US surveillance programmes like X-Keyscore, NSA Quantum, and NSA ANT are existing examples of the level of sophisticated threats existing in the cyber domain. It is clear that India is the fifth largest snooped country through Prism programme. However, it is not clear if the country is developing any defences against such programmes in the future. It is also unclear if the country has the capability to face threats from cyber weapons like Stuxnet and customised cyber tools like the ones listed in NSA ANT catalogue (refer Chapter 6). At present it would not be an exaggeration to state that the country is almost unprotected to highly sophisticated and precisely engineered and targeted covert or overt cyber attacks.

In addition to the above mentioned high profile threats, the number and variety of cyber attacks on individuals and organisations in the country are also on the rise every year. Annual reports of subsequent years from the different cyber security agencies like CERT-IN stand proof for the same.

Figure 7.9: Cyber security incidents recorded by CERT-IN from 2005-2015

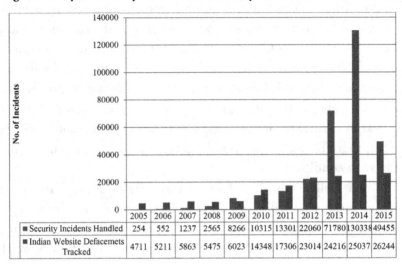

	2005	2006	2007	2008	2009	2010	2011	2012	2013	2014	2015
■ Security Incidents Handled	254	552	1237	2565	8266	10315	13301	22060	71780	130338	49455
■ Indian Website Defacemets Tracked	4711	5211	5863	5475	6023	14348	17306	23014	24216	25037	26244

Source: Data compiled from Annual Reports of CERT-IN from 2005-2015

According to CERT-IN there are varieties of cyber attacks that are carried out on individuals and organisations of the country and the most reported forms of cyber attacks are Phishing, Network Scanning/ Probing, Virus/ Malicious Code, Website Defacements, Spam, Website intrusion and Malware Propagation. It is needless to say that the number of incidents of each type of cyber attack is showing an upward trend every year. This trend of increasing cyber incidents in the country clearly indicates not only the vulnerability of the country's cyber security, but also challenges the various cyber security initiatives undertaken at various levels by India. It should also be noted that there are thousands of other cyber security infringements, intrusions and various other attacks which had gone unreported to the security agencies but have created some sort of damage to the target.

Bridging the Gap

At this juncture, taking an overview of the cyber security threat landscape of India, few questions that come up on the cyber security arrangements of the country are:

- Despite the various cyber security initiatives by the government at regular intervals, why is there an upward trend in the number of cyber security incidents in the country?
- What more can be done to check and reduce the vulnerabilities of the country's cyber space in order to make it more safe and secure?

The cyber world, unlike the real world is beyond any geographical barriers created by international borders and therefore, being a huge entity, threats can originate from any part of the world. Hence, it becomes difficult for one country to tackle all these threats as there are many technical barriers involved in it associated by the legal hurdles. Keeping in view the fact that global cyber space is still largely an ungoverned space, it increases the chances for cyber threats to spread easily in the networks across the world.

In addition to this, despite the existence of various agencies like CERT-IN, NTRO, NCIIPC, etc, in the country, it remains unclear whether India has the ability for early warning and detection of large scale cyber attacks as there has not been a single case disclosed in any public domain where these agencies have been able to detect or warn the country's networks before an attack takes place. Unfortunately, in the cyber forensic phase, the country's abilities are technically limited not only due to lack of knowledge of advanced technologies but more because of lack of expert human resource and legal restrictions due to the non-availability of 'smoking gun evidence' of any cyber attack. According to 'National Cyber Security Policy', India needs around 500,000 cyber security experts at various levels and for different organisations to secure the cyber space of the country. But, there is no clarity regarding the current strength of cyber security experts available in the country. However, it is only a speculation that the country has around 20-25 percent of the desired strength. Finally, the lack of any major Research and Development in the field of cyber security in the country is also a major factor contributing towards the growing trend of cyber threats to the country's cyber space.

Based on the understanding of the various technical, policy level decisions and institutional and legal initiatives taken by the country in the cyber domain it could be stated that India is ready with a full-fledged reactionary mechanism in securing and safeguarding the country's networks from cyber attacks. It is time for the country to move ahead in establishing a pro-active approach towards cyber security by drafting policies and acquiring advanced technology for cyber deterrence, early warning and detection, and real time monitoring and mitigation of national level networks. Bilateral and multilateral agreements between countries for cooperation at global and regional group level related to sharing of cyber security related technology are definitely a step in the right direction for enhancing cyber environment in the country. Additionally, as the domain is highly technical which is becoming more complex every day, the country has to keep pace to grow through this technical path with domestic resources by nurturing the technical talents in the country and by grooming the technical community to work in the national interest.

Apart from this, the country could also take certain long term and short term measures in order to secure its cyber space. The possible long term strategy could be to enhance cyber governance, develop indigenous hardware and software manufacturing capability and implementing more state sovereignty over the country's cyber resources (refer Chapter 8). A few short term/ immediate measures that the country could undertake are as follows:

- Immediate attention has to be given to human resource development which would increase the number of experts who can effectively manage the cyber security of the country. The government has a 'National Security Database', in which many ethical hackers of the country have registered voluntarily to come to country's aid during critical situation, which is a welcoming act. However this resource alone would not be enough for a country as huge as India. Therefore, conducting nation-wide talent hunts could be a method through which the government can identify and promote prospective talents (refer chapter 2) which could also avoid brain drain and creation of rogue warriors in the field.

- The country's Rand D activities towards cyber security should be given utmost priority with a view to develop more innovative technologies. Successful R and D activities in cyber security can also help in reducing the number of cyber security incidents. Moreover, more focus is necessary towards early warning, detection and state of the art cyber forensics mechanisms.
- The country could also concentrate more specifically on the implementation of the existing policies on cyber security. Policies such as the National Cyber Security Policy should be implemented to the maximum extent possible. For instance, appointment of Chief Information Security Officer (CISO) at various NCIIs and other organisations was a key recommendation given in the NCSP and it has to be implemented as soon as possible. Identification and listing of NCIIs across the country has to be completed without delay and these infrastructures have to be put in place along with the cyber security mechanisms charted out in the guidelines for protecting NCIIs.
- CERTs at all levels and all the departmental CERTs like Railway CERT, Military CERTs, etc. must develop appropriate information sharing and coordination mechanisms.
- Due to the existence of several agencies with overlapping functions and many departments in various ministries which look into matters of cyber security, coordination between these agencies becomes tumultuous as well as confusing. In order to streamline this chaotic situation, a country-wide command and control structure for managing cyberspace has to be formulated encompassing all the organisations, agencies and government departments responsible for cyber security at various levels. A viable solution could be setting up the proposed 'National Cyber Security Coordination Centre (NCCC) which has already been allotted Rs 800 Crores as soon as possible to identify duties and responsibilities for smooth functioning and better coordination among departments and officials.
- Another important task would be to find the means and methods in which the upcoming military cyber command and the civilian cyber

command could effectively interact to facilitate information and intelligence sharing and coordination.

- It is a well known fact that the country's private sector has a pool of talent in the cyber domain. They also possess the technological capability of a higher quotient than the public sector. Therefore, Public Private Partnership (PPP) should be explored to the maximum possible extent in order to achieve an ideal comprehensive security in the cyber space. In 2012, a small initiative was taken by the government to analyse the public private partnership in the cyber security and a committee was formed. This joint working group came up with a report on a roadmap for PPP. This initiative has to be taken forward to its full extent to achieve the desired results.

- In the interim period the country has to come up with its 'National Cyber Security Doctrine' with clearly defined national strategy for cyberspace and it has to be implemented effectively.

- Another intermediate measure could be on the legal front, where the country's IT laws have to be made more precise and it should be amended from time to time in order to keep up with the fast changing atmosphere in this domain.

- Finally, since cyber is a field that empowers not only the states but every user who uses this technology, it becomes the responsibility of every user in this virtual space to be aware of the threats and challenges to the security of the domain. It is only due to lack of awareness most of the cyber crimes are taking place resulting in huge economic loss. Therefore, the role of government in this aspect could be to create awareness among the public through various public awareness programmes about the common threats and best practices for everyday computing. Social media could be used by the government to spread awareness about cyber security to the public.

Addressing these issues may not assure a comprehensive cyber security environment for the country but it will definitely enhance the level of security to the country's cyber environment several notches above the existing level. In order to further enhance the level of security, the country may carry out certain long term measures which are discussed in the following chapter.

Notes

1. "Top 20 countries with the highest number of Internet users", http://www.internetworldstats.com/top20.htm, accessed on October 11, 2016.
2. Aradhana Aravindan, "Once the preserve of the youth, IT staffing enters middle age", *Reuters*, January 29, 2014, http://in.reuters.com/article/2014/01/29/india-technology-ageing-idINDEEA0S02720140129, accessed on February 11, 2015.
3. "Annual Report 2014", Indian Computer Emergency Response Team, Ministry of Communications & Information Technology, Government of India, February 27, 2015.
4. V.Rajaraman, "*History of Computing in India (1955-2010)*", Supercomputer Education and Research Centre, Indian Institute of Science, Bangalore, 2012, p. 15.
5. n.4., p. 16.
6. Ibid.
7. n.4, pp. 16-18.
8. n.4, pp. 16-18.
9. Ibid., p. 18.
10. n.4, pp. 16-18.
11. Government of India, Report of the Electronics Committee (Bhabha Committee), Bombay, 1960.
12. Ibid.
13. R. Narasimhan, "Meaningful National Goals in Computer Development, Production and Use", *Proceedings of the National Conference on electronics*, TIFR, Bombay, 1971, pp. 371-378.
14. C.R. Subraminan, *India and the Computer – A Study of Planned Development* (New Delhi: Oxford University Press, 1992).
15. S. Ramani, "R and D in Software Technology at the National Centre for Software Technology, 1960-2001", in *Homi Bhabha and the Computer Revolution*, edited by R.K. Shyamasundar and P.A. Pai, (New Delhi: Oxford University Press, 2011), pp.17-49.
16. Sudha Nagaraj, "New Domain Name Registration Policy Soon", *The Economic Times*, 26 October 2004, http://articles.economictimes.indiatimes.com/2004-10-26/news/27403856_1_domain-name-internet-corporation-icann, accessed on February 20, 2015.
17. N.Seshagiri, "National Informatics Centre: Evolution and its Impact", in *Homi Bhabha and the Computer Revolution,* edited by R.K. Shyamasundar and P.A. Pai, (New Delhi: Oxford University Press, 2011).

18. The main processing unit of AREN system was the first micro-programmed computer, developed in India. This computer was the central control unit for the Mobile Electronic Telephone Exchange, which was developed at TIFR under the guidance of Prof. P V S Rao and Prof. M V Pitke. The processor was developed using Bit-Slice Microprocessors (AMD Am 2901) and under the control of 60-bit Word Horizontal Micro-program of 512 words; basic design and development was done in a record time (from September 1, 1977 to December 27, 1977). The computer used a Non-Restoring Division Algorithm, which was eventually used by IIT-Bombay in its IBM-370 emulation project and also by M/S Motorola (USA) in their MC 6802 Microprocessor. The rugged version of the computer was used heavily by the Indian Army. TIFR again pioneered in developing this indigenous technology, thus providing a leading role for the technological development for the Indian Defence. The know-how of this computer was transferred to the Department of Electronics, ECIL, ITI, and Indian Army. Bharat Dynamics Limited (BDL) started a new department for producing a rugged version of this computer. M/S Tata Electric Company developed non-rugged version of this computer, which were used extensively at the Cyclone Warning Radar Centre at Chennai as the main processing unit. http://www.tifr.res.in/~sanyal/national.html, accessed on February 22, 2015.

19. n. 4, p. 27.

20. Lt. General P.C. Katoch, "Tactical Communication system Programme of Indian Army", *SP's MAI*, Vol 4, Issue 20, October 16-31, 2014, http://www.spsmai.com/military/?id=3252&q=Tactical-Communications-System-Programme-of-Indian-Army, accessed on February 21, 2015.

21. n. 4, p. 28.

22. S.Ramadorai, "The TCS Story...and beyond", (New Delhi: Penguin India, 2011).

23. Om Vikas and L.Ravichandran, Computarization in India: A Statistical Review, *IPAG Journal* Vol. 16, No. 03, December 1978.

24. Ibid.

25. Report of the Committee on Automation, Ministry of Labour & Rehabilitation, Government of India, (New Delhi: 1972).

26. Government of India, "Case History of computer Import", Report of the Review Committee on Electronics, New Delhi, September 1979.

27. C.R. Subramanian, *India and the Computer – A Study of Planned Development*, (New Delhi: Oxford University Press, 1992), p. 289.

28. n.4, p. 29.

29. n.4, p. 31.

30. n.4, p. 32.

31. n. 27, pp. 352-362.

32. n. 27.

33. Dinesh Sharma, *The Long Revolution – the Birth and Growth of India's IT Industry*, (New Delhi: Harper-Collins, 2009).

34. n. 4, p. 41.

35. n. 4, p. 33.
36. Paula Chakravarthy, "Telecom, National Development and the Indian State: A Post colonial Critique", *Media, Culture and Society*, Vol. 26, No. 2, 2004, pp.227-249.
37. n. 33, pp. 144-156.
38. n. 4, p. 34.
39. n. 4, p. 39.
40. n. 4, p. 43.
41. Department of Telecommunication, *National Telecom Policy 1994*, (New Delhi: Ministry of Communications, 1994).
42. Rakesh Basant and Uma Ravi, "Labour Market Dependence in the Indian Information Technology Industry: An explanatory analysis", IIM Ahmedabad, 2004, http://www.iimahd.ernet.in/publications/data/2004-06-06rakesh.pdf, accessed on January 18, 2016.
43. Press release on "Highlights on Telecom subscription Data as on March 31, 2016", *Telecom Regulatory Authority of India*, Press Release No 34/2016, May 25, 2016.
44. Ibid.
45. "IT and ITeS Industry in India", http://www.ibef.org/industry/information-technology-india.aspx, accessed October 13, 2016.
46. "Prime Minister to Launch Digital India Week on the First July", *Press Information Bureau*, Ministry of Communication and Information Technology, Government of India, June 27, 2015.
47. http://www.dot.gov.in/about-us/vision-mission, accessed February 13, 2015.
48. http://deity.gov.in/content/vision-mission, accessed August 13, 2016.
49. http://www.cert-in.org.in/, accessed on February 13, 2015.
50. E.Dilipraj, "PPP – Opening of a New Avenue in India's Cyber Security", *CAPS Issue Brief, 80/12,* December 24, 2012.
51. E.Dilipraj , "India's Cyber Security 2013: A Review", *CAPS Issue Brief,* 97/14, January 27, 2014.
52. Ibid.
53. Ibid.
54. "GI Cloud Initiative (Meghraj)", *Department of electronics and Information Technology,* Ministry of Communication and Information Technology, http://deity.gov.in/content/gi-cloud-initiative-meghraj, accessed February 20, 2015.
55. "Annual Report 2014", *Indian Computer Emergency Response Team*, Ministry of Communications & Information Technology, Government of India, February 27, 2015.
56. "Annual Report 2013", *Indian Computer Emergency Response Team*, Ministry of Communications & Information Technology, Government of India, March 31, 2014.
57. http://ces.iisc.ernet.in/hpg/envis/doc98html/miscbarc69.html, accessed on February 22, 2015.
58. Ibid.

THE NEED FOR STRATEGY
IN CYBERSPACE

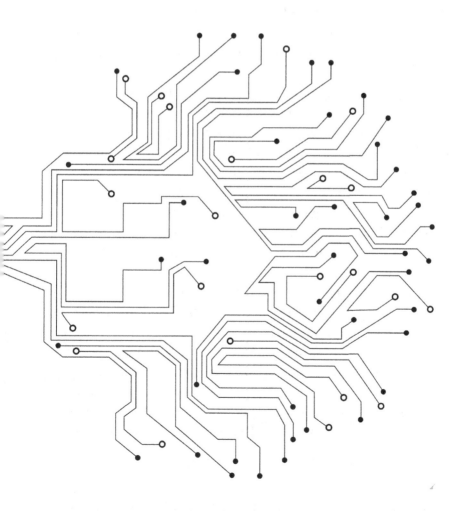

We have so far examined different aspects of the cyber world such as understanding the cyber world as a zone of conflicts, the various threats caused by different players like hackers, terrorists and non-state actors and also the use of covert cyber capabilities by nation states like the US and China through the seven chapters. The kind of threats existing deep within the cyberspace in the form of dark web around the globe through the internet was also discussed in detail. Chapter 7 dealt exclusively in understanding the cyber environment in India and studying its cyber history, current cyber milieu by analysing the various threat perceptions to the country's cyber resources. The chapter concludes with a few recommendations as short term strategies for enhancing India's cyber space. The concluding chapter 8 of the book would identify few long term strategies that when effectively implemented could enhance the country's cyber environment by ensuring better safety and security from the various threats that were discussed and then sum up the findings so far.

It is observed that the biggest problem or complication cyber world is facing at present is not of its being a universal domain but being a domain which is still highly unregulated. For a domain which is clearly three decades old, the existing regulations are clearly not sufficient. The global cyber community is more focused in enhancing and upgrading the technology which is being used but found wanting when it comes to taking coherent measures to stabilise and secure the domain in spite of understanding the growing threat perceptions. This is evident from the fact that new advances and further upgradation in technology are taking place daily and as a result new threats are emerging very often while safety and security related developments are put in the back burner and are not so often in the news. Therefore, there is an urgent need to rectify this scenario and a pragmatic solution has to be found to regulate the cyber space to the extent possible.

Regulation of cyber space is however not a onetime activity but rather an ongoing process similar to cyber governance. Elaborating further, cyber governance *per se* could be seen as a more global activity and regulation of cyberspace is more domestic i.e. within the country. While the countries around the world have collectively started to discuss seriously about cyber governance, every country should now start looking into the issue of regulating its own cyberspace. To make it more coherent in conventional terms, it could be stated that the countries around the world have agreed to certain norms of management of air space in a collective approach, but that does not stop any country from regulating its own airspace by declaring no-fly zones, no-low flying zones, authorising airlines operators, issuing licences, building airport infrastructure, etc. Likewise, in cyberspace too, a country could regulate and thereby establish the state's sovereignty over its own cyberspace. Unlike, airspace domain, cyber space is filled with more global players than domestic players in the form of tech giants, internet giants, etc., whose activities could also be regulated along with regulating the user activities.

The regulation of cyberspace is rather not a new concept but it is a concept which is not implemented often by countries except a few such as China (see Chapter 5, section: "Cyber Environment of China" for more information on regulation of China's cyberspace). Although, the Chinese system of regulating the cyberspace is more authoritarian in nature, it has implemented this strategy to suit its national interest. There are a few other countries which take initiatives to regulate their cyberspace from time to time. Some highlighting incidents occurred in the past on the efforts made by different countries for regulating their respective cyberspace are as follows.

• In December 2015, the Brazilian court blocked WhatsApp, a mobile based messaging application, for a period of 24 hours in Brazil after the company refused to hand over the content of communications between alleged drug dealers involved in a drug trafficking case. Apart from this, on March 1, 2016, Brazil's Federal Police arrested Facebook's Latin American Vice President Diego Jorge Dzudan for failing to comply with the court orders to help investigations in a drug case that involves WhatsApp, owned by Facebook.[1] Brazil is one of the countries which openly voice its views on keeping the data of the country in domestic servers. In this case, as the company did not comply with the Brazilian court orders the country attempted to punish the company thereby expecting some form of regulated service from the Multi-national company in the future.

- One more country which has strict regulations in cyberspace, apart from China, is Iran. In fact, Iran's cyber monitoring and censorship technologies are purchased from China. In May 2016, Iran's Supreme Council of Cyberspace made new regulations by asking all the foreign messaging companies active in the country to transfer all data and activity linked to Iranian citizens to the country in order to ensure their continued activity.[2] Though this move by the Iranian government has been welcomed by neither the tech companies, nor the users in Iran, the country nevertheless is following its regulation to suit its national interest.

- Being the cradle of cyber technology, the US companies enjoy a sort of monopoly in many aspects of the cyberspace including operating systems. This pattern has continued in the age of mobile phones too where the three most popular mobile OS used around the world are Google's Android, Apple's iOS and Microsoft's Windows mobile OS. However, the US is exploiting the monopoly of its companies to conduct its covert cyber operations on other countries by manipulating the operating systems. In order to avoid being a victim of such covert cyber operations and also to challenge the US monopoly, Russia is developing its own mobile operating system. The Russian company Open Mobile Platform has been chosen for the project and the project is under way. The new operating system being developed by Russia is a Linux-based OS developed on top of the Sailfish OS, an open source platform.[3]

- While Russia is working on its version of mobile operating system, China on its part has already executed a similar strategy by developing its own version of operating system for personal computers known as *Kylin* (麒麟) operating system. The operating system was developed indigenously by the National University of Defence Technology since 2001 and there are nearly four versions for public use. This is again a strategy adopted by China to regulate the operating systems market in the country and also to avoid exploitation through foreign developed OS by China's rivals through covert cyber operations.

- The Infocomm Development Authority, a government agency under the Government of Singapore has announced that from May 2017, public servants in the country will be blocked from accessing the internet on computers at work. The agency stated that this change was necessary to ensure more secure working environment and to stop any potential leaks from e mails from the work premises and shared documents amid heightened security threats.[4] In the age where sensitive information has become the target, Singapore government's regulation could be seen as an effort to contain data leak from its government offices.

- In June 2016, the Cyberspace Administration of China has imposed new regulations on distribution of mobile apps. The list of criteria that the app stores and app developers must meet when operating in China are:

  - App providers must verify users' identities by requiring their mobile numbers or other information.
  - Providers should protect their users' information and cannot use the information without their consent.
  - Providers should improve censorship and punish anyone releasing illegal information through warnings, closing the accounts or suspension of service.
  - Providers are forbidden from collecting user's location data and reading their contacts stealthily.
  - Providers are also banned from pirating the products of its rivals.
  - Providers must record user logs and keep the information for at least 60 days.

These regulations by China on app distributors are only to be seen as a new move by the Chinese government to tighten its control over the internet especially the mobile apps. However, similar regulations barring the negative ones on censorships could provide many other countries like India a regulated distribution of apps where the situation now is chaotic.

- Post Snowden revelations, it is clear that government agencies of different countries around the world are desperate in putting secret backdoors in the network of other countries, devices and software (see Chapter 6 for more information). In order to avoid such instances, Bulgaria has passed legislative amendments to its Electronic Governance Act that require all software written for that country to be fully open-sourced and developed in the public Github repository.[5] This means that whatever computer software, code, databases and programming interfaces the government procures will be freely available for others to read, modify and use thereby enabling public sourcing for fixing bugs in the government software.

The above mentioned experiences of different countries in regulating their respective cyberspace at different levels are only examples of what is happening around the world. However, with some exceptions like China, the efforts of other countries are limited to few aspects of cyberspace which dilutes the purpose of regulation to a large extent. With regard to India, the matter of cyberspace regulation is a rare occurrence but has huge potential to bring order in a tumultuous space if implemented. India could take a cue from the efforts undertaken by various countries in regulating their respective cyberspace and formulate its own strategy in order to stabilise the country's cyberspace and also to ensure better safety and security.

To start with India could look into the feasibility of publicising it's indigenously built operating system "Bharat Operating System Services (BOSS)"[6]by recommending the government agencies to operate their systems with duel OS by installing BOSS as a standby to the existing operating system. This might enable wider public reach and publicity for the OS and when the OS is competent enough in the future, the government might also look at the possibility of switching all computers being used in government offices to BOSS in multiple phases.

The country might also consider encouraging Indian App developers to develop new messaging apps for domestic consumption with localised servers and encourage the public to use the same which would enable data of Indian users to stay within the country and it would also be easy for Indian government agencies to acquire data whenever required for any legal procedures.

Moreover, as a strategy in the long run, regulation could also be implemented effectively through enhancing and better monitoring of Indian cyberspace. Monitoring the cyberspace of a country is a necessary evil and it cannot be fully rejected claiming it to be a complete misconduct. Any country has the right to monitor its own cyberspace but it has to be ethical in nature. Effective checks and balances should be in place within the framework of monitoring service to ensure ethical behaviour. The country could also be transparent about its monitoring practice which would help in enhancing the trust and confidence among the public and also act as deterrence against those involving in malpractices. Effective monitoring of cyberspace, if done, might help in identifying terrorist activities in cyber domain against the country and help in curbing the same. Monitoring in real-time might also prove successful in foiling the plot of malicious hackers in their data breach operations against the country's critical infrastructure. Also, monitoring the country's networks might enable the agencies to know and identify new malwares and fix them before they could cause any serious damage to the country's cyber resources.

Cyber monitoring, however, is a double edged sword and when a country diverts its cyber monitoring capabilities against other countries it leads to conflicts of breach of state sovereignty in cyberspace. In the age of information, where the countries are competing in the race of 'Global Information Supremacy', monitoring and covert breach of each others' networks have become a common phenomena. Therefore, any country which aims to be a global power like India is forced to develop its own defences against such covert cyber capabilities of other countries and if possible can also develop its own offensive covert cyber capabilities to suit its national interest.

In order to secure the civilian cyberspace, India might also consider the option of establishing a fully fledged 'Cyber Police Force' as a paramilitary organisation, as a long term strategy, provided the country has enough human resource for establishing the same. As it is undeniable that dependence on cyber technology for everyday life is increasing in the future and more new threats would emerge in addition to the existing ones, it is prudent to have a specialised and exclusive police force that could concentrate specifically only on cyber domain for a country as huge as India. Such a force would act as a real deterrence against the various forms of cyber crime targeted against the country and might also act as a supplementary force to the military cyber command.

The regulatory measures discussed above as well as several more such ones can be undertaken by the Indian state for stabilising its cyberspace in the long run. Apart from this, India also needs to focus in another area in order to achieve a robust and secure cyberspace, which is the enhancement of capability in the country's computer hardware sector. Although the country has a superior IT industry, the capability is mostly focused in the software sector (see Chapter 7 for more information) and the hardware sector continues to remain as a weaker link. It is in this area, that India need to invest in development of indigenous computer hardware industry to reduce the country's dependence on imports, which would in turn reduce the country's vulnerabilities for hardware exploits.

The most immediate task in this direction is to establish a full-fledged semi-conductor industry utilising the 'Make-in-India' initiative and the Foreign Direct Investment (FDI) options. This policy initiative could be used in its favour by encouraging Indian companies to collaborate with foreign companies for establishing their semiconductor and other computer hardware factories in India. Considering the acute need for developing computer hardware capability, Indian government could also consider the option of establishing a 'Department for Cyber Development' to give special focus and funding to the sector thereby ensuring proper monitoring and manufacture of computer hardware. Successful plan of developing an indigenous hardware industry in the country would not only enhance the country's cyber environment but will also establish India as an unquestionable cyber power in the world.

Nevertheless, it would be unwise and an act of over expectation to think of a fool-proof cyber environment after successfully implementing the long-term recommendations listed out in this chapter and the short-term recommendations charted out in the previous chapter. It has to be understood that all these strategies and even more such measures, even if implemented successfully cannot eradicate the practice of hacking, abolish the existence of deep and dark web or stop countries and non-state actors from using covert cyber capabilities to target their rivals. In fact in course of time hackers would become even smarter, countries would develop and build more new covert cyber capabilities and cyber weapons, and the deep and dark web would find more new technologies like 'Ripple'[7]—an anonymity network in making, to mask their locations and operate in the cyber underworld. However, implementation of these long-term and short-term strategies may ensure a more stable and robust cyber environment for the country that would be several notches secure with reference to the existing one. It may also enable India to be a cyber power of the world and could project the country as equals among the global players. It may ensure a safe and secured cyber domain for the future generations of this country that would be highly depended on the domain. Finally, a secured and technically superior cyberspace in India would not only enhance the lifestyle of every Indian but also elevate the status of India in the global platform.

If creation of the world is the work of God, then humans have achieved godly status by creating the cyber world. No God would leave his/her creation unprotected, insecure and to destroy itself. Therefore, as the creators of the cyberworld it is the collective responsibility of humans to secure the cyberspace and to keep it protected, safe and secure for future generations to evolve digitally.

Notes

1. "PF cumpre mandado de prisão em desfavor do representante do Facebook no BR", *Notices,* Federal Police of Brazil, March 1, 2016, http://www.pf.gov.br/agencia/noticias/2016/03/pf-cumpre-mandado-de-prisao-em-desfavor-do-representante-do-facebook-no-br, accessed on June 20, 2016.
2. "Iran orders social media sites to store data inside country", *The Reuters,* May 29, 2016, http://www.reuters.com/article/internet-iran-idusl8n18q0in, accessed on June 24, 2016.

3. Mohit Kumar, "Russia to get rid of Android and iOS by launching its own Mobile Operating System", *The Hacker News*, June 6, 2016, http://thehackernews.com/2016/06/russian-mobile-os.html, accessed on June 24, 2016.

4. "No Internet for Singapore Public Servants", *BBC*, June 08, 2016, http://www.bbc.com/news/world-asia-36476422, accessed on June 24, 2016.

5. Chris Merriman, "Bulgaria passes law requiring all government-developed software to be open source", July 7, 2016, http://www.computing.co.uk/ctg/news/2464089/bulgaria-passes-law-requiring-all-government-developed-software-to-be-open-source, accessed on July 10, 2016.

6. BOSS (Bharat Operating System Solutions) is a GNU/Linux distribution developed by C-DAC, Chennai in order to benefit the usage of Free/Open Source Software in India. BOSS GNU/Linux is a key deliverable of NRCFOSS. It has enhanced Desktop Environment integrated with Indian language support and other software. The software has also been endorsed by the Government of India for adoption and implementation on a national scale. The operating system is currently in its sixth version and has been tested positively to stand strong against different kinds of cyber attacks.

7. Researchers from the *Massachusetts Institute of Technology (MIT)* and the École Polytechnique Fédérale de *Lausanne (EPFL)* have created a new anonymity network, which they claim fixes some of Tor's weak points. Dubbed Riffle, the anonymity network promises to provide better security against situations when hackers introduce rogue servers on the network, a technique to which TOR is vulnerable. Riffle maintains users' privacy as long as at least one of its server remains safe.

APPENDICES

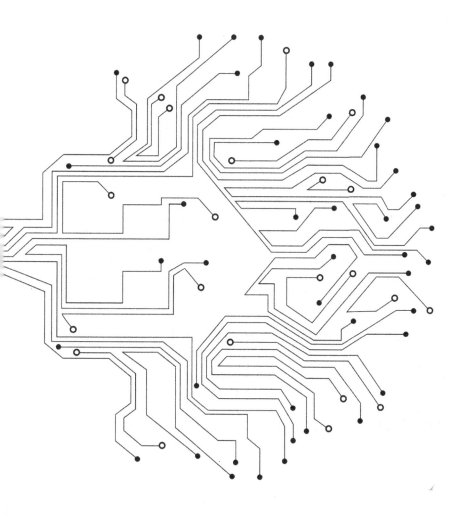

Appendix 1

Particulars of devices developed by Phone Phreaks for Phreaking

S. No.	Name of the Device	Function of the device
1	**(2600 Box)** *(another name for the Blue Box).*	*see Blue Box.*
2	**Acrylic Box** *(aka Extended Bud Box).*	The purpose of this box is to get Three-Way-Calling, Call Waiting, programmable Call Forwarding, and an easier way of extended Bud Boxing, stealing them from the fortunate ones on your block. **Created by The Pimp.**
3	**ALF Box.**	A tone generator for the Apple IIe with an ALF Music Synthesizer Card. **Created by Sir Briggs of the SouthCentral Discount Waremeisters (SCDW) of Texas.**
4	**Aqua Box.**	Every true phreaker lives in fear of the dreaded F.B.I. 'Lock in Trace.' For a long time, it was impossible to escape from the lock in trace. This box does offer an "escape route", by lowering the voltage on the phone line. **Concept by: Captain Xerox.** **Plans by: The Traveler.**
5	**Assassin Box** *(sometimes mispet as assasin box, asassin box, asasin box).*	A box designed to scare, harm, or kill people at the phone by a shock of electricity right in the ear as soon as the victim starts dialling a number. This box was designed, because its authors, after trying a Day-Glo Box for some weeks, "were bored and decided to move on to telephone terrorism." **Linked by Grim Reaper.**
6	**[Beagan Box]** *(sometimes mispelt as Began Box)* *[similar to Beige Box, Beige Box Revisited, Day-Glo Box].*	*see Beige Box.* **Concept and Design: Black Box.** **Beta Testing: Lord Reagan.**

S. No.	Name of the Device	Function of the device
7	**Beige Box** *[similar to Beagan Box, Beige Box Revisited, Bud Box, Day-Glo Box].*	A home made a lineman's handset, also known as REMOBS (REMote OBserving Systems). With a Beige Box you can do the following things: "Eavesdropping; Long distance, static free phone calls to phriends; Dialling direct to Alliance Conferencing (also static-free); Phuking up people; Bothering the operator at little risk to yourself; Blue Boxing with a greatly reduced chance of getting caught; Anything at all that you want, since you are an extension on that line". **Invented by The Exterminator and The Terminal Man** **Date: Friday, May 17, 1985.**
8	**[Beige Box Revisited]** *[similar to Beagan Box, Beige Box, Day-Glo Box].*	*see Beige Box* **by Mercenary** **Year: 1992 or later.**
9	**Black Box.**	A Black Box is a device that is hooked up to your fone that fixes your fone so that when you get a call, the caller doesn't get charged for the call. This is good for calls up to 1/2 hour, after 1/2 hour the phone Company gets suspicious, and then you can guess what happens. The original box was created in the USA. There are modified versions for other countries. **Original author unknown** **UK Black Box by K.S.Reach of The Hackers Academy (March 1988)** **Greek Black Box by Fabulist and Enigma (year 1992)**
10	**Blast Box**	A blast box is, is a really cheap amplifier (around 5 watts or so), connected in place of the microphone on your telephone meant to talk to someone on the phone who just doesn't shut up.
11	**Blast Box II**	Similar to the Blast Box, but designed to blow up other people's computers, instead of their ears.
12	**Bleeper Box** *[UK version of the Blue Box]*	The United Kingdom's own version of the Blue Box, modified to work with the UK's phone system. Based on the same principles. However, British Telecom uses two sets of frequencies, foreword and backwards.

S. No.	Name of the Device	Function of the device
13	Blotto Box.	For years now every pirate has dreamed of the Blotto Box. It was at first made as a joke to mock more ignorant people into thinking that the function of it actually was possible. This box quite simply, can turn off the phone lines everywhere. **Originally conceived by King Blotto** **Created by The Traveler**
14	Blue Box *(aka 2600 Box).*	The mother of all boxes. The first box in history, which started the whole phreaking scene. Invented by *Al Gilbertson* (Original name unknown). **Year: early 1960s.**
15	(Blue Con Box) *(short name for the Blue Conference Box).*	*see Blue Conference Box.*
16	**Blue Conference Box** *(aka Blue Con Box).*	A Blue Box and a Con Box combined.
17	**Bottle-Nosed Grey box** *[selective version of the Rainbow Box].*	This box will do damage to only your phone, the line between you and your enemy and your enemy's MODEM, whereas the Rainbow Box just takes everything out. **by The Dolphin that came from Belmont.**
18	**[Brown Box]** *(aka Opaque Box)* *[similar to Con Box, Party Box, Three Box].*	**Created by The Doc.**
19	Bud Box.	This box is quite similar to a beige box, except this is a portable unit. It is extremely handy for free voice calls and tapping a near by house's line. **Invented by Dr. D-Code & The Pimp of The Slaughtered Chicken.**
20	Busy Box.	This box is attached to the outside of the person's house, in their telephone box. It makes it so that when any phone inside that house is picked up, no dial tone is heard, and no calls can be received, or sent. This is good for lame BBS's as they tend not to call out much, and it will remain undetected for a longer period of time. **Invented by Black Death.**

S. No.	Name of the Device	Function of the device
21	**Charging Box** *(aka Light Box).*	This box is used to indicate when a call is being charged for and when it is not. Once installed, the box has two lights, a green one and a red one. Green means free and red shows that you are being charged. **Created by Stinky Pig Productions (a UK team).**
22	**(Chart Box)** *(short name for the Chartreuse Box).*	*see Chartreuse Box.*
23	**Chartreuse Box** *(aka Chart Box, Obnoxious Box).*	Your telephone line is a constant power source. This box is designed to allow you to tap that power source and give you up to 12 volts (more if you use a transformer). **Created by Wonko The Sane.**
24	**Cheese Box.**	This box (named for the type of box the first one was found in) turns your home phone into a pay phone. It can be used together with a Red Box to make free calls. Created by Otho Radix.
25	**Clear Box.**	This box works on "post-pay" payphones (a kind of payphone that could be found in Canada and in rural United States), in other words, those phones that don't require payment until after the connection has been established. If you don't deposit money, you can't speak to the person at the other end, because your mouthpiece is cut off -- but not your earpiece. (Yes, you can make free calls to the weather, etc. from such phones.) With this box the user is able to speak to the other person for free. The clear box thus "clears" up the problem of not being heard. **Originally published on the July 1984 issue of 2600 The Hacker's Quarterly.**
26	**Con Box** *(aka Conference Box)* *[similar to Brown Box, Party Box, Three Box].*	This box allows you to connect two lines in your house to give 3 way type service, creating a party line.
27	**(Conference Box)** *(expanded name for the Con Box).*	*see Con Box.*

S. No.	Name of the Device	Function of the device
28	Copper Box.	Uses cross-talk feedback to try to damage sensitive equipment of a phone company. More a method than a real box. **Concieved by The Cypher** **Year: 1986.**
29	Crimson Box *(sometimes mispelt as Chrimson Box)* *[similar to Green Box (2), Orange Box, Hold Box, Hold On Box, White Box (2), Yellow Box (2)].*	This box is a very simple device that will allow you to put someone on hold or make your phone busy with a large amount of ease. You flip a switch and the person can't hear you talking. Flip it back and everything is peechy. It doesn't have a led to show when hold mode is on. **Created by Dr. D-Code** **Year: 1985.**
30	Dark Box: Multi-Purpose Network Manipulation Unit.	This box's basic design allows you to call anywhere on earth without fear of being billed or traced. **Created by Cablecast 0perator of the Dark Side Research Group** **Year: 1987.**
31	[Day-Glo Box] *(aka DayGlo Box)* *[similar to Beige Box].*	This box lets you place calls for free with no time limit, no possibility of a wiretap, and the calls can be placed from anywhere in the world. **Conceptualized by John F. Kennedy.**
32	Diverti Box.	Cited in the "Blotto Box" document. Probably used to divert a phone call. **Created by The Traveler.**
33	Dloc Box.	Call/receive on two lines, with the option to conference them. **by The Dark Lords of Chaos: Prowler, Apprentice, Pro Hack, Zeus, Tarkmeth, Blackstoke, Lazer.** **Date: October, 3 1988.**
34	DNA Box.	Not actually a box but a project of the Outlaw Telecommandos to hack cellular phones, in the early era of those devices (1989). **Issued on February 1989.**

S. No.	Name of the Device	Function of the device
35	(Extended Bud Box) (another name for the Acrylic Box).	*see Acrylic Box.*
36	Fuzz Box.	This box duplicates the tones of coins dropping down the phone chute, and thereby allowing the user to place calls without paying for them.
37	Gold Box [similar to X-Gold Box].	When you put a gold box on two phone lines it lets anyone who calls one of the lines call out on the other. So when the phone company traces the line it will tell them that you're calling from the line you hooked the gold box up to. **by Dr. Revenge, cosysop of Modem Madness.**
38	Green Box	This box generates tones for Coin Collect, Coin Return, and Ringback. It must be used by the CALLED party.
39	[Green Box (2)] [similar to Crimson Box, Orange Box, Hold Box, Hold On Box, White Box (2), Yellow Box (2)].	A hold button. *see Crimson Box.*
40	(Grey Box) (another name for the Silver Box).	*see Silver Box.*
41	[Hold Box] [similar to Crimson Box, Green Box (2), Orange Box, Hold On Box, White Box (2), Yellow Box (2)].	A hold button. *see Crimson Box.*
42	[Hold On Box] [similar to Crimson Box, Green Box (2), Orange Box, Hold Box, White Box (2), Yellow Box (2)].	A hold button. *see Crimson Box.*

S. No.	Name of the Device	Function of the device
43	Infinity Box (*sometimes mispelt as Infiity Box*).	When the phone number of a telephone containing an infinity box device is dialled and a certain note is blown into the phone from a honker, keyof-c, harmonica, the bugged phone does not ring, and what's more, enables the caller to then hear everything said in the room that the phone is located in. As long as the caller wants to stay on the phone, all is open to him or her. If the phone is lifted off the hook, the transmitter is disconnected and the "bugged" party receives a dial tone as if nothing was wrong with the line. **Description by Iron Man of The Crack Shop from the original "Infinity Transmitter" by Manny Mittleman.**
44	Jack Box.	A device to generate tones created starting from a phone keypad.
45	Jolly Box.	A software written in 8086 assembly which generates several phone tones ("Multi-Frequenz-Demon-Dialer for Global Access"). **Code by Jolly Roger** **Updated by by Zaphod Beeblebrox of Control Team** **Date: probably 1993 or earlier.**
46	(Light Box) (*another name for the Charging Box*).	*see Charging Box.*
47	Loud Box.	Makes your voice louder over the phone line. Especially meant for use in conference calls. **Designed, written and built by Mr. Bill**
48	Lunch Box (*aka Tap Box*).	The Lunch Box is a very simple transmitter used for eavesdropping. It is quite small and can easily be put in a number of places. **Created by Dr. D-Code.**
49	Magenta Box.	When you call up line one from your house you will get a dial tone almost immediately. Using DTMF you can dial anywhere that the person who owns line 2 has service to. Which means you can direct dial alliance, Australia, and your favourite BBS for FREE. **Designed by Street Fighter.**

S. No.	Name of the Device	Function of the device
50	Magenta Box (2).	A portable ringing generator which, if connected to a phone line, will make the phone on the end of it ring. It works by using a relay as a vibrator to generate A.C. which is then stepped up by a transformer and fed through a capacitor into the phone line to make the phone ring.
51	Mauve Box.	Generates a magnetic field to tap the nearest phone conversation (somehow similar to the TEMPEST -- Van Eck radiation -- system to tap video screens). **Created by Captian Generic with Help from The Genetic Mishap** **Date: November, 24 1986.**

52	Meeko Box.	A multi-purpose box with the following features:
		  1. *It is able to record telephone conversations with excellent quality.*
		  2. *It is able to play a source directly into the phone line.*
		  3. *It can keep the phone line open.*
		  4. *You can box without using a phone, and headphones (requires a modem).*
		
		Designed by Meeko of Hi-ReS UK
		Year: 1994.

53	Mega Box.	A cable re-router to hook up a second line in your house.
54	Modu Box *(aka Modula Box).*	A second phone plug attached to an existing one. **Designed by Magnus Adept.**
55	**(Modula Box)** **(expanded name for the Modu Box).**	*see ModuBox.*
56	**[Music Box]** **[similar to Pink Box (2)].**	It's basically a Pink Box (2) without the led. *see Pink Box (2).* **Created by Aluminium Gerbul.**
57	Mute Box.	This box lets the user receive long distance calls without being detected.

S. No.	Name of the Device	Function of the device
58	Neon Box *(aka Record-o-Box)* *(erroneously used as an alias for the Blast Box II)* *[similar to Sound Blaster Box, Rock Box, Slug Box].*	A device that adds a normal jack interface to a telephone, allowing to send music or tones into the phone line, or to record conversations using the microphone input of a recorder. This kind of box can be commonly found in a phone shop. **??anterior to April 1994.**
59	Noise Box *[similar to the Scarlet Box].*	It is a device you can attach to a victim's phone line so that an abnormal amount of noise will be present on the line at all times, which would make data transmissions almost impossible and voice communications annoying, to say the least. **by Doctor Dissector of Phortune 500.**
60	(Obnoxious Box) *(another name for the Chartreuse Box).*	*see Chartreuse Box.*
61	Olive Box.	An alternative ring for your phone, with a light that also flashes when the phone rings. by Arnold, sysop of Hobbit Hole AE (HHAE) East Branch.
62	(Opaque Box) *(another name for the Brown Box).*	*see Brown Box.*
63	[Orange Box] *[similar to Crimson Box, Green Box (2), Hold Box, Hold On Box, White Box (2), Yellow Box (2)].*	A hold button. *see Crimson Box.*
64	Paisley Box.	A multi purpose box that combines the functions of several boxes, including blue, beige, and blotto. Among other things can seize operator lines and remotely control all TSPS and TOPS consoles. **by Blade of the Neon Fucken Knights.**
65	Pandora Box.	A device that generates a high intensity sound to produce pain. A similar device (usually called "phasor") is commonly sold in security shops for personal defence. **by Dr. Rat of Rat Labs, S.F., CA** **Year: 1986.**

S. No.	Name of the Device	Function of the device
66	[Party Box] *[similar to Brown Box, Three Box, Con Box].*	This box allows free three-way calling, connects two phone conversations at once, without any static or excess wiring, or even having two phone lines. **Created by Greyhawke of The Dark Knights (TDK)**
67	**Pearl Box** *[similar to Pearl Box 2 - Advanced Pearl Box].*	This is a box that may substitute for many boxes which produce tones in hertz. The Pearl Box when operated correctly can produce tones from 1-9999Hz. As you can see, 2600, 1633, 1336 and other crucial tones are obviously in its sound spectrum (yet you'd need two Pearl Boxes to generate combined tones, such as the ones of the dialpad). Created by Dr. D-Code Year: before than 1989.
68	**[Pearl Box 2 - Advanced Pearl Box]** *[similar to Pearl Box].*	A Pearl Box made in an easier and cheaper way. Created and Tested by Dispater Date: July, 1 1989.
69	**Pink Box.**	Pink box allows you to hook two separate phone lines together to have three way calling with hold on either line, and well as bringing a dial tone into the conversation with someone and allowing them to dial the number touch tone, and it will connect three way, and when they hang up, it will disconnect three way calling, no more need to play with the hook for 3 way.
70	**Pink Box (2)** *[similar to Music Box].*	The function of a "Pink Box" is to add hold button that allows music or anything else to be played into the telephone while the person is on hold. This Modification either be done right in the telephone as a separate box. This kind of box can be commonly found in a phone shop.
71	**Plaid Box.**	Turns a pulse phone line into a touch phone capable line.
72	**(Portable Gray Box)** *(another name for the Portable Grey Box).*	*see Portable Silver Box.*
73	**Portable Silver Box** *(aka Portable Grey Box).*	A battery operated Silver Box that can fit in a pocket for use in payphones or wherever. **by The Phone Phantom.**

S. No.	Name of the Device	Function of the device
74	Puce Box.	This box emits vaporous LSD. Line noise may cause strychnine formation.
75	Purple Box.	This box allows switching between two phone lines, putting one of them in hold. A led shows which line is on hold. **Created by The Flash** **Date: February, 26 1986**
76	Rainbow Box *[non selective version of the Bottle-Nosed Grey box].*	Connects the electric line to the phone line blowing up everything. Odds are you will take out every phone in the neighbourhood and get caught. **by The Dolphin that came from Belmont.**
77	Razz Box.	This box allows you to tap your neighbours line without your neighbour knowing it. You can also make free phone calls. **Written by The Razz and Released by The Magnet of Crime Ring International** **Date: November, 12 1988.**
78	**(Record-o-Box)** *(another name for the Neon Box).*	*see Neon Box.*
79	**Red Box** *[similar to the Red Box Whistle].*	The Red box basically simulates the sounds of coins being dropped into the coin slot of a payphone. The traditional Red Box consisting of a pair of Wien-bridge oscillators with the timing controlled by 555 timer chips.
80	**[Red Box Whistle]** *[similar to the Red Box].*	A phreak in the Midwest has extensively tested a method of red boxing which uses nothing more than a pair of brass or aluminum whistles. This method is very similar to the original blue boxing. **Reported by THE RESEARCHER.**
81	**Red Green Box** *[combines a Red Box and a Green Box together].*	This is a device that generates the tones for red boxing and green boxing. **by Pink Panther.**

S. No.	Name of the Device	Function of the device
82	Ring/Busy Box.	When connected to a phone line, this box will cause a busy signal anytime a call is made to that particular line. They can still use their phone to make outgoing calls. **by M0rtaSkuld, dedicated to The Emporer.**
83	[Rock Box - Basic] *[similar to the Rock Box - Advanced, Neon Box, Sound Blaster Box].*	The Rock Box channels the music from the stereo out to the phone line via the headphone output. It also can record conversations. **Created and Designed By Video Vindicator of the Shadows of IGA.**
84	[Rock Box - Advanced] *[similar to the Rock Box - Basic, Neon Box, Sound Blaster Box].*	The Rock Box channels the music from the stereo out to the phone line via the headphone output. It also can record conversations. The Advanced version has a more complex wiring and a better audio quality. **Created and Designed By Video Vindicator of the Shadows of IGA**
85	[Scarlet Box] *[similar to the Noise Box].*	The purpose of a Scarlet box is to create a very bad connection, it can be used to crash a BBS or just make life miserable for those you seek to avenge. **Written and Created by THE PIMP**
86	Silver Box *(aka Grey Box)* *[similar to Solid State Silver Box].*	The silver box transforms keys 3, 6 , 9, # to operator's keys A, B, C, D.
87	[Slug Box] *[similar to the Neon Box].*	A slug box is a recording box that stops and starts the tape recorder when a connection is made. **Date: May, 14 1990.**
88	Solid State Silver Box *(can be shortened as SSSilver Box)* *[similar to Silver Box].*	This box uses an integrated circuit to generate the tones rather than converting a phone keypad.
89	(SSSilver Box) *(short name for the Solid State Silver Box).*	*see Solid State Silver Box.*

S. No.	Name of the Device	Function of the device
90	[Sound Blaster Box] [similar to Neon Box, Rock Box].	A device that adds a normal jack interface to a telephone, allowing to send music or tones into the phone line, or to record conversations using the microphone input of a recorder. Better than Neon Box. **by ShadowHawk** **Date: March, 31 1994.**
91	Static Box.	This box keeps the voltage regulated so that you can avoid static, this allow a more stable line for high speed modem (which at that time meant 2400bps). In a certain way it's the opposite of boxes like the noise box. **Created by The Usurper and The Raver of the Lords of Twilight.** **Date: Originally released on November, 21 1986; second release on December, 27 1987.**
92	Switch Box.	With the Switch Box you can put one or both phone lines on hold with visible indicators of each lines status; conference call with two people; change a phone from line #1 to line #2; and lastly, make one phone line physically dead to outside world. **by Autopsy Saw.**
93	Sword Box.	The sword box is just essentially a bud/beige/day-glo box with enhancements and modifications. The structural differences in the sword box make it better however, and thus safer for you to use. **by Grim Reaper/STS** **Date: November, 22 1987.**
94	Tan Box *(it's not the short name of the Tangerine Box, which is a different box).*	It allows you to make recordings from a phone line, and it will only record once the victim's phone is picked up. It's like a Neon Box combined with a Beige Box.
95	Tan Box (2) *(it's not the short name of the Tangerine Box, which is a different box).*	It serves as a phone ringer. You have two choices for ringers, a piezoelectric transducer (ringer), or a standard 8 ohm speaker.

S. No.	Name of the Device	Function of the device
96	(Tanger Box) *(short name for the Tangerine Box).*	*see Tangerine Box.*
97	**Tangerine Box** *(can be shortened as Tanger Box. Can't be shortened as Tan Box, which is a different box).*	Enables you to plug it in, then listen to the conversation, without them hearing a click or anything... plus a jack for headphone, or tape. **by Happy Harley.**
98	**(Tap Box)** *(another name for the Lunch Box).*	*see Lunch Box.*
99	**[Three Box]** *[similar to Brown Box, Party Box, Con Box].*	Use one line, another line, or both... like a con box, but better because it uses LEDs for which line you are on.
100	**Urine Box** *(aka Zap Box).*	It basically creates a capacitative disturbance between the ring and tip wires in another's telephone headset. **by Wolfgang von Albatross of the Underground_Elite Date: March, 2 1986.**
101	**V-Box.**	Detect voltage changes in phone lines (used for taps).
102	**Violet Box.**	This box allows making calls from payphones with just one coin, avoiding the line from being released, when time is up. **by The Kez.**
103	**[White Box (2)]** *[similar to Crimson Box, Green Box (2), Orange Box, Hold Box, Hold On Box, Yellow Box (2)].*	A hold button. *see Crimson Box.*
104	**White Gold Box.**	A White Box and a Gold Box combined. **Created by The Traveller**
105	**Yellow Box.**	This box can switch a payphone from working to out of order and vice-versa. by CAPTAIN HOOK.

S. No.	Name of the Device	Function of the device
106	[Yellow Box (2)] [similar to Crimson Box, Green Box (2), Orange Box, Hold Box, Hold On Box, White Box (2)].	A hold button. see Crimson Box.
107	(Zap Box) (another name for the Urine Box).	see Urine Box. The scheme and description is the same for the urine box, but it's attributed to another author. by KiLLg0re Trout [BULge].

Source: http://www.aboutphone.info/lib/phreak/boxes-2.html, accessed on February 12, 2016.

Appendix 2

A sample of active onion websites' URLs in the Tor network during the period of this study

Category	Name of the Website/ Webpage	URL
Wikis And Introduction Points	Hidden Wiki	http://zqktlwi4fecvo6ri.onion/wiki/index.php/ Main_Page(new) or http://kpvz7ki2v5agwt35.onion/wiki/index.php/ Main_Page(old)
	Wikileaks	http://zbnnr7qzaxlk5tms.onion/
	Tor Links .onion Link List	http://torlinkbgs6aabns.onion/
	OnionDir - Deep Web Link Directory	http://dirnxxdraygbifgc.onion/
	ParaZite	http://kpynyvym6xqi7wz2.onion/links.html
	Liberty Wiki	http://455sdmsz3oa5w3xx.onion/wiki/index. php?title=Main_Page
	Onion Wiki	http://cu7yjdxqw37yjv5n.onion/
	Cepa Hound	http://onionsumqbpcrsnu.onion/
	French Deep Web	http://fdwocbsnity6vzwd.onion/
Search Engines	Duck Duck Go	http://3g2upl4pq6kufc4m.onion/
	Torch	http://xmh57jrzrnw6insl.onion/
	Tor Search	http://kbhpodhnfxl3clb4.onion/
	Ahmia.fi	https://ahmia.fi/search
	Grams	http://grams7enufi7jmdl.onion/
E-mail and Chat Services	Dark Nexus	http://e266al32vpuorbyg.onion/
	Tor Box	http://torbox3uiot6wchz.onion/
	Mail Tor	http://mailtoralnhyol5v.onion/src/login.php
	Mail2Tor	http://mail2tor2zyjdctd.onion/

Category	Name of the Website/ Webpage	URL
Social Networks	Galaxy	http://hbjw7wjeoltskhol.onion/
	Hell Online	http://u4uoz3aphqbdc754.onion/
	TorBook	http://torbookdjwhjnju4.onion/
	Twitter Clone	http://npdaaf3s3f2xrmlo.onion/
Miscellaneous Information, tutorials, etc	Intel Exchange	http://rrcc5uuudhh4oz3c.onion/
	Tube Amp Building	http://tubeshavbpvdniap.onion/
	The Explosives and Weapons Forum	http://parazite.nn.fi/roguesci/
	Tor Graphics	http://6tgwhhqryumqtbpv.onion/
	Bugged Planet	http://6sgjmi53igmg7fm7.onion/index.php?title=Main_Page
	The Tor Library	http://am4wuhz3zifexz5u.onion/
Black Market (Drugs and Weapons)	Silk Road	http://silkroad6ownowfk.onion/login
	Black Market	http://dgoega4kbhnp53o7.onion/
	Israel Service	http://israeliwht6bzuqb.onion/
	Portman Cigars	http://oo5w7anwuqybxhdj.onion/
	Only. Cigs	http://cigs7cviqbi4bvuy.onion/
	Urban Leaf	http://pn5lq46gq4kb46rf.onion/
	Mr. Nice Guy	http://niceguymn4plorwb.onion/
	Derek 4 Real	http://derek4real.bviaqyj6obc54vhn.onion/
	UK Guns and Ammo Store	http://tuu66yxvrnn3of7l.onion/
	Sweet Leaf	http://weedemvltt36vfkx.onion/
	eStadion	http://5qqwqsqictvper25.onion/
	Pandora Open Market forums	http://bl3j73taluhwidx5.onion/
	DeDope	http://kbvbh4kdddiha2ht.onion/
	Black Market	http://z67uv77ridgc2q6n.onion/shop.php
	Executive Outcomes	http://5zkfuvtrpotg2nzd.onion/

Category	Name of the Website/ Webpage	URL
Other Dark Pages (Assasins, Hitman, hackers, Middle man, fake Ids, etc)	Creditcards Paypal Market BlackMarket SilkRoad Hidden Wiki Underground - Selling creditcards and Paypalaccounts	http://kio5ei7cuj2bp6z4.onion/blackmarket/
	Apples 4 Bitcoins	http://tfwdi3izigxllure.onion/
	Hitman Network	http://ybp4oezfhk24hxmb.onion/
	The Assasination Market	http://assmkedzgorodn7o.onion/
	Fund The Islamic Struggle Without Leaving a Trace.	http://teir4baj5mpvkg5n.onion/
	Password Recovery	http://imgbifwwqoixh7te.onion/#!EICE8iO!wNKR 02gdjF1Huf2uN6f4Fz1NRYt3MXZ2lAnH7hBt
	Rent a Hacker	http://2ogmrlfzdthnwkez.onion/
	Old Man Fixer's Fixing Services	http://yth5q7zdmqlycbcz.onion/
	Samsung Store	http://storegsq3o5mfxiz.onion/
	Code Green	http://pyl7a4ccwgpxm6rd.onion/w/index.php/ Main_Page
	The Human Experiment	http://xqz3u5drneuzhaeo.onion/users/ experiments/
	Fake Passport. onion	http://fakepasvv3holddd.onion/

Source: Accessed using the Tor browser bundle in May 2014.

Appendix 3

Evolution of Stuxnet Versions

Version	Date	Description
0.500	November 3, 2005.	C and C server registration
0.500	November 15, 2007	Date of submission to a public scanning service
0.500	July 4, 2009	Date on which Infection was stopped
1.001	June 22, 2009	Main binary compile timestamp
1.100	March 1, 2010	Main binary compile timestamp
1.101	April 14, 2010	Main binary compile timestamp
1.x	June 24, 2012	Infection was stopped

Source: Geoff Mcdonald, Liam O Murchu, Stephen Doherty & Eric Chien. "Stuxnet 0.5 – The Missing Link", Symantec, version 1.0, February 26, 2013.

INDEX